W9-CFW-960

TRIPS AND TREKS:
A GUIDE TO OUTINGS IN NEW JERSEY AND BEYOND!

BARBARA HUDGINS

The Woodmont Press
P.O. Box 108
Green Village, N.J. 07935

© 1983 by Barbara Hudgins. All rights reserved. No part of this book may be reproduced in any form without the permission of the author.

This is an enlarged and expanded edition of "Trips and Treks: A Guide to Family Outings in the New Jersey Area" by Barbara Hudgins, © 1980. Some of the material in this book first appeared as part of the newspaper column, "Trips and Treks" in the *Chatham Press, Summit Herald, New Providence/Berkeley Heights Dispatch* and in the *Journal of Chatham, Madison and Florham Park*.

If a copy of this book is not available at your local bookstore, you may order one by sending $6.95 pp. to:

The Woodmont Press
P.O. Box 108
Green Village, N.J. 07935

ISBN 0-9607762-1-4
Printed in the United States of America

DEDICATION

To Webster, Lani and Robert who trudged through countless amusement parks and reconstructed villages to help me with my book.

ACKNOWLEDGEMENTS

Much gratitude and thanks to:

All the driving companions who searched out New Jersey's nooks and crannies with me. In particular: Gail Davies, Sheila Di Marsico, Bill Mawhinney, Marilyn Kennedy, Linda Kimler, Alexandra Knox, Betty Murphy, and the Wemple family.

All those who shared their expertise with me, especially Ken Benson and Bonnie Lacey.

Those who helped with the book production beyond the call of duty, particularly: Mary Lou Nahas for copyreading, Jack Krug for editorial help, Kathy Hughes for book design of the first edition, and Linda Kimler for pictures and general support.

I would also like to thank tour leaders Sandy Brown and Nicki Kessler for making the bus tours I took with them so informative and interesting.

FOREWORD

This book grew out of an advertising agency assignment I was given several years ago. I was to put together a small booklet on the towns of New Jersey which would include area attractions. As I researched in libraries I noticed that the shelves were stocked with tour guides to New York and Philadelphia while the New Jersey guide section was small in comparison. The guides I did find were either too specialized or simply outdated.

The advertising agency assignment was never completed but in the meantime I began to take trips with my family in the New Jersey area, using several standard books as my guide. I discovered that the places I visited were often quite different from what I had been led to expect. My personal visits to various attractions became the basis for a column in several local newspapers entitled "Trips and Treks".

In putting the articles together to create the first edition of my book (1980) I found, alas, that there were gaps in categories. So for the convenience of the reader, in both that edition and this one, I did what most guidebooks do as a matter of course — I included listings for several sites I had not personally seen. This is particularly true of the short listings such as planetariums and nature centers, where a visit to three or four assured me of their value and their similarity. Of course all entries have been checked for hours and prices by telephone. For the most part, however, this is a personal book based on visits with my family or on group tours to an amazing variety of places as I expanded my horizons to gardens, flea markets and walking tours in this second edition.

I have learned many things on my trips and treks — I have learned the history of homes and the psychology of groups — but above all I have learned to wear good walking shoes and to bring my own sandwich along whenever possible.

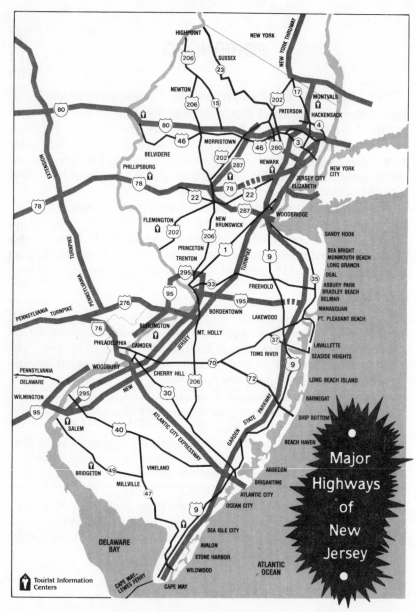

Courtesy N.J. Div. of Travel & Tourism

Map of New Jersey, showing major highways.

CONTENTS

Unique Towns, Places to Browse,
Guided Walking Tours
(Atlantic City, New Hope, Hoboken, etc.) 1

Where Washington Slept, Ate and Fought 21

Homes of the Rich and Famous 39

Restored and Reconstructed:
Colonial, Federal and Victorian
Villages, Mills, Farms and Homes 59

Museums of All Kinds 79

The Classics 117

Theme Parks, Amusement Parks,
Boardwalk Amusements 129

Zoos, Aquariums, Wildlife Refuges,
Nature Centers 145

The Outdoor Life: Ski Areas,
the Jersey Shore, etc. 161

The Garden Variety 177

Flea Markets and Outlets 189

Other Outings:
(Wineries, Planetariums, Racetracks) 203

Index 217

Regional Index 227

NOTE

1. Hours and prices listed in this book are as up to date as possible. However changes occur constantly according to the whim of the owner or the budget cuts of state funds. Always telephone or check newspaper advertisements before you set out.

2. The following attractions are not included in this book because they are **not** presently in operation:

   The Gingerbread Castle, Hamburg
   The Morris County Railroad, Newfoundland
   N.J. Antique Auto Museum, Wall Twp.

UNIQUE TOWNS,
PLACES TO BROWSE,
GUIDED WALKING TOURS

Photo: Courtesy N.J. Div. of Travel & Tourism

In This Chapter You Will Find:

Atlantic City
Princeton
New Hope, PA.
Lahaska, PA.
Chinatown, N.Y.

Guided Walking Tours for:
  Soho
  Other N.Y. Walking Tours
  Hoboken
  Paterson
  Plainfield
  Bordentown
  Burlington
  Mount Holly
  Salem
  Gloucester County
  Philadelphia

←

A new skyline emerges at Atlantic City.

ATLANTIC CITY

The back streets are still desolate and run down, but the Boardwalk is booming and the clink of money is heard all over town as Atlantic City re-emerges from the doldroms. It will take a long time before condominiums and classy shopping areas really dominate — for now parts of the Boardwalk seem to be in a constant state of demolition and halted construction. But once you enter the casino-hotels, you are in a world of mirrored glass and plush carpets, chorus girls and high-priced drinks — a little bit of Las Vegas swept up on the Northeast's shoreline. Here is what you will find at the new Atlantic City:

Parking: Lots range from $5 in the winter to $12 and above in the summer. Valet parking is available at the hotels if you are staying over or using the casino. This costs from $5 to $8, according to the season. One new wrinkle in the off-season gimmicks offered by the casino-hotels is free valet parking for 3 hours. Not a bad idea as gimmicks go, since parking space is one of the most sought after commodities in town.

Transportation: Once you have parked your car, the best way to get around town is take the small jitneys that operate along Pacific Avenue. They come frequently and cost 60¢. The famous tram still traverses the Boardwalk. Although it moves at a snail's pace and costs $1 per one-way trip, it does give you a chance to view the new boardwalk scene in relative comfort. The tram travels from Resorts at North Carolina Ave. to the Golden Nugget at Boston Ave. and back again.

Bus Tours: Still the favorite way for most people to make a one day visit — fares vary from point of embarkation. It costs $15 from north Jersey and the casinos give you $10 back in the form of quarters (although this amount shrinks drastically in the heavy summer months). You must stay for 6 hours if you take a bus tour. Many people take a sandwich along on the bus trip down, then eat at the hotel buffet just before the return trip. These casino-subsidized buses travel to Atlantic City every day of the week. When groups charter their own buses, they often get a package which includes buffet and show.

The Hotels: Prices are high: $75 to well over $100 a day in the sparkling new hotels. However, if you don't mind visiting A.C. when the chill winds blow, there are some very reasonable weekend and weekday packages available from the big hotels. These include room and dinner. Once the summer season hits, though, be prepared to pay through the nose. Actually almost every shore resort in Jersey has a bus tour to A.C. several nights a week, so it is not necessary to stay in town in order to play in town. There are also many older motels in town along Pacific and Atlantic Avenues. Although their accomodations are neither sparkling nor new, they are no worse than many shore resort sand-in-the-carpet motels and they are comparatively reasonable. For a list of hotels and motels and recent prices write to: *Atlantic City Convention and Visitors Bureau*, 16 Central Pier, Atlantic City, N.J. 08401.

The Casinos: If your idea of a casino is garnered from the movies and you expect evening dresses and tuxedos, leisurely gaming tables and James Bond types floating around, forget it. This is supermarket gambling, where little old ladies with shopping bags hover over the slot machines, longshoremen and bewildered bus groups from Delaware wander around in a vast hall of glass, chrome and green and the hotel employees all seem to have taken a vow of silence. Roulette and blackjack and craps tables are placed cheek by jowl and rows of slots glisten in the artificial light. It's all very confusing. If only the casinos had one central information booth where people could ask the most obvious questions. Even the signs for restrooms, coatcheck, restaurants, etc. are not as clear as they could be.

Most hotels have free gaming guides in the lobbies or casinos but these small brochures only give the most basic information and the odds. If you plan to play a table game you really should read up on the game first and practice a bit before you visit A.C.

As for slot machines — you change your paper money into coins at the elevated change booth in the slot area. But to transform a bucketful of coins into dollars you must hike over to the Coin Banks, usually located way across the room.

Food: There are many excellent restaurants in Atlantic City. From the old *Knife and Fork Inn* (outside the Boardwalk area) to the new French and English restaurants such as *Camelot* in Resorts and the *Palm Court* at Caesar's. The better restaurants absolutely require reservations. However, the daytripper will more likely land up at the buffets (which vary in quality and price) at almost any hotel. There are also 24-hour coffee shops which are mediocre and a few New York style delis which are good — I particularly like the one on the casino floor of Park Place. For those who are absolutely broke, there are a number of hot dog vendors outside the casinos and a few pizza and ice cream stands along the Boardwalk.

Entertainment: First class shows, chorus girls and big name stars appear at all the hotels, and this, above all, has brought a certain zing to the resort. No, things do not go all night as they do in Las Vegas, but at least there is some life here after 6 p.m. Besides the big shows, there are lounges with brassy singers, lounges with tinkling pianos, boxing matches and all sorts of tournaments. Teenagers will find video game rooms in the hotels and some on the boardwalk also. And the Steeplechase Amusement Pier still has rides and arcades as in pre-casino days.

For those who want to venture beyond the Boardwalk, there are a few summertime attractions. One is **Lucy, the Margate elephant**, an architectural oddity that is six stories high complete with howdah. You can walk through Lucy (although the original rooms are gone) with a guided tour during the summer for a fee. It's located at 9200 Atlantic Ave., in Margate — two towns down from A.C. and open weekends May and Sept., daily from June 21 to Labor Day.

On the inlet side, Atlantic City offers **Historic Gardner's Basin** which was supposed to be a miniature fishing village a la Mystic, Connecticut. A restaurant, a few shops and a genuine 130 foot square-rigger, "The Young America" which takes passengers on a sail, are the attractions. All this was set up at the traditional boating and fishing area of A.C., the inlet. However, nearby Capt. Starn's Pier is closed and as you drive over to Gardner's Basin you pass a section of the city so blighted it looks like World War II took place yesterday. These factors have cut down on possible tourism. There are special events here, however, and during the summer there seems to be some action. Call 609-348-2880 first.

Other standard sidetrips from Atlantic City are the winery tours at Renault and Gross' Highland Winery, the Historic Towne of Smithville and Wheaton Village, all of which are mentioned elsewhere in this book. And, of course in the summertime, there is always The Atlantic City beach.

DIRECTIONS: Garden State Parkway to Exit 40 and 38S.

PRINCETON

Shades of F. Scott Fitzgerald! Golden lads and lasses walking the well-clipped paths between venerable University Halls while russet leaves flutter overhead from rows of sturdy trees. Time, scholarships and the inclusion of girls have changed the atmosphere at this Ivy League bastion somewhat. But still for a trip to a true University town that combines history, culture and a typical collegiate Gothic architecture, nothing beats a visit to Princeton.

For many, the trip to Princeton means either a show at the popular McCarter theater or football at Palmer Stadium. For everyone else there is still plenty to do and see. And the best way to see the campus sights is to take the free tours offered by the *Orange Key Guide Service*. Just go to the John Maclean house, on campus in time for the tours which leave at 10 AM, 1:30 PM, and 3:30 PM weekdays and Saturdays. Sunday tours are 1:30 and 3:30 PM. The telephone number is 609-452-3603 but it is not necessary to reserve in advance. Here are some campus sights included in the tour:

1. **Nassau Hall:** Built in 1756, this Georgian stone structure has survived pillage and fire (by the British, not the students) over the years. It served as a barracks and hospital for troops of both sides during the Revolutionary War. In 1783 Congress met here and drafted the Constitution while Princeton was still the Capitol. It now serves as an administrative office for the University. A painting by Charles Willson Peale of Washington at the Battle of Trenton is to be found here.

2. **Firestone Library:** A beautiful two-million volume library built in 1948, it is the embodiment of the Collegiate Gothic style. Major collections include the papers of F. Scott Fitzgerald, Adlai E. Stevenson, John Foster Dulles, Woodrow Wilson and other famous graduates. A changing exhibit of rare books is also on display.

3. **Woodrow Wilson School of Public and International Affairs:** Guides will show you the outside of this striking building, one of the few modern structures on campus. Designed by Minoru Yamasaki, it includes a reflecting pool and the Fountain of Freedom by James Fitzgerald.

4. **The University Chapel:** Built in a Gothic design by Ralph Adams Cram in 1928, it is the third largest University chapel in the country, seating 1800. A 16th Century carved oak pulpit and some of the finest stained glass to be seen this side of the Atlantic Ocean make the Chapel an outstanding part of the Princeton trip.

5. The Putnam Sculptures: These are a series of massive metal and stone sculptures thrown around the campus as if a giant had decided to distribute his toys among the college buildings. Almost all are abstract in design and they stick out like sore thumbs among the ivy-walled buildings. You can't miss them so you might as well examine them. Sir Henry Moore, Jacques Lipchitz, Louise Nevelson and Pablo Picasso are among the biggies represented there.

6. The Prospect: A Tuscan villa built in 1849, it is now used as a Faculty Club and not open to the public. However, the formally designed garden to the rear is open for browsing and is very pleasant.

Not included in the tour, but an important stop, is the **Princeton Art Museum** (open Tuesday - Saturday 10-4; Sunday 1-5. Summertime it is best to call 609-452-3787 to check on hours.) This is a first-rate small museum and wonder of wonders — it's free! Paintings include a generous sampling of Italian Renaissance and French Baroque. Downstairs you'll find a good collection of Chinese Bronzes as well as artifacts from Central and South America. A top collection of prints and a separate medieval room that includes part of the stained-glass window from the Cathedral at Chartres are also "must sees". Special changing exhibits are of a high order.

Besides the university, Princeton has pleasant shopping along Nassau Street and many good restaurants (among them *"Lahiere's"*, *"The Nassau Inn"* and the *"Alchemist and Barrister"*). You might also want to look at The *Princeton Cemetery* at Wiggins and Witherspoon, which holds the remains of Aaron Burr and Grover Cleveland among its many notables. The *Princeton Battle Monument*, a fifty-foot structure, stands imposingly at Nassau and Mercer Streets, while a walking tour of the area will take you past many lovely old houses. Two outstanding historic buildings, *Morven* and the *Bainbridge House* have separate listings in this book. The children's museum room of the Bainbridge House is a favorite spot for little ones. *Princeton Battlefield Park* is also listed separately.

The *McCarter Theater* runs a full program of professional plays, movies, ballet and concerts from September to June. There are also a good number of fairs and community doings going on. However much of Princeton's activity is geared to the school season, so call first to see what's open if you're planning to visit during the summer or holiday seasons.

DIRECTIONS: Route 206 or 27 to Princeton. The University is on Nassau Street.

NEW HOPE, PENNSYLVANIA

There are a number of small towns in the United States that seem to survive simply by being picturesque. A combination of natural beauty, historical significance and the establishment of an art colony (followed inevitably by a writers' colony and a rustic theater) creates that certain atmosphere that brings the tourists out in droves. Whether the original tourist impetus was the antiques in the historical part of town or the artworks in the art colony, the more that people arrive the more craftshops, antique stores, boites, boutiques and charm-laden restaurants open.

Provincetown, Key West, Taos — some have become over-burdened by the hippie-drug culture. But New Hope, Pennsylvania, remains the cultural and picturesque capitol of Bucks County and beyond. And on any fall weekend the narrow sidewalks of this sophisticated oasis set in Pennsylvania farm country are simply jammed. People come to shop, browse or just wallow in the atmosphere.

In the 1920's landscape painters settled here, bringing with them the excitement of the creative world. By the Thirties, Bucks County had become well known as a quiet weekend haven for novelists, poets and playwrights. And in 1939 a grist mill in the center of town was transformed into the **Bucks County Play-house**. The opening program was "Springtime for Henry" with Edward Everett Horton, and the playhouse has remained a stalwart of the "Straw Hat Circuit" ever since. The season now begins in late spring and extends well into fall. Since the theater offers family musicals and matinee performances it is one of New Hope's biggest draws. (Telephone: 215-862-2041)

Another summer season attraction is the **New Hope Mule Drawn Barge Ride** which offers a one-hour ride down the old canal works. It is a slow and easy way to see the town. It departs from the barge landing at New Street and usually several rides are offered during the afternoon. Call 215-862-2842 for details.

Historic house lovers will enjoy the **Parry House Mansion** at South Main and Parry Streets. Guided tours of ten rooms that run the gamut from Colonial to early 20th Century are available. The rooms were furnished by a professional interior decorator and each reflects a period — Federal, Victorian, etc. — in the history of the house. It's quite well done. The house is open from May to October on Fridays, Saturdays and Sundays from 1-4 PM. Tours are $1.50 for adults, 50¢ for children and free to those under six. Call 215-862-2194 for additional information.

But even without these extras there is plenty to see in New Hope. Stroll along the leaf-strewn streets and visit the shops if you are interested in antiques. There are plenty of shops featuring memorabilia in town, and if you collect old sheet music, military hats or miniature dolls, you'll find much to pick from.

Art galleries can be found on Main Street, Mechanic Street and Route 202. Phillips Mill just two miles outside of New Hope, hosts an art festival and has galleries too. Besides the standard landscape of Pennsylvania red barn country you can find modernistic sculpture and paintings also. The kids will be more interested in the toy shops, the knickknack shops and the candy shop (from whence the aroma of chocolate-dipped strawberries wafts over town).

One of the charms of visiting a quaint, riverside town is eating in a quaint, interesting restaurant, and there are plenty of them in New Hope, most along the main drag. Whether you opt for the casual *Mother's*, the glossy *Hacienda*, the formal *Logan Inn* or the cutesy *Picnic Basket*, you will be satisfied. The better places fill up on weekends, though, so you'd better make reservations as soon as you hit town. There's a variety of night spots in and around town also.

DIRECTIONS: Route 202 across Delaware River, then 32S; or 179 or 29 to Lambertville and cross bridge.

LAHASKA, PENNSYLVANIA

Having gone as far as New Hope, you might as well go the extra four miles on Route 202 to Lahaska and the Peddler's Village. The road is dotted with antiques shops which is what brought this area to prominence in the first place. **Peddler's Village** is one of those reconstructed shopping malls that combine the brick walks and lamps of the 18th Century and very pretty landscaping with astute 20th Century commercialism. In fact, it is very similar to the Historic Towne of Smithville, except there are no "authentic" Colonial homes and no "authentic" Colonial craftspeople — just nice scenery and a great big waterwheel to give the proper atmosphere.

Many people who visit New Hope like to go on to Lahaska to eat since The Peddler's Village features one of those Colonial restaurants that has several different eating and drinking areas (not all are always open, though). Still in all, you can be pretty sure of finding a decent meal here without too long a wait. The Village also includes 42 shops which sell china, leather, contemporary furniture, children's clothes, hand-crafts and so on, together with enough cheese, nut and candy shops in insure you don't leave the grounds without buying something.

A number of new shopping areas have sprung up close to Peddler's Village: The Yard, with its California look, a small discount mall and the flea market. More about this in the chapter on Flea Markets.

LOCATION: Routes 202 and 263, Lahaska, Pennsylvania
HOURS: 10 am - 5 pm daily for shops, Fridays until 9 pm. Some shops are open Sunday 1-5 pm. Restaurants open later.
TELEPHONE: 215-794-7055

CHINATOWN, NEW YORK

There are many unique neighborhoods in nearby New York, but the one that stands out as the last of the true ethnic neighborhoods is Chinatown. Although there are some modern towers rising up in the area, most of Chinatown is still packed with six-story tenements that nestle within them a huge variety of shops and restaurants. Pagoda-shaped telephone booths, a Chinese movie house and the *Chinese Museum* at 8 Mott Street (open 10 AM to 5:30 PM daily) add touches of the Orient. But it is the smell of spices in the streets, the gnarled looking vegetables in the grocery shops and the tinkling brass bells in the curio shops that gives Chinatown its special flavor.

Most of all it is the restaurants that pull the crowds to Chinatown. You can find hot and spicy Northern cooking, the traditional (to New Yorkers) Cantonese cuisine, and the new tea shops that serve dim sun lunches. Sunday is the big day for tourists so it gets awfully crowded but weekdays it's just blah. Try Saturday or get there early on a Sunday if you want to find a parking space. This is the closest you'll get to a foreign country without leaving the United States.

DIRECTIONS: Use Holland Tunnel. Keep straight on Canal Street to Pell Street. Chinatown lies in general area between Pell and Mott Streets in lower Manhattan.

GUIDED WALKING TOURS

There are two kinds of walking tours. One is the self-guided type where you begin with a map and brochure, (usually provided by the local historic society) and hoof it yourself. The other is the pre-arranged group tour wherein you reach your destination by bus or car and then proceed *en masse* down the street, following a highly knowledgeable leader who tells you what you are seeing. Group tours often include one or two private houses where you enter by special permission.

Here is a sampling of some of the many guided and self-guided tours available. While most group tours require a pre-arranged schedule and a group of at least ten, others are open to whomever shows up.

THE SOHO TOUR

This excursion is particularly popular with residents of New Jersey because Soho is comparatively new territory on the New York art scene. Soho is that section of lower Manhattan that is bounded by Houston, Sullivan, Canal and Broadway, with its boundaries ever widening. Although this basically industrial area has undergone a great transformation in the last fifteen years, there are still piles of garbage on the street and an occasional wino in a doorway, so traveling *en masse* is practical.

On a nice spring weekend, though, the streets of Soho are jammed with browsers. The art galleries have their doors open, (unlike the Madison Avenue galleries where you must be buzzed in) and many are on street level. The boutique shops and Art Nouveau restaurants are filled and the whole area has a carnival air. People with pink hair and black jackets or Mork from Ork costumes roller skate, walk dogs or simply stroll around.

Enter into this colorful scene a group of thirty New Jerseyans dressed in suburban pantsuits and cloth coats and following a young man from the *Cast Iron Society* who is pointing out mansard roofs and wrought-iron grillework. Naturally, all eyes are riveted on this non-motley crew and many an arty bystander follows along. As a matter of fact, the particular group I was in stopped traffic several times as cars and passersby gaped at the intracies of late 19th Century urban architecture, not knowing quite why.

For groups who prefer gallery tours to architectural ones there are several ways to plan it. One is through your local museum curator; another is through the Municipal Art Society or specialized art tour groups. In the galleries of Soho you can find Pop Art, Neon Art, abstract, post-Modernism and whatever is the fad at the moment. Besides the galleries, the most popular stops are:

Urban Archaeology, 137 Spring St. — It's a store, not a museum, but it attracts browsers with its fascinating collection of old building remnants. Stone gargoyles, bathroom sinks outfitted with gold-plated fixtures, old doors and pediments are strewn around the place. And you can probably find one of those turn-of-the-century mirrored bars that land up in your local quaint pub eventually.

Museum of Holography, 11 Mercer St. — Something new and exciting. Holography is three-dimensional laser photography. Open Wed. - Sun., 12-6 PM. Adults: $1.50; Children & Seniors: 75¢.

Dean & DeLuca, 121 Prince St. — Okay, so this is where we all landed up. It sells a combination of gourmet kitchenware, gorgeous looking breads, and a variety of cheeses and delicacies. You can probably find the same thing in New Jersey but somehow it seems more exciting down here. Also more expensive. I paid one dollar for one croissant — and that's a lot of dough. Some crust!

CONTACT: Friends of Cast Iron Society, 235 E. 87th St., N.Y.C., Tel.: 212-369-6004. (This group runs a very limited number of tours. Other tour groups are listed in the next article.)

OTHER NEW YORK WALKING TOURS

Since New York is a center for art and theater and New Yorkers are traditionally preoccupied with being "In", it is only natural that some of the most popular tours here are of the behind-the-scenes variety.

Lincoln Center, for instance runs escorted tours through Avery Fischer Hall, the State Theater and of course the Metropolitan Opera House. Call 212-877-1800 for reservations and information.

Radio City Music Hall, 6th Ave. & 49th St., now has its own tour through the backstages and rehearsal halls of this newly refurbished institution. Given daily, the tour costs $5.95 and takes

2½ hours. Call 212-246-4621 for reservations. Groups limited to 15 at a time.

And there is the **Rockefeller Center Tour** (mentioned in another chapter) which includes both a quick look at the Music Hall and a stop at the top of Rockefeller Center. Call 212-489-2947.

For those interested in the backstage machinations of the Capitalist world, the **New York Stock Exchange**, 20 Broad Street in the Wall Street area, has been conducting free tours on a regular daily basis for years. Call 212-623-5168 for further information.

A private group called **Art Tours of Manhattan** runs half and full day excursions to Soho, 57th Street and other areas of interest to art lovers. These are escorted trips to galleries, museums, artists' studios or whatever you wish. A half-day group tour of Soho, for instance, costs $10 a head. This outfit also arranges for behind-the-scenes fashion tours and will take care of lunch arrangements for you. (You foot the bill naturally.) Call 212-254-7682.

A well-publicized walking tour group is the **Municipal Art Society**. They offer a variety of trips to Greenwich Village, Upper Fifth Avenue, Brooklyn Heights, etc. During good weather they leave once a week (it used to be Sundays) from a predetermined spot. Rain automatically cancels these pre-set tours. As for arranged group tours call them at 212-935-3639.

HOBOKEN WALKING TOUR

This is a typical walking tour. I happened to take it under the auspices of the Summit YMCA which chartered the bus. We began our tour at the *Erie Lackawanna Terminal* (officially the Conrail Terminal) a most familiar landmark to thousands of commuters. But this time, instead of rushing from the train to the PATH station, our group followed the tour guide through Byzantine passageways and marvelled at the bannisters, the halls, the ceilings. We glimpsed the old ferry slips and listened to the lore of Hoboken.

The city was a major shipping port in World War I and remained so until after World War II. It was made famous in a way by Marlon Brando in "On The Waterfront", a movie about crooked maritime unions. In fact, the person on whom the Brando character was based still hangs around the railroad terminal and was pointed out (surreptitiously) by the guide.

But on to revitalized Hoboken, where lowly brownstones are being reconverted into showplaces for living, and real live artists are settling down and giving the town some tone. We boarded our bus again and journeyed to a street close to the terminal. Here we found a row of "gentrified" houses that stood out from the Spanish bodegas and ordinary tenements close by.

The guide took us through a home which, though narrow as most townhouses are, was still resplendent with paintings, rugs and modern decor. The owner, a pilot, was absent, but he was certainly most generous to allow a bunch of thirty strangers to traipse through his living quarters. And yes, the beds were made and the towels perfectly hung.

Outside again, we returned to the waterfront for a stroll along the river path which was lined with green serpentine rocks. We passed Stevens Institute of Technology, which was high above us, and enjoyed the view of Manhattan. But were we to see the home of Hoboken's most famous citizen? No. The guide mentioned that Frank Sinatra's boyhood home was not in the best neighborhood, so the tour leaders did not bother with it.

We ended up at the *Madison Hotel Victorian Saloon* at 14th and Washington for a farewell drink. This is one of those quaint, mirrored, 60-foot oak bar "bistros" that are a dime a dozen in New York but seem like a gift from heaven when they appear on Jersey's urban scene.

Tours can vary, of course, according to taste and interests. The Hoboken Environment Committee also runs a fabulously successful house tour in autumn wherein individuals pay their money and visit the designated brownstones and duplexes on their own.

> CONTACT: Hoboken Environment Committee, Box M-252, Hoboken, NJ 07030. Telephone: Claire Waters, 201-656-4488.

PATERSON TOURS

Do-it-yourself tours, guided group tours, visits to the variegated ethnic churches or simply a walking tour of the public statues of Gaetano Federici — these are some of the many tour posibilities you find in the city of Paterson. This industrial city is proud of its history as one of the earliest manufacturing sites in the United States. Its tours emphasize the historic district of The Society for Useful Manufactures.

The **Great Falls of Paterson,** a spectacular waterfall completely surrounded by concrete and urban landscape, is the focal point of the S.U.M. Tours. The Society for Useful Manufactures' Historic District covers the area of mills and plants that were once the heart and breath of the city. Paterson's Golden Age began early in the 19th Century when power from the falls created an industrial bonanza. **The Colt Mill** with its cotton duck sails for the Navy, the **Rogers Locomotive Works** (now a combination museum/office building) where the Iron Horses that crossed the plains were built, and the silk mills that made Paterson the center of that industry are included in the tour. Many of these brick and stone edifices are in various states of rehabilitation.

The **Great Falls Development Corporation** runs tours that take you to the scenes of Paterson's industrial past, but they also will custom-tailor tours to the interests of the group. This outfit also runs the annual Labor Day celebration based around this urban waterfall. The three-day gala includes tightrope walking, jugglers, and other goings-on.

CONTACT: Grace George, Great Falls Tour Office, 80 McBride Ave., Paterson, N.J. 07501. Telephone: 201-881-3896

THE PLAINFIELD TOUR

At the turn of the century Plainfield boasted of over one hundred millionaires living within its pleasant precincts. Huge, rambling Victorian homes with wraparound porches, dormer windows, turrets and gables sat behind well-tended lawns. They were the homes of New York financiers, lawyers and physicians. It was the height of Plainfield's glory.

Years later, during the turmoil of the 1960s, the town seemed to hit the depths. Urban riots, deteriorating housing stock, middle-class flight — all the ingredients were there for total destruction. But it didn't happen. Today Plainfield is alive and well and back into graciousness.

Tours are available to reserved groups only and cover several sections of the city. The Van Wyck Brooks tour (which our group took) covers one of the pleasantest sections of town. Many of the large homes here have been restored to combine a Victorian shell with a modern ambience. One house, with giant ceilings, stained glass window and ornate bannisters, had been divided into five apartments. A single apartment here was equal to one large suburban home. And the decor, with wall-length murals and stained glass coffee tables, was enough to make any Home Furnishings editor salivate with glee.

Many other homes visited had been restored with great verve or with a careful eye to authenticity. And the stroll from one block to the next, past towering trees and quiet lawns, made us think we had indeed returned to the 1900s. Our group was treated to brownies and lemonade and it seemed almost a shame that the setting for our repast was a backyard patio and not one of those great wraparound porches that seem to be made for lemonade socials and wicker rocking chairs.

CONTACT: John Grady, Plainfield Heritage, Inc., 201-757-2415 (Groups only)

BORDENTOWN WALKING TOUR

One of the most historical towns in New Jersey, Bordentown, is no longer the Quaker enclave it once was. Nor is it the large metropolis (the major boat and coach stop on the route to Philadelphia) of yore. Several famous citizens once made their abodes here — among them Clara Barton, Thomas Paine, Francis Hopkinson (another Revolutionary notable) and Joseph Bonaparte, brother of Napoleon. There are many Quaker buildings still standing and the homes of the famous are here but are private for the most part. And even though the town — which depends heavily on the Ocean Spray cannery for income — is heavily working class, there is still an aura of quaintness and history here.

Self-guided walking tours begin with a brochure from the Historical Society. You can also book guided tours from the same place. The advantage of the guided tour is that certain buildings will be opened up for you. The tour I took started at the **Old City Hall**, headquarters for the Historical Society. Among the rooms to be noted are the one-room courtroom upstairs and the four-cell jail downstairs. The jail demonstrates how economically space was used in the old days. The guide gives some history of the town in the small front room of the courthouse, which also serves as the Society's book & gift shop.

Once outside, our first stop was the **Gilder House** (actually we all hopped in a car and drove there — you don't always walk on walking tours). As we entered the front hall we noticed an elaborate rendition of a family tree that traced the line from Samuel Bunting to the Reverend Gilder for whom the house is named. But it is the furniture from Joseph Bonaparte's estate that creates the most interest here. An elaborate buffet, a blue couch with eagles and a gold-trimmed tea set in the Empire style are some of the remnants this rich and proud French family left in this small New Jersey town. The guide also pointed out a painting of sheep by artist Susan Waters. She is another Bordentown native whose fame is growing with the stronger appreciation of American itinerant painters.

From the Gilder House we proceeded to the **Clara Barton Schoolhouse**, a prime historical site in the town. Actually Miss Barton taught here for a very short time but she made quite an impact on the town. Up to that time middle-class children went to private school while public schools were considered to be for paupers. Miss Barton had to persuade the local schoolchildren to attend. There was no fee but each child was required to bring a stick of wood to keep the woodstove going. The small red brick building has benches and a raised platform where the teacher sat (in the back of the room, not the front).

Houses included on the self-guided walking tour are: Friends Meeting House (open 10-2 except Mondays), Shippen House, Francis Hopkinson House, Thomas Paine House, Joseph Borden House and the Bonaparte Park Garden House which is on the grounds of the Divine Word Seminary on Park Street. While these are private they are often opened up for Bordentown's *"Open House Tour"* which takes place around mid-October.

CONTACT: Bordentown Historical Society, P.O. Box 182, 302 Farnsworth Ave., Bordentown, N.J. 08505. Telephone: 609-298-1740 (12-3 PM except Mondays).

BURLINGTON

Another town that saw its heyday years ago at a time when it was the capitol of West Jersey and a stronghold of Quakerism is Burlington. Among the many buildings that still stand are the **Friends Meeting House**, the **Revell House**, and the **Ulysses S. Grant House**, plus several prominent churches.

A very active Historical Society operates a museum here comprised of five houses. One is the house once rented by the family of America's first novelist and is named, appropriately, **The James Fenimore Cooper House,**" although the writer only spent the first thirteen months of this life here. **"The Captain James Lawrence House"** is right next door and is dedicated to memorabilia of the War of 1812 hero who is best known for his words, "Don't Give Up The Ship!". These side-by-side homes are located at 457 and 459 High Street. **The Pearson How House** (453 High St.) the **Alice Wolcott Museum** and the **Delia Pugh Library** make up the rest of the museum's holdings. The Historical Society is open on Wed. 1-4 and Sun. 2-4 and by appointment. You may call them at 609-386-4773 if you are interested in visiting the museum complex.

Aside from its historical district, Burlington also offers the home base of the *Burlington Coat Factory*, a well-known outlet house on Route 130 and a small mall of outlet shops called *The Burlington Mart.*

A brochure for a self-guided walking tour of the historical district is available from City Hall. You can also make arrangements for guided group tours from there.

CONTACT: Dr. Nicholas Kamaras, City Hall, Burlington, N.J. 08016. Telephone: 609-386-3993

MOUNT HOLLY

The county seat of Burlington was a center of Quakerism in New Jersey. This quiet little town has several buildings of note on its walking tour. You may obtain a pamphlet for the self-guided tour from: *Township Hall*, 23 Washington St., Mt. Holly, NJ 08060. Telephone: 609-261-0170.

Among the noteworthy buildings are: the **Burlington County Prison-Museum,** designed by Robert Mills, architect of the Washington Monument, the **Mill Street Hotel,** the **John Woolman Memorial** and a restored 1759 schoolhouse where Woolman, the famous Quaker abilitionist once taught.

A few miles outside of Mt. Holly there stands the historic mansion of **Smithville** (not to be confused with the historic town of Smithville in Atlantic County). This large columned house includes a museum of bicycles and is open for tours Wednesdays and Sundays from April through November. Telephone: 609-261-5068.

SALEM

An historic courthouse, an old Quaker burying ground and more than 60 refurbished 18th Century homes and buildings along Market Street are points of interest in this settlement that dates back to 1675. The 500-year old Salem Oak is also to be noted. **The Historical Society Headquarters** (79-83 Market Street) is open from 9:30-4 Monday to Friday. Here you can find exhibits of period furniture and glassware. Contact: Greater Salem Chamber of Commerce, 104 Market St., Salem, N.J. 08079. Telephone: 609-935-1415 or 609-935-7510.

GLOUCESTER COUNTY

For those who wish to see the many historical buildings in the small towns of Gloucester, the County Historical Society has prepared a map which lists 48 of them and gives a short history of each. Many are privately owned, but **Hunter-Lawrence House** at 58 North Broad St., Woodbury is now a museum and open to the public. It is also headquarters of the **Gloucester County Historical Society** and you may write there for the map. Telephone: 609-845-4771.

PHILADELPHIA TOURS

Probably the best known self-guided tour is that of Independence National Historical Park (Independence Mall) which is treated in the chapter entitled *"Classics"*. The map you pick up at the Visitors Center includes all the buildings run by the National Park Service plus other sites such as the *Besty Ross House* (Arch and 3rd Sts.) and *Elfreth's Alley*. Other popular tours in Philadelphia are:

UNITED STATES MINT: Within the downtown historic area (it's located at Arch and 5th Sts.) is the building where the coins we use are produced. No, they don't give free samples, but you can buy special sets and commemorative coins from the sales counter in the lobby. Self-guided tours are continuous and last about 45 minutes. Free. *Hours:* 9 - 4:30, Mon. - Friday. *Telephone:* 215-597-7350.

FAIRMOUNT PARK HISTORIC HOUSE TOURS: Fairmount Park cuts a wide swath through Philadelphia on both sides of the

Schuylkill. It includes within its many acres, not only the usual play-grounds, pools and tennis courts, but such major attractions as The Philadelphia Zoo and the Philadelphia Museum of Art.

In the 18th century, the park was a center for country homes of the gentry who wanted to escape the epidemics of the crowded "city". Eight of these homes have been restored and are now open to the public. They include John Penn's *Solitude*, Robert Morris' *Lemon Hill*, and such Georgian classics as *Woodford* and *Mount Pleasant*. The houses, which are scattered about the park, are furnished with authentic antiques and hark back to the time when Philadelphia was the most important colonial town in the world. Guided tours for groups can be arranged beforehand to emphasize history, decorative arts or gardens. In early December, a special Christmas tour features the houses decorated in the manner of the 18th and early 19th centuries.

Individuals may also tour the homes ($1 for adults, 50¢ for children). Since the days each house is open vary, you must call 215-878-7930 first. For the special guided tours call 215-PO3-8100.

For general information on Philadelphia Tours and other attractions, write: Philadelphia Convention and Visitors Bureau, 1525 J. F. Kennedy Blvd., Philadelphia, Pa., 19102.

See Also: *Cape May* under the "Jersey Shore" section of the chapter, "The Outdoor Life".

WHERE WASHINGTON
SLEPT, ATE AND FOUGHT

Photo: Courtesy N.J. Div. of Travel & Tourism

In This Chapter You Will Find:

Jockey Hollow
Washington's Headquarters (Ford Mansion,
    Revolutionary War Museum)
Dey Mansion
Wallace House
Dutch Parsonage
Rockingham
The Old Barracks, Trenton
Washington Crossing State Park, New Jersey
Washington Crossing Historic Park,
    Pennsylvania
Valley Forge
Monmouth Battlefield State Park
Convenhoven House
Red Bank Battlefield
Indian King Tavern
Boxwood Hall
Buccleuch Mansion
Von Stueben House
Other Revolutionary War Sites

←

Once in a while, the troops still muster. Here, a reenactment at Jockey
Hollow, Morristown

JOCKEY HOLLOW

The winter of 1779-1780 was the coldest in a century. On December 1, 1779, General George Washington entered Morristown and took up residence at the home of Mrs. Jacob Ford, Jr.

Meanwhile, four miles away at Jockey Hollow, 10,000 men chopped down six hundred acres of oak, walnut and chestnut trees to build hundreds of huts along the slopes of the "hollow". Severe snowstorms hindered their work and delayed the supply of meat and bread they needed to survive. Starvation confronted the army, which also suffered from inadequate clothing, disease and low morale. So terrible was the winter of the second Morristown encampment that many troops finally mutinied.

But the history books only tell you about Valley Forge. Why? Because New Jersey has simply never had a very good public relations man. Not until recently, anyway.

Today there are only four reconstructed huts on the site which is administered by the National Park Service. However, the Visitor's Center at the parking lot area gives full information about the encampment. If you go beyond the main desk you find a mini-theater where an eleven-minute film begins at the touch of a button. The story of typical foot soldiers huddled in a simple hut waiting for the rations and money that took so long in coming is unfolded. After the film, you can move on to the mock-up of the soldiers hut and see the straw beds, muskets and clothing used at the time.

From the Information Center, proceed out the back door to the **Wick Farm** where a Park Service employee is always in residence. The farmhouse was occupied by both the Wick family (owners of the farm that included Jockey Hollow) and General Arthur St. Clair and his aide. A vegetable and herb garden, a well and a horse barn surround the wooden cottage.

Inside the smoky cabin, a Ranger dressed in Colonial garb will be cooking, melting down candles or performing some chore in the main front room. What you learn depends on how talkative this person is. On one trip, when I asked the girl who was tending a pot over the open fire what she was doing, she answered, "Cooking lunch" and that was that. However, during a later visit, I discovered a "soldier" who was completely into his 18th Century role. He told me he was from the Pennsylvania Regulars, he was watching the hut while General St. Clair was out and that the government hadn't paid him in three months. (I assume he was not talking about the Reagan administration.) A tour through the house shows the little bedroom of Tempe Wick, the General's office and bedroom. There are no signs however, to tell you which is which.

From the Wick House proceed to the open slopes called the Pennsylvania line. There the simple huts and some hiking trails await. Summer weekends from 11 to 4 a soldier in period costume performs outdoor duties. Free.

HOURS: 9-5 Daily. May be closed Mon. & Tues. in winter. Closed major holidays.
LOCATION: Take 202 to Tempe Wick Road (south of Morristown). Follow signs.
TELEPHONE: 201-543-4030

WASHINGTON'S HEADQUARTERS, MORRISTOWN

For another look at the details of military life, hie over to the **Ford Mansion** and **Revolutionary War Museum** which is part of the overall National Historic Site called "Washington's Headquarters". It's a short drive away. You must enter through the museum and there you will find all the paraphernalia — surgeon's tools, mess kits, muskets and cleaning rods — that accompanied the troops. The display of 18th Century weaponry is considered one of the best in the country. There are also very graphic dioramas, sketches and audio-visuals that show the poor condition of the ragged army at Jockey Hollow. Some period costumes brighten the museum.

Don't miss the fifteen-minute movie shown periodically in the museum auditorium. A professional film which was shot on location both here and in Jockey Hollow, it contrasts the warmth and food available to officers at the mansion with the hungry, freezing men camped four miles away. A lively ball scene was filmed in the central hall of the Ford Mansion which is right next door to the museum.

The Mansion itself is a solid frame colonial house — by no means a mansion in the modern sense. As you enter the long central hallway you notice how well such halls were suited to the line dances such as the Virginia Reel. The Ford home was offered as headquarters to the General by Mrs. Jacob Ford, Jr., a widow with four children. The Ford family lived in two rooms while Washington and his staff occupied the rest of the house. The furnishings shown are authentic to the period and many are true Ford family pieces. Beds include the canopied master bed used by Washington. Highboys, chest-on-chests, wall maps, and lots of straw mattresses are all to be noted. There are uniformed National Park Service people around to answer questions but there are no guided tours as such unless arranged for groups.

Despite the rigors of the Morristown encampment, the Ford Mansion looks like a warm, homey, yet comparatively elegant abode for the chief of staff. It was here also, on May 10, 1780, that the Marquis de Lafayette was welcomed. He brought news that France would send a second expedition to help. And Alexander Hamilton, at that time Washington's aide-de-camp, used his time in Morristown to court Betsy Schuyler who was staying at the nearby Schuyler-Hamilton House.

HOURS: 9-5 daily. May be closed Mon. & Tues. in winter. Closed major holidays.
ADMISSION: Adults $.50; children and Seniors, free.
DIRECTIONS: Route 287 to Exit 32A to Morris Avenue East. Follow signs for Washington's Headquarters.
TELEPHONE: 201-539-2016

DEY MANSION

A solid Dutch farmhouse built in the early Georgian style, the Dey Mansion was Washington's headquarters for three months during the summer and fall of 1780. Furnishings reflect the status of the Dey family who were quite well-to-do. An unusual feature of this northern house is the separate kitchen. (There is a breezeway between it and the main house for use during the colder months.) According to the guide the separate kitchen was practical for if the place caught on fire it would not take the rest of the house with it!

After an inspection of the well-stocked kitchen, you may tour the house which has two floors of well-kept furnishings and many family portraits. The third floor attic is a museum in itself with a hodge-podge of collectibles that range from colonial antiques to 19th Century ice-skates.

Outside is a very pleasant garden and grape arbor with a few picnic tables placed about. You are so close to the neighboring golf course (for this historic site is part of a county park) that you might get a golf ball in your iced tea. On the right hand side of the house is a small barnyard where a few chickens and rabbits reside. There are also several outbuildings in various states of repair.

HOURS: Tues., Wed., Fri.: 1-4. Sat.: 10-12 & 1-4. Sun.: 10-4
ADMISSION: Adults: $1.00. Under 15, free.
LOCATION: 199 Totowa Rd., Wayne, Passaic County
(part of Preakness Valley Park).
TELEPHONE: 201-696-1776

THE WALLACE HOUSE

Washington's headquarters during the winter encampment at Middlebrook (1778-79) is a two-hundred year old clapboard Colonial now hidden away on the back streets of Somerville. (Well, not hidden, exactly, but you have to look sharp for the sign if you're coming from the north.) Once you discover the back street, you will find that the guide who administers The Wallace House also takes care of the Old Dutch Parsonage across the street. So if you knock and no one answers, wait a while—he might be at the other house. He will usually leave a sign advising you of the fact, if he does cross the street. On busy days there are volunteers who help out.

The headquarters itself is a nine room, solidly built wood structure with wide plank floors that creak curiously under modern weight. Although the furnishings are not those actually used by Washington and his staff, they are all of the period. A four-poster bed with tatted canopy stands in the room where Washington probably slept. There are also campaign trunks and the typical toiletry articles there. The rooms for the aide-de-camp and lieutenants (among them, Alexander Hamilton) are furnished less handsomely with simple trundle beds and straw mattresses.

The dining room does not look large but it is said up to thirty people ate there when General and Mrs. Washington entertained. They must have been awfully crowded. The Wallace House may have been the best home in the area, but the rooms are small and cramped compared to the high, airy drawing rooms at Mount Vernon. One can see why Washington was constantly pining for his old Virginia home. And although Martha spend part of the winter here she did manage to return to her Southern home once or twice. However the house has both a drawing room and a sitting room. The latter was Martha's private preserve.

The winter of 1778-79 was rather mild, much pleasanter than those at Valley Forge and Morristown, and the encampment at Middlebrook was marred by much less disaster. Food, however, was never plentiful, so when the Washingtons entertained, they did so sparsely. Incidentally, Washington paid $1000 to rent this house — the only time he had to pay for his headquarters in New Jersey. Free.

HOURS: Wed.-Fri. 9-12 & 1-6. Sat.: 10-12 & 1-6. Sunday 1-6.
LOCATION: 38 Washington Place, Somerville, Somerset County. One block east of Route 206.
TELEPHONE: 201-725-1015

THE OLD DUTCH PARSONAGE

This house was the home first of Pastor Frelinghuysen, minister of the Dutch Reformed Church. The bricks that built the house were brought over as ballast from Holland. Later it became the home of Rev. Jacob Hardenburgh, who married Frelinghuysen's widow. Hardenburgh was one of the "Fighting Pastors" of the Revolutionary War who condemned the British from the pulpit. He was a frequent host to General and Mrs. Washington when they lived close by during the Middlebrook Encampment. The house has since been moved so it is now across the street.

The parsonage contains several authentic relics and is rather well furnished, with a certain Dutch look. The guide takes you through each room, explains its historic significance and gives a quick history of the Frelinghuysen family. Many of the furnishings, including a 1780 secretary, were donated by this family.

LOCATION, HOURS, ETC.: Same as Wallace House.

ROCKINGHAM

A little beyond the quaint town of Rocky Hill, which in itself looks like it has slept since the Revolution, lies Rockingham. It was here that Washington stayed in 1783 while the Constitution was being hammered out at nearby Nassau Hall in Princeton. Actually both George and Martha stayed here and entertained extensively. It is best known as the house where the "Farewell Address to the Armies" was composed.

A medium-sized colonial with front porch, the house was once part of a fine estate of 360 acres with barns, stables, coachhouse and granary. Now it has been removed from its original site (because of dynamiting in a nearby quarry) and is set a little ways off Route 518 in such a way that it takes a hardy traveller to find it. Not only that, but with its peeling paint and desolate air it hardly looks like the house one sees in pictures. Perhaps it will be repainted by the time you see it.

Well, inside it's better. (You may have to knock several times to get inside during the off season. There are not too many visitors in winter and the guide keeps things locked up.) Of course rooms were never huge in these New Jersey colonials but the ten rooms in Rockingham are good sized. The furniture is handsome. Period pieces include Chippendale sets, burnished bureaus, canopied beds and antique tea services. The Blue Room study where the Farewell Address was composed is left with the ink stand and green cloth still on the table. Free.

HOURS: Wed. - Fri.: 9-12 & 1-6. Sat.: 10-12, 1-6. Sunday: 1-6
LOCATION: Route 518, Rocky Hill, Somerset County
TELEPHONE: 609-921-9935

THE OLD BARRACKS, TRENTON

If you are expecting an old, dilapidated military structure when you hear the name "Old Barracks" you are in for a surprise. Outside, the fieldstone building with its narrow balcony that runs the length of the second story, looks in top-notch condition. The lawns and hedges are a gardener's delight. Not only is the Old Barracks well kept and well administered but the building itself is well laid out and beautifully furnished. From the main room on, you will find china, Chippendale furniture and silver from the Colonial and Federal periods that are as good as any found in the many restored homes in New Jersey.

The Barracks have quite a history. Just before the building was saved from demolition the rooms were being used as a "Home for the Relief of Respectable, Aged and Indigent Widows and Single Women." Before that the building had been chopped up into a

Washington Crossing State park commemorates Washington's famous crossing of the Delaware River on Christmas night, 1776.

The "Old Barracks" in Trenton is well preserved both on the outside and the inside.

Photos: Courtesy N.J. Div. of Tourism

series of private dwellings (hence all those well-furnished rooms). Before that it was a hospital for wounded American soldiers in the Revolutionary War. And before that — well, the famous crossing of the Delaware on Christmas Day by Washington was for the express purpose of surprising the Hessian mercenaries who were sleeping off their Christmas cheer in this self-same barracks.

Originally, the Barracks were built in 1758 during the French and Indian War because American colonists objected to the billeting of British troops in private households. Later, in 1776, the British and Hessian mercenaries used it until the Americans gained control. Then the building went through a series of ups and downs until the Old Barracks Association saved it around 1899. They persuaded the State to help and finally in 1902 the Association ceded their part of the Barracks to the State with the proviso that the Association should control and manage the building forever.

And what a difference that has made. Unlike other State Historic Sites, they don't close down for lunch here, and you can be pretty sure they will be open when they say they're open. The tour guides are knowledgeable and well versed in their speeches. The rooms shown include a replica of a British barracks room with three-tiered bunk beds filled with straw and mannequins busy at soldiers' work. Another room depicts an officer's drawing room while the bedroom features a canopied bed and maple cradle (presumably for accompanying wives and children). Also at the Barracks you can view a magnificent dinner service, mementos of Washington, a collection of firearms (including a blunderbuss and early muskets), and a huge diorama of the Battle of Trenton. Gift shop, too, of course.

HOURS: April - Oct. Daily 10-5; Sunday 1-5. Nov. - March
Daily 10-4:30; Sunday - 1-4:30
ADMISSION: Adults: $.50; Children: $.25
LOCATION: South Willow St. at West Front St., Trenton
TELEPHONE: 609-396-1776

WASHINGTON CROSSING
STATE PARK (N.J.)

This popular park, covering 807 acres that stretch from the banks of the Delaware in Titusville, commemorates the crossing that led to the most important victory of the war's early years. On

Christmas night 1776, General Washington crossed the icy Delaware with 2,400 men, artillery and supplies. The crossing took nine hours and men and officers converged on this spot on the Jersey side. The ensuing surprise attack gave a sweet taste of victory to the discouraged American troops.

Now, at the park, you find a Visitor Center filled with information on the battle, the uniforms and muskets of the times. There are a variety of exhibits and some audio-visuals.

Outside there are open fields for frisbee throwing, a nature center (you must take a rocky road to get there), an open air ampitheater for summer shows and all sorts of picturesque picnic groves. Near the Delaware River there is a monument marking the spot and two historic houses. One of these, the **Ferry Museum** has guided tours.

LOCATION: Routes 29 and 546, Titusville, Mercer County.
HOURS: Park: 9 A.M. to dusk. Visitor Center & Ferry Museum: Summer, Wed. - Sun.: 10-5; Winter: 1-4
TELEPHONE: 609-737-2515

HISTORIC WASHINGTON CROSSING PARK (PA.)

Across the river the site of the embarkation is the focus for a large park that stretches up the Delaware River and includes several sections. In the first section, a modern Visitor's Center offers brochures, a theater for a film about the crossing and tickets for three historical buildings within the park. Two of these buildings are within easy walking distance. The first is the **McKonkey Ferry Inn** where Washington and his staff met and ate just before the crossing. It is fixed up as a travelers inn with tables set with pewter and bar and grill. Quite close to it is the **Durham Boat House** with a reproduction of the famous boats that were used to cross the men. Across the street, **Homewood** is another reconstruction, this time of an 1816 house with fine quality Federal furnishings.

Travelling north you come upon another section of the park which includes a wildflower preserve, the high observation tower on Bowman's Hill and the **Thompson-Neely House** (which is an original structure built of Delaware River ledgestone and looking as authentic as all get out). Tickets for all three historic houses are reasonable and of course you get a guided tour through each. One thing about Pennsylvania, they are very exact about what is a true historic house and what is a replica. One guide even told me it took them twenty years to get New Jersey to stop calling that white clapboard house across the river the McKonkey House.

Lots of picnic pavilions, walking paths and driving roads throughout the park.

> **HOURS:** (Daylight Savings) Grounds 9-8; Buildings Tues. - Sat. 9-5; Sun.: 12-5. (Standard Time) Grounds: 9-4:30. Buildings Tues. - Sat.: 10-4:30. Sun.: 12-4:30.
> **ADMISSION:** Buildings only: Adults $1.00.
> **DIRECTIONS:** Take bridge from Titusville, N.J., drive north on Pa. 32 for other sections of park.
> **TELEPHONE:** 215-493-4076

VALLEY FORGE

It is known as "The Crucible of Victory" because the 10,000 men who emerged from the harsh winter had coalesced into an efficient, well-trained fighting force. The encampment lasted from December 19, 1777, to June 19, 1778. It is now commemorated at this huge 2200 acre park which is so vast you must start with a map or a tour bus.

The Visitor Center, where you can procure both, also offers a slide show and a small museum of Revolutionary swords and military equipment. It is here that you can board the buses (warm weather only). The bus tour which stops at key sites features a taped narration as you go along. Even better, you can rent or buy a tape narration as you drive along yourself. Among the important sites you will pass on the scenic drive are the Memorial Arch, the earthen fortifications, statues of Anthony Wayne and Von Steuben, and of course, the soldier's huts.

When staffing permits, costumed soldiers are at hand to welcome you at **Washington's Headquarters**, the **Isaac Cotts house**, **General Varnum's headquarters** and the soldier's huts. They help to point out the hardships the soldiers endured. A friend's child was properly awed by the sacrifices of the Revolutionary soldiers when he saw one of the simple huts reconstructed here. "They didn't even have portable radios," he told his mother.

For modern day visitors there are picnic grounds, bicycle trails, snack bar and souvenir shop and lots of beautiful scenery. The park is free.

HOURS: Daily except Christmas 8:30-5. For buses: Memorial Day - Labor Day leave every 20 minutes. April, May, Sept., Oct. 3 times daily.

AUTO-TAPE
TOUR: Available April - Oct. from 9-2; tape and player rental: $5.00 (or you can just buy the tape for $5.00 and keep it)

TELEPHONE: 215-783-7700

LOCATION: Visitor Center — Junction of PA 23 & 363, Valley Forge, PA

MONMOUTH BATTLEFIELD STATE PARK

Although it was not a complete victory, still the Battle of Monmouth proved that American troops, honed by the winter at Valley Forge, could hold their own against British soldiers. Today's park was the scene of a hot day's battle with a general who ordered a retreat (and was later reprimanded by Washington) and a lady named Molly "Pitcher," who became a heroine according to legend.

The fields of close-cropped rolling hills are empty at Monmouth Battlefield, but a large new Visitor's Center gives you the necessary information. Three audio-visual screens offer the story of the battle from the night before to the day after. And a relief map set with tiny lights displays the position of the opposing forces. Press a button and the lights move and "shoot" each other to the sound of rifle fire on the accompanying audio track. So much for the show.

There is a small gift shop in the Center where you can also pick up a map of the battlefield and other historic sites. Also a refreshment counter and a picnic area are part of the building. If you drive around following the map, you will find the **Craig House** (which may or may not be open) where the wounded were cared for; **Tennant Church**, a good-looking shake-sided Colonial building which was close to the battle; and **Molly Pitcher's well**. Free.

HOURS: Daily, 9-4. Longer hours in summer.

LOCATION: Route 9 to Route 33, just west of Freehold, Monmouth County

TELEPHONE: 201-462-9619

COVENHOVEN HOUSE

One of the four historic houses administered by the Monmouth County Historical Association, it is significant for its role in the Battle of Monmouth. Henry Clinton, commander of the British troops at the battle, stayed at the home from Friday, June 26 until Sunday, June 28, 1778. After the battle, he and his troops left Freehold and returned to New York.

The main section of the home is in Georgian style and is furnished according to a 1790 inventory of William A. Covenhoven, the well-to-do farmer who owned the property.

HOURS: June - October: Sat., 10-4; Sun.: 1-4
ADMISSION: Adults: $1.00; Seniors: $.75; Children: $.50; under 6 free
LOCATION: 150 West Main Street, Freehold
TELEPHONE: 201-462-1466

RED BANK BATTLEFIELD

A small but decisive battle to defend Fort Mercer took place here on October 19, 1777. The Hessian army received many casualties at the hands of the American Army, which, up until this point had known mostly defeat. Since the Fort guarded the Delaware River and prevented British ships from entering occupied Philadelphia, the freedom of Fort Mercer was quite important. Although British ships eventually went through, the Red Bank victory helped France to decide to join America in her fight against the British. The site is not to be confused with the town of Red Bank in Monmouth County on the ocean side of New Jersey. The park contains old cannons and an historic house that is open for tours when guides are available (usually Memorial Day to Labor Day). Picnic areas. Free.

HOURS: Daily, 9-6
LOCATION: 100 Hessian Ave., National Park, Gloucester County
TELEPHONE: 609-845-4318

INDIAN KING TAVERN

Set in the little town of Haddonfield, which looks as if it stepped out of the 18th Century, this public house, or tavern, was the site of frequent meetings of the New Jersey State Legislature during the

Revolutionary War. Among the rooms the guide shows off are the colonial kitchen, the toy room, and the bedroom where Dolly Madison slept. (Her uncle was a one-time owner of the tavern). Groups by appointment only. Children under 12 must be accompanied by adults. Because there is ongoing restoration to the building it is best to call first before visiting. A State Historic Site. Free.

HOURS: Wed. - Fri.: 9-11:30 & 1-5:30. Sat.: 10-11:30 & 1-5. Sun.: 1-5:30.
LOCATION: 233 Kings Highway, Haddonfield, Camden County.
TELEPHONE: 609-429-6792

BOXWOOD HALL

Also known as the Boudinot Mansion, this very nicely furnished colonial house is not far from the main drag in Elizabeth. Built in 1750, it was the home during the Revolution of Elias Boudinot, president of the Continental Congress. George Washington had lunch here on the day he embarked for New York and his inauguration as President. House furnishings include both colonial and empire style. State Historic Site. Free.

HOURS: Wed. - Fri. 9-12 & 1-6. Sat.: 10-12 & 1-6. Sun.: 1-6.
LOCATION: 1073 East Jersey St., Elizabeth.
TELEPHONE: 201-648-4540

BUCCLEUCH MANSION

A handsome Georgian mansion in various states of repair, the house is set inside of Buccleuch Park on one of those treelined streets that is practically part of Rutgers Campus in New Brunswick. Originally built in 1739, White House Farm, as it was then known, was sold to an English Army officer in 1774.

The house was confiscated by the Americans in 1776, but by December the British troops re-occupied New Brunswick. The bannisters still retain the marks of soldier's musket barrels from the time of this occupation, which lasted until 1777. After the war, Colonel Charles Stewart, Commissary General of the Revolutionary Army, became the owner. At this time White House Farm was visited by Washington, Hancock and Alexander Hamilton, who all loved the setting.

Much of Buccleuch Mansion's furnishings today are of 19th century origin. Of particular note is the striking wallpaper in both the downstairs and upstairs hallways. Rooms include a Victorian parlour and a drawing rooms with Queen Anne pieces. You can also inspect the bedrooms (including the one where Washington slept), a toy room, a craft room with spinning wheel, and an attic filled with assorted "significa," including side-saddles, hoops for hoopskirts and two centuries of whatnots. Free. (Donations accepted).

HOURS: Last Sun. in May thru Last Sun. in Oct.; Sat. & Sun. 3-5 PM. Group tours by appointment.
LOCATION: Easton Ave. to Buccleuch Park, New Brunswick, Middlesex County
TELEPHONE: 201-846-1063

VON STEUBEN HOUSE

A Dutch Colonial home built in 1695 and further added to in 1752. The house was confiscated by the Americans during the Revolutionary War because the owners (the Zabriskie Family) were loyal to the British crown. It was later presented to Baron Von Steuben for his aid during the war. Notice the colonial furnishings with emphasis on local craftsmen. Some fine specimens include a New Brunswick kas, a Hudson Valley kas, an old settle, etc. The upstairs garret is maintained as a museum by the Bergen County Historical Society and includes Indian artifacts, dolls, toys and such. Free.

HOURS: Wed. - Sat. 10-12 & 1-5; Sun. 2-5
LOCATION: Main Street, River Edge, Bergen County (take River Edge exit from Route 4)
TELEPHONE: 201-487-1739

OTHER REVOLUTIONARY WAR SITES

Among the many other historic sites and buildings associated with the Revolutionary War are:

PRINCETON BATTLEFIELD STATE PARK: A short, decisive battle was fought here on January 3, 1777 just a week after the famous crossing of the Delaware. General Hugh Mercer was mortally wounded during this battle. Free. *Hours:* 9 AM to dusk. *Location:* Mercer St., Princeton.

BRANDYWINE BATTLEFIELD STATE PARK: This battle was a defeat for Washington's forces. It took place on September 11, 1777, and is commemorated by dioramas and audio-visuals at the Visitor's Center. There are also two historic houses within the park. One was Washington's Headquarters and the other was used by the Marquis de Lafayette. Free. *Hours:* Daily May 30 -Labor Day. Weekends thereafter. *Location:* Route 1, Chadds Ford, Pennsylvania. *Telephone:* 215-459-3342

DRAKE HOUSE: During the battle of the Watchung Mountains, Washington used this house as his command headquarters. Although there is a colonial bedroom where he is supposed to have rested, the house was later remodeled. It now reflects the Empire and Victorian styles as well as the basic colonial. Closed summers. *Hours:* Wed. & Sun.: 2-5 PM *Admission:* $.50 *Location:* 602 West Front St., Plainfield, Union County. *Telephone:* 201-755-5831

FORT LEE PARK: View of the Hudson and reconstructed gun batteries on the site of the old fort which was built to defend the river against invasion. Only 33 acres here, but there are guides and a Visitor Center with museum, maps, audio-visuals, etc. Observation tower gives view of George Washington Bridge. Free. *Hours:* March - Dec. Wed. - Sun.: 9:30-5 (for Visitor Center). *Location:* Hudson Terrace, Fort Lee, Bergen County. *Telephone:* 201-461-3956

HANCOCK HOUSE: Scene of massacre of American troops by attacking British Rangers. 1734 house has period furnishings. Free. *Hours:* Wed. - Fri.: 9-12 & 1-6, Sat.: 10-12 & 1-6. Sun.: 1-6. *Location:* Route 49, 5 miles south of Salem, Salem County. *Telephone:* 609-935-4373

CANNONBALL HOUSE: Named for the cannonball that struck it during the Battle of Springfield, 1780. Information and mementos of the battle are present. *Hours:* Sun. 2-4, Sept. - June. *Admission:* $.25. *Location:* 124 Morris Ave., Springfield, Union County. *Telephone:* 201-467-3580

SCHUYLER-HAMILTON HOUSE: Colonial home where Alexander Hamilton courted Betsey Schuyler. *Hours:* Tues. & Sun. 2-5 PM *Admission:* Adults: $.50, Children under 12, free. *Location:* 5 Olyphant Place, Morristown, Morris County. *Telephone:* 201-267-4009

See Also: *"Nassau Hall," "Morven," Independence Hall* and several of the colonial homes mentioned in the chapter on "Restored Villages and Homes."

HOMES OF
THE
RICH AND FAMOUS

Photo: Courtesy Newark Museum

In This Chapter You Will Find:

Nemours
Hyde Park
The Vanderbilt Mansion
Edison Labs — Glenmont
Speedwell Village
Grover Cleveland Birthplace
Ballantine House
Lambert Castle
Ringwood Manor
Skylands
Lyndhurst
Sunnyside
Boscobel
Macculloch Hall
Morven
Bainbridge House
William Trent House
Walt Whitman House
Pennsbury Manor

←———

Dining room of the Beer Barons: Ballantine House, Newark

NEMOURS

The fabulous homes of the super-rich are America's equivalent of the palaces and castles of Europe. And no home is more palatial than Nemours, the former residence of Alfred I. DuPont. Located outside Wilmington in the increasingly popular Brandywine Valley area, Nemours is the latest in a series of DuPont Estates now open to the public.

The mansion, built in 1909, is a modified Louis XVI French chateau. The landscaped gardens are in the French formal style and include marble statues, cascading fountains and a series of terraces and stairways to please the eye. In fact, the hand of Louis XVI seems to lie everywhere in Nemours — a tribute as much to the Gallic origins of the DuPonts as to the possibility that American millionaires in 1910 must have known the era of conspicuous consumption was about to end. A few years later the income tax and World War I helped destroy any notion of an American aristocracy. Like the French kings before them, the DuPonts may have realized this was the last chance to flaunt their riches.

There was also Alfred's desire to outdo his cousin Pierre's Longwood Gardens. A schism had developed in the family over Alfred's divorce from his first wife. A battle over the family fortune, alienated children, a mad love affair, a remarriage — this is the stuff that best-selling novels are made of. I heard about it on the tour bus going down; at Nemours they don't breathe a word of scandal. And actually it was the third wife — a beautiful young woman whose portrait enhances many of the rooms — who was mistress at Nemours.

Once you enter the chateau, you are led by a tour guide into a home of vast elegance. The gold and white dining room boasts ornate moldings on walls and ceilings, Rococco style paintings and a chandelier worthy of the Phantom of the Opera. The reception room, living room and other public rooms are equally fabulous with inlaid ceilings, marble tiled floors, rich oriental rugs and carved walls. Furniture includes both genuine antiques like George Washington's chair and fine copies of Louis XVI furnishings.

You rarely see the kitchens of "great homes" but at Nemours there's a downstairs tour of the restaurant-sized cooking area with its empty pantry and huge pots. A dumbwaiter is set up with a breakfast tray of Spode china as if ready to be sent up to the bedroom of Mrs. DuPont. Also, downstairs is the bowling alley (no, it's not automatic, they used real pin boys), the billiard room (with a table the size of a bowling alley) and the furnace room (ingeniously set up by Alfred himself, who was an engineer).

The second floor contains the bedrooms of husband, wife, and guests. Mrs. DuPont's room opens through French doors to a large balcony which offers a perfect view of the formal gardens below.

The guides who escorted us through had an almost proprietary air about Nemours. When a man asked about the cost of all this, the guide sniffed, "We don't discuss money here." And I made the social gaffe of mentioning the second wife. I was told sternly that the only Mrs. DuPont mentioned at Nemours was the third Mrs. DuPont. However, our group was treated to orange juice on the terrace, a tray of rosebuds and a free packet of postcards.

After the house tour you may either board a mini-bus for a tour of the gardens or walk around yourself. Fountains and pools, colonnades and balustrades, marble Cupids and Dianas, velvet lawns and clipped hedges create a mini-Versailles here.

Nemours doesn't exactly admit hordes of people, only 19 to a tour (they expand for bus groups) and only four tours a day. Reservations are suggested for individuals and required for groups. No children under 16. No picture-taking inside the mansion. And mind your manners — this here is DuPont territory!

> **HOURS:** May - Nov.: Tues. - Sat.: tours at 9, 11, 1 & 3. Sunday tours: 11, 1 & 3
> **ADMISSION:** $4.00
> **LOCATION:** Rockland Road (inside Alfred I. DuPont Institute) Wilmington, Delaware
> **TELEPHONE:** 302-573-3333 or write: Reservations Office, Nemours Foundation, P.O. Box 109, Wilmington, Delaware 19899

HYDE PARK

For people who lived under Franklin Delano Roosevelt's administration there is either a deep love for the man who dominated the White House from 1932 to 1945 — or an abiding hatred. As President during the great Depression and World War II, Roosevelt was both blamed and praised for cataclysmic changes in American life. For those who are too young to remember, the excellent television series "Franklin and Eleanor" has brought renewed interest in the Roosevelt family and in the family home, Hyde Park.

Now a National Historic Site, the Hyde Park complex consists of the family home, the beautiful grounds on a high, green hill overlooking a clean Hudson River and the **Roosevelt Library and Museum.** The admission price also includes entrance to the *Vanderbilt Mansion* two miles up the road, an excellent example of the millionaire's palaces of the Gilded Age.

Starting at the Roosevelt home, you enter from a parking lot which is lined with apple trees still bearing fruit. The white, classically proportioned country house is not overly large and can accomodate only 50 people at a time. However, there is an easy traffic flow since you do not have to wait for a tour guide to take you through. Instead, you may move about as you like, using the cassette tape recording as your guide. The cassette was recorded by Eleanor Roosevelt and gives you an interesting insight into family life in the inimitable accents of that voice.

Upon entering the main hall you see the heavy furnishings that characterized a country home of the 1890's. Some of the furniture here was damaged by the fire that hit in January, 1982. Further on, the pretty Dresden Room, is brightened by the colorful floral drapes and upholstery picked out by Sara Roosevelt in 1939 shortly before the King and Queen of England visited. The whole house, in fact, shows much more the influence of Franklin's mother, Sara, than of his wife.

Upstairs the boyhood bedroom and FDR's bedroom contain the memorabilia we expect. Favorite pictures, the leash and blanket of the Scottie (Fala) on his own chair, and books and magazines that were scattered there in March, 1945, are still present in Roosevelt's room.

Next to the home is the FDR Library. The museum section contains gifts from foreign rulers, cartoons, photographs, and a passing picture of both the Depression and World War II. Special exhibits on both Franklin and Eleanor are here plus the wooden wheelchair Roosevelt used. Outside on the quiet green lawn next to the rose garden are the graves of both FDR and Eleanor.

HOURS, ETC.: See Vanderbilt Mansion.

VANDERBILT MANSION

If the Roosevelt home radiates quiet wealth, the Vanderbilt Mansion exudes conspicuous consumption. A marble palace in the style of the Italian Renaissance, it is set on large estate grounds where swans paddle about on a meandering stream. Inside, the

Mansion's furnishings are closer to French Rococco than Italian Renaissance. The huge marble reception hall opens to both the dining room and drawing room. The dining room, which seated 30, and the beautifully furnished drawing room were the scene of gala balls. A small side room called the Gold Room was the gathering place for guests to sip sherry before dinner. This room attracts tourists to its gold leaf decoration. The ceiling painting depicts scantily clad maidens floating in the azure sky.

If the downstairs chairs all look like thrones, then the upstairs bedrooms of Mr. and Mrs. Vanderbilt were certainly fit for a king and queen. Walls of embroidered silk and a bed with a marble gate around it are features copied from a French queen's bedroom to outfit the one Mrs. Vanderbilt used. As for Frederick's room — he merely had a canopy with a crown above his bed and true Flemish tapestries hanging on the walls. It all goes to show what you could do if you had money in the pre-income tax days.

The mansion with its marble and finely turned Circassian walnut and the quiet, heavily treed grounds all help to recreate the splendor of a bygone era. No guided tours, by the way, but National Park Service personnel give informal talks at specific times. Check at Visitor's Center where you can also pick up brochures and buy postcards.

> **HOURS:** Daily 9-4:30. Closed major holidays.
> **ADMISSION:** (For both houses): Adults: $1.50; Children, Seniors: Free
> **LOCATION:** Hyde Park, N.Y. Take Garden State Parkway to N.Y. Thruway to Exit 18. Cross Mid-Hudson Bridge, then Route 9N for 7 miles. Follow signs for either house.
> **TELEPHONE:** 914-229-9115

THE EDISON LABS

For many area schools a trip to the Edison Labs is *de rigeur* around the 4th or 5th grade. Therefore parents get the idea that this is strictly a children's tour. So while troops of camera-toting Japanese and Germans tramp through the facilities at West Orange, there are still local residents who have never set foot inside the laboratory where Edison worked for 44 years.

Indeed, if my husband, the scientist, hadn't dragged me there when we first moved to the Garden State, I never would have troubled to go. The second time around, it was myself, under the influence of an Architectural History course, who insisted we see *Glenmont*, Edison's elegant Victorian home that is an oft neglected part of the tour. After all, where else can you find a perfectly intact sample of Haute Victoriana for a mere fifty cents?

Actually, both buildings comprise the **Edison National Historic Site**. Headquarters are on Main Street and Lakeside Avenue in a rather busy area of West Orange. You buy the tickets there, make your reservations for the Glenmont tour (which is given on the hour in Llewellyn Park a few blocks away) and begin your tour of the Labs. All tours are guided by National Park Service personnel. Our particular guide was quite personable although her talk seemed geared to ten-to-twelve year olds. (Probably the influence of all those school groups passing through.)

First stop: The phonograph room which displayed various models of Edison's prized invention. Naturally the group was treated to audio effects — from Edison's voice reciting "Mary Had A Little Lamb" in tinfoil to a 1922 comedy routine about King Tut recorded on an inch-thick wooden record.

From audio, one goes to visual. In the next room we watched the first feature motion picture — "The Great Train Robbery." A few years ago the National Park Service showed this movie in the *Black Maria* (a replica of the original tarpaper studio). But in order to accommodate the swelling number of tourists, the film is now shown in a large central room, along with a film about Edison. "The Great Train Robbery," by the way, is of interest not only because it is the first Western. This early 1900's silent picture was filmed locally using the talents of laboratory workers and the trains of the Erie Lackawanna. The actors may have passed on to the Great Beyond, but I believe the passenger cars are still traversing the Conrail tracks. You may even recognize a few of them.

The chemical labs, machine shop and junk storage bins are also part of the extensive one and a half hour tour. Grand finale is the golden oak library where Edison's desk, cot and 10,000 volumes still stand. Even the six-foot wall clock remains stopped at 3:27 — the time on October 18, 1931, when Edison died.

HOURS: 9-5 Daily. May be closed Mon. - Tues. in winter.
ADMISSION: Age 16-62: 50¢; Otherwise, free.
LOCATION: Main St. & Lakeside Ave., West Orange, Essex County
TELEPHONE: 201-736-0550

Photo: Courtesy N.J. Div. of Tourism

Glenmont, the home of Thomas Edison, lies in Llewellyn Park, a private "suburb" within West Orange. The house was purchased complete with the furnishings of the former owner, because Edison did not want to waste time with interior decoration.

GLENMONT

One must get in the car and drive to Llewellyn Park, a secluded section of town only minutes away where the Edison family home, Glenmont, stands. Since tours of this elegant home, set on sweeping laws, are given only once a hour, it's best to be on time — but not too early. The guide doesn't open the door until the exact time of the tour, and there's no place to stand but outside, whatever the weather.

The house itself is very warm. It is filled with carved oak woodwork, oriental rugs, wild animal skins, stained glass windows and a sunny Conservatory worthy of an English manor house. One finds rich fabrics and tile floors, pianos, pipe organs and paintings, and of course a gentleman's library filled with leather-bound tomes. The upstairs bedrooms are simpler although all beds seem to be of the massive six-foot headboard variety.

The guard carries a tape recorded tour narrated by Edison's daughter. It is personal and anecdotal and makes the tour much more meaningful. After the house tour, one may visit the greenhouse, potting shed and other out-buildings on this 13½ acre estate. It is a pleasant glimpse not only of a famous man's home, but of an unhurried, elegant era.

HOURS: Wed. - Sun. 12-4. Tours are on the hour. Get tickets at the Edison Labs main office.

SPEEDWELL VILLAGE

Every 19th Century technological breakthrough led to further inventions. And Speedwell Village in Morristown, is the scene of one of the most important American achievements. It was here that Samuel Morse and Alfred Vail spent years perfecting the electro-magnetic telegraph. And that invention gave rise to the later inventions of radio, television and more. Perhaps some inventor today will find inspiration from the exhibits at Speedwell Village. School children and adults should enjoy it anyway.

One thing you learn from a visit to this green and pleasant compound: you do not have to be a scientist to be an inventor. Samuel Morse was a portrait painter by profession. At the *Vail House* (the main building of the complex) you can see the portraits Morse painted of the senior Mr. and Mrs. Vail. These were painted in 1837 when the elder Vails were becoming restless with their son and non-paying sometime guest. The invention was taking too long to pay off. Morse's gift was in the way of a consolation prize.

The original Vail money came from their Iron Works. Many of the buildings are devoted to artifacts concerning the making and molding of iron machinery. In the *Homestead Carriage House* there is a collection of wooden patterns. The wet sand molds formed by these patterns were used to create the iron gears, waterwheels and parts for locomotives that were the main industry here. The foundry was best known for its early steam engines. In fact, the steam engine for the first trans-Atlantic steamship was built here.

At the *1849 Carriage House* you will find a one-horse open sleigh (without the horse, of course) and a number of butter churns on permanent display. *The Granary* displays hand-crafted wooden farm tools and an exhibit of 19th Century ice harvesting equipment. And the Vail House itself is a fine example of a comfortable mid-19th Century home.

But it is at the *Factory*, originally built for cotton weaving, that you will find the most information about the telegraph. Vail and Morse held the first public demonstration of this new wonder here in 1838. An exhibit of documents, models and instruments illustrates the invention and development of the telegraph. A slide presentation tells you the story if you just push the button next to the screen.

The story, by the way, is that Alfred Vail, a student of the ministry at NYU, came back to visit his Alma Mater and saw Fine Arts Professor Samuel Morse demonstrate the electro-magnetic invention. Alfred became entranced and offered Morse space and money (which came from his father and brother) to perfect the telegraph. Vail became Morse's junior partner, but by prior agreement he received very little credit and no share of the future earnings of the Western Union Company.

Speedwell Village is situated on an old homestead of the Vail family across from a picturesque dam where a Vail factory once stood. Six buildings are presently open to the public. There are tables for picnicking, too.

HOURS: Winter by appointment only. April - Oct.: Weekends, 1-5. May - Sept.: Thurs., Fri.: 12-4. Weekends: 1-5.
ADMISSION: Adults: $1.00; Children: 50¢
LOCATION: Route 202 (Speedwell Ave.) at Cory Road, one mile north of Morristown Green, Morris County.
TELEPHONE: 201-540-0211

GROVER CLEVELAND BIRTHPLACE

Grover Cleveland, the only United States president to be born in New Jersey, spent his first year in this pleasant Manse. The clapboard house was built in 1832 for the pastor of the First Presbyterian Society. Two years later, Reverend Richard F. Cleveland obtained that position. Grover was born in 1837, but by the following year the pastor had retired and moved his family to Buffalo.

The house, which is a State Historic Site, therefore boasts a melange of furniture. The open hearth kitchen reflects the earlier 1830 period when life in the country was still fairly simple. However, a number of later pieces from Cleveland's presidency reflect the richer, more ornate world of the 1880's. A large chair and rocker from the White House term plus several other pieces show both Cleveland's girth and his station in life.

The caretaker of the Manse is happy to act as guide and to point out the photographs, medals, sheet music, etc. that have been collected about Cleveland. A portrait of Mrs. Cleveland, a beautiful young woman whom he married when she was 21 and he 49, adorns the house and the guide bubbles with anecdotes about her. No heavy history here. No talk of Pullman strikes and gold panics and oppressed workers. What you learn is good Presidential gossip. Frances was Grover's ward and she turned down his marriage proposal several times before she finally said yes; she was the youngest First Lady ever; their first baby, Ruth, became the namesake of a still popular candy bar, etc., etc.

After his second term (Adlai Stevenson was his Vice-President) Cleveland retired to Princeton. He became friends with Woodrow Wilson, then President of the University. They are both buried, incidentally, in the Princeton Cemetary.

All the downstairs rooms of the "Old Manse" are open to the public and include the well-filled living room; a bedroom with high-backed bed, cradle and quilts; a den with lots of memorabilia and a roll-top desk; and the earlier, pre-Victorian kitchen. My companion, herself the daughter of a minister, was impressed with the house as a pastor's residence. So was the original congregation that built it in 1832 and thought the construction price of $1490 a little steep. The house, by the way, is set on a busy street in Caldwell and is easy to miss since it's not really very large despite its phenomenal 1832 price. Free.

HOURS: Wed.-Fri.: 9-12 & 1-6; Sat. 10-12 & 1-5; Sunday 1-6
LOCATION: 207 Bloomfield Ave., Caldwell, Essex County
TELEPHONE: 201-226-1810

THE BALLANTINE HOUSE

One of the pleasures of visiting the Newark Museum is the presence of the Ballantine House right next door. You enter this opulent late Victorian townhouse from an interior passageway in the museum proper. The house was restored to its original lustre only a few years ago. And while only the first floor is open to the public and you cannot go into the rooms, you can see perfectly through the glass walls and you can enter partially. It is a marvelous job of restoration with the colors brighter and the furniture cleaner than it probably ever was in its heyday.

On the way in, you read about the Ballantines, a Scotch family who rose from poor immigrants to wealthy beer barons within a span of two generations. Since a townhouse on Washington Park was the sure sign of success in Newark, John Ballantine commissioned this spacious, seventeen-room, three-story, Renaissance-Revival house to be built in the mid 1880's.

In the High Victorian period the term "interior decoration" was taken literally and every inch of space is covered, plastered, panelled, draped, ensconced or otherwised prettified. The dining room, for instance, features oak and cherry parquet floors, mahogany woodwork, a ceiling of molded papiermache panels between painted plaster beams and walls of leather-looking paper. Add to that a brick and wood fireplace, small stained glass windows, tapestried chairs and table sparkling with white linen and you get a scene of solid bourgeois luxury that was meant to impress the guests.

Other rooms on view are the rich, red-toned library, the delicate French-style drawing room and the somber reception room. The large hallway where you walk also serves to show off special exhibits of Tiffany glassware or Belleek ceramics. And at Christmas time, a tree full of ornaments and holly decorations are added to this already richly decorated home. A magnificent stained glass window with its rising sun presides over the stairwell leading to the second floor. The Ballantine House provides not only insights into Victorian highstyle living but an understanding of why later generations opted for bare, modern, unadorned lines in rebellion against all this decoration. Free.

HOURS: 12-5 PM daily
LOCATION: (Enter through Newark Museum) 49 Washington Street, Newark
TELEPHONE: 201-733-6600

LAMBERT CASTLE

Situated high on a bluff in the Garrett Mountain Reservation overlooking Paterson, Lambert Castle is more impressive from the outside than from within. Built by silk manufacturer Catholina Lambert in the heyday of 19th Century opulence, it appears as a brownstone Medieval castle with rounded towers and crenelated turrets — just perfect for longbow archers to repel the invading hordes.

However, it was not the invading hordes that undid Lambert, but the silk strike of 1913 together with a decline in the American silk trade. Bankruptcy loomed and many of Lambert's prize possessions — European paintings and fine furnishings — were sold to pay debtors. He retained the house, though, until his death in 1923.

The view from Lambert Castle is spectacular, encompassing both the city of Paterson with its many church domes and spires and the mountains beyond. But once inside the Castle you find that only the first floor is open to the public and only a handful of opulent furnishings remain. The place is run by the *Passaic County Historical Society* and is half museum, half historic house. The ballroom has been cut down in size because a new ceiling now covers the high-domed original. There are photographs showing how the home once looked, plus an interesting 13-foot clock in the shape of a woman, a giant walnut sideboard and a stained glass window. But not much else to remind you of the grand past. There is also the everything-but-the-kitchen-sink historical museum memorabilia here — somebody's collection of spoons (including what must be the largest tablespoon in the world), pictures of the Great Falls, details on famous sons of Paterson and so forth. There are some plans afoot to make further restorations of the Castle.

HOURS: Wed. - Sun. 1-4 (for museum).
ADMISSION: Adults: 50¢. Children free.
LOCATION: Valley Road. Garrett Mountain Reservation, Paterson, Passaic County.
TELEPHONE: 201-345-6900

RINGWOOD MANOR

If they ever film a Chekhov play in New Jersey, Ringwood Manor would make the perfect setting. This rambling manor-house set on a rise overlooking a small lake where ducks paddle about is a prime example of the Victorian country house. Actually the house was originally the residence of Martin Ryerson an ironmaster and relics of the old iron forge days still dot the landscape. Short cannons and iron chains are placed about at intervals.

But it is the expanded manor with a porte-cochere design by Stanford White, that gives Ringwood its high Victorian look. As the country home first of Peter Cooper, the industrialist and philanthropist who founded not only Cooper Union but the short-lived Greenback Party as well, and then of his son-in-law Abram S. Hewitt, Ringwood became a pleasant haven filled with antiques, and cottage furniture. Approximately 30 rooms are open to the public (the house contains well over 50) and bedrooms with lace curtains, parlors filled with paintings, heavy oak stairways and bronze chandeliers create a pleasant ambience. The walls are also filled with mementos of the Cooper-Hewitt family: newspaper articles and cartoons on politics both national and local, for Peter Cooper ran for President when he was 85, and Hewitt was Mayor of New York.

Outside on the grassy lawn and beyond, visitors picnic or meander around the wide grounds with its gardens and play-grounds. The manor is in one corner of a huge state park high in the Ramapo mountains. Each section of the park has its own toll gate and parking fee ($1 weekdays, $2 weekends). While Shepherd's Lake is recreational and therefore the most popular area, another historic section of *Ringwood Manor State Park* is:

SKYLANDS

A 44-room mansion in the Jacobean style which looks like an English castle. No furnishings inside but there are handsome carvings on the walls, the ceilings and the fireplace. Skylands is best known for its gardens (see Garden section) but it is also the scene of weddings for brides who like a touch of class in their nuptials. Tours are given on the first floor of Skylands during the summer season.

> **HOURS:** Park - daily. MANOR HOUSES: Memorial Day - Labor Day: 10-4 Tues. - Fri. (Weekends: 10-4:30)
> **ADMISSION:** Parking Fees $1 weekday, $2 weekend each section, during warm weather
> **LOCATION:** Route 17 past N.Y. State line to Sloatsburg Road
> **TELEPHONE:** 201-962-7031 or 7047

LYNDHURST

Just a few minutes south of the Tappan Zee Bridge and run by the National Trust for Historic Preservation, this Gothic "castle" was the summer home of Jay Gould. The crystal greenhouses were once the foremost indoor gardens in America although they are now empty. The house, with its turreted towers and manicured lawn is often used in commercials and advertisements as an example of the good life.

Visitors are taken through the home by a tour guide and are shown, among other things: an ornate dining room with enough carved woodwork to fill a Gothic church; the butler's pantry which reminds one of the "Upstairs, Downstairs" days when people really had butlers; and the huge drawing room with its many landscape paintings, its stained glass windows and view of the Hudson. Much of the interior is wood or plaster painted to look like stone to enhance the Medieval effect. This is not unusual in homes built in the Gothic Revival style, although it seems to disappoint many tour groups who expect more of Jay Gould.

HOURS: Because of severe cuts in funding, hours are down. Call first.
ADMISSION: Adults: $3.00; Seniors & students: $2.00
LOCATION: U.S. Route 9, Tarrytown, N.Y., ¼ mile south of Tappan Zee Bridge
TELEPHONE: 914-631-0313

SUNNYSIDE

Home of Washington Irving, America's first internationally famous author. Built in a whimsical manner to suit Irving's individual taste, the early 19th Century house is a cross between the Dutch and the quaint. It is built on the banks of the Hudson with lovely grounds, swan ponds and a Visitor's Center where a film on the *Sleepy Hollow Restorations* (of which this is one) is shown. Guided tours only. Because the rooms and hallways are small, and the tour takes time, there are long lines here on summer weekends. Best to go during the week. Sleepy Hollow Church and graveyard are nearby.

DIRECTIONS: Take Tappan Zee Bridge to New York, then Route 9 south to Sunnyside Lane.
ADMISSION: Adults: $4.00; Seniors: $2.50; Children under 6, free.
HOURS: 10-5 Daily
TELEPHONE: 914-631-8200

BOSCOBEL

A stately Federal mansion set on the banks of the Hudson River (it was moved 15 miles from its original location), Boscobel was built by Morris Dyckman in 1808. The house is completely restored and refurbished (in fact it was refurbished twice!) and reflects an authenticity of period.

A large central hall, sweeping stairway, patterned wallpaper, Duncan Phyfe furniture, china, glass, silver and a bevy of whale oil lamps reflect an era of early and gracious wealth. The wide lawns, the rose garden and the view of West Point across the river all add to the ambience of quiet gentility. Guides take you through the home, but you may peruse the outdoor scenery on your own. A small gift shop is located in a separate building.

      HOURS: Daily except Tues. Closed Jan. & Feb. Tours: 10-3:30
                         Closed major holidays
ADMISSION: Adults: $4.00; Children 6-14: $2.00; under 6, free
 LOCATION: Garrison, N.Y. on Route 9D, 8 miles north of Bear Mt.
                         Bridge
TELEPHONE: 914-265-3638

MACCULLOCH HALL

Unfortunately, this 1808 Federal structure has very limited public hours, because the furnishings within are quite handsome. Oriental rugs throughout, huge Waterford crystal chandeliers brought over from the millionaire Twombly estate (now Fairleigh Dickinson campus), and an original portrait of Washington by Rembrandt Peale are among the eclectic collection of the mansion's last owner.

There is no attempt to furnish each room according to a specific period, but you will see quality cupboards, china, and crystal of the 18th and 19th century throughout the house.

Macculloch Hall also houses two small rooms dedicated to **Thomas Nast,** the famous cartoonist whose vitriolic cartoons helped to topple the corrupt Boss Tweed regime. Nast was a Morristown resident (his home is practically across the street, but privately owned) whose drawings became classics. His depiction of Santa Claus is the one we now use as the standard and he also created the donkey and elephant as symbols of the two political parties. The Nast room includes cartoons, paintings, drawings and awards.

The house is shown by guided tour (allow a half-an-hour at least) but you may wander through the pleasant garden by yourself.

HOURS: April - Nov. Sun. only 2-4:30 PM
ADMISSION: Adults: $1.00; Students over 12 & Seniors: 50¢
LOCATION: 45 Macculloch Ave., Morristown, Morris County. (2 blocks west of South St.)
TELEPHONE: 201-538-2404

MORVEN

Until December 1981, this lovely Georgian mansion was the official home of New Jersey's governor. Now that Drumthwacket has taken over that honor, Morven will be administered by the *N.J. Historical Society* as an historic house and possibly a museum.

Morven is not really a large house and one feels that previous governors must have had trouble accomodating guests here. The dining room is only of moderate size and one cannot imagine large state dinners here. That is probably why the surrounding five acres with those verandas and gardens were often used for summer parties.

Furnishings in the brightly hued living room and elsewhere are either authentic or period pieces donated over the years. The Stockton family, whose portraits dominate Morven, owe this grand colonial house to Richard Stockton the Elder who began building it in 1701. His grandson, known as Richard the Signer (because he signed the Declaration of Independence) and his wife Annis, named the residence Morven. Morven was the name of the home of King Fingal, a character in the tremendously popular, and absolutely fake, "The Lays of Ossian."

In 1777, General Cornwallis seized Morven, used it as his headquarters, then looted and burned it. In 1783, Elias Boudinet, a Stockton brother-in-law used it as his residence. It was here that American leaders came to celebrate the signing of the Peace Treaty with Britain.

Burned twice, enlarged over the years, the house was finally rehabilitated in 1955 by the New Jersey State Legislature to be used as a Governor's mansion. The high calibre of its furnishings and the clean look of its wallpaper and paint make Morven one of New Jersey's outstanding historical homes. One only hopes it remains so in the future, now that it will no longer receive special attention as an official residence. Visiting hours may be broadened once the Historical Society gets things set up. Free.

HOURS: Tues.: 1-3 PM. Possible more in summer.
LOCATION: 55 Stockton St., Princeton

BAINBRIDGE HOUSE

This small brick building is wedged between stores and movie houses on the well-traversed Nassau Street and stands practically opposite the iron gates of Princeton University. The one-time home of Captain William Bainbridge, a hero of the War of 1812 and a commander of the U.S.S. Constitution, it serves now as headquarters for the Princeton Historical Society. Luckily, this particular historical society keeps its house open to the public much longer than most. A typical small home of the well-to-do family of the late 18th Century, it features period furnishings in the downstairs rooms plus changing exhibits.

Parents appreciate the Bainbridge House because of the one-room Children's Museum on the first floor. Although the exhibits are historical, they are still of the touch and feel variety (such as an old-fashioned store or different types of shoes). There is also a surprisingly well-stocked souvenir and book shop here. Free (donations accepted). School trips also scheduled for children's section.

HOURS: Daily, 12-4. Closed major holidays.
LOCATION: 158 Nassau St., Princeton, Mercer County
TELEPHONE: 609-921-6748

WILLIAM TRENT HOUSE

The founder of Trenton, so to speak, because his house and property were known as "Trent's Town," William Trent built his stately home in 1719. It was later the residence of four governors. "A genteel brick dwelling house, three stories high, with a large, handsome staircase and entry," according to an early observer, it is one of the best restorations in New Jersey. In the Georgian style with 18th Century English furniture and many early American pieces. Some of the William & Mary and Queen Anne furnishings here are equal to what you would find in Colonial Williamsburg. Guided tours by knowledgeable volunteers.

HOURS: Weekdays: 10-4; Sunday: 1-4
ADMISSION: Adults: 50¢; Children: 25¢
LOCATION: 15 Market St., Trenton
TELEPHONE: 609-989-3027

WALT WHITMAN HOUSE

A narrow row house in Camden contains the rooms where the poet who sang of America lived out the last eight years of his life. Accumulations of furniture (much of it the landlord's which Whitman took over along with the house), photographs and memorabilia are here. Whitman had had a paralytic stroke and much of what is in the house was given to him by friends during this invalid period. A bathtub kept in the upstairs bedroom is typical of the many gifts his friends collected for him.

Four rooms are open, two downstairs, two upstairs. The downstairs rooms are filled with books, manuscripts and photographs (Whitman was the most photographed writer in America at that time). A painting by Thomas Eakins, hats, locks of hair, etc. are just a portion of the memorabilia. A guide will show you around. Since this is a State Historic Site, it is always a good idea to call first — state houses are sometimes closed for renovations. Free.

HOURS: Wed. - Fri. 9-12 & 1-6; Sat. 10-12 & 1-6. Sun.: 1-6
LOCATION: 330 Mickle St., Camden
TELEPHONE: 609-964-5383

PENNSBURY MANOR

Here is a complete recreation, on the original site, of the beautiful Manor House built by William Penn on the banks of the Delaware. Located 25 miles above Philadelphia in what was then a wilderness, the estate includes many outbuildings such as a bake and brew house, a smoke house, ice house and stable. Although everything was built from scratch in the 1930's, great care was taken to follow the letters and journals of Penn regarding this self-sufficient estate.

There are two striking things about Pennsbury Manor. One is the earliness of the period. The house was built in the late 17th Century (Penn lived there only from 1699 to 1701), so the furnishings reflect the heavy Jacobean hand. And the tour guides look as if they came from the pages of Mother Goose with their tunics and high black hats — quite different from the ubiquitous mob caps and wool shawls of the typical colonial reconstruction.

The other is the surprising elegance of this Quaker household. Although nothing is lavish, still the furnishings are richer than one would expect of a Quaker leader.

As the guide points out, although William Penn was a great believer in the equality of men, he was still the Proprietor, entitled to receive an annual fee from each settler for each parcel of land sold. He had, after all, received the Charter for Pennsylvania from King Charles II. He also came from a wealthy background and apparently relished good furniture.

After a tour through the bedrooms, parlors and countingrooms of the Manor, a tour through the grounds is in order. First to the barge-landing where a handsome replica of the ornate barge that Penn used to travel down to Philadelphia is moored. (Actually it looks more like a large gondola than a modern-day flat barge.) Then there is the herb garden, the barnyard with its peacocks and hens, and the brew house where it is supposed great vats of ale were mixed and where huge ovens held the bread to be baked for the estate.

The grounds include orchards and gardens. Walnut, hawthorn and hazel trees, fruit trees and rosebushes created a little corner of England in the new wilderness of America.

HOURS: Daylight Savings Time: Weekdays: 9-5; Sun.: 1-5.
Otherwise: 10-4:30; 12-2:40. Always closed Mondays.
May be closed Jan. & Feb.
ADMISSION: Adults: $1.50; Children under 12 free. Seniors: $1.05
LOCATION: Bordentown Road, near Levittown, Pa.
TELEPHONE: 215-946-0400

See Also: *Winterthur* ("Restored and Reconstructed"), *Longwood* and *Duke Gardens* ("The Garden Variety") and specific homes of the prominent, such as *The James Fenimore Cooper House* in the chapter on "Walking Tours."

RESTORED AND RECONSTRUCTED COLONIAL, FEDERAL AND VICTORIAN VILLAGES, FARMS, MILLS AND HOMES

Photo: Courtesy N.J. Div. of Travel & Tourism

In This Chapter You Will Find:

Waterloo Village
Van Cortlandt Manor
Philipsburg Manor
Clinton Historical Museum Village
Historic Towne of Smithville
Wheaton Village
East Jersey Olde Towne
Batsto
Allaire Village
Historic Cold Spring Village
Liberty Village
Longstreet Farm
Fosterfields
Israel Crane House
Miller-Cory House
Other Historic Houses in New Jersey
Winterthur
The Hagley Museum

← A colonial spinster at work. This one at the Historic Towne of Smithville.

WATERLOO VILLAGE

One of the largest of the restored Colonial Villages in New Jersey, Waterloo Village is set on acres of mountain greenery beside the Musconetcong River. Run by a public, non-profit organization, the village adheres to a non-commercial image. The artisans are authentic — the potter makes clay candlesticks — and he gives you a good history of pottery in the old days, too. The blacksmith really hammers out horseshoes at his forge. There is little hawking of food and souvenirs.

Another image that Waterloo is pushing is that of the new Tanglewood. For, every weekend from June through August, there are evening concerts right outside of the historical area. Separate tickets are required for the concerts, which range from classical to bluegrass.

The village complex covers over 5,000 acres and includes buildings ranging from a tiny 1740 duplex to a solid 1870 mansion. Since Waterloo prospered both during the Revolutionary War and later during the era of the Morris Canal and Sussex Railroads, the houses reflect the colonial, federal and the later Victorian styles.

When it comes to guides and artisans, however, we are back to colonial times. Everyone dresses in the doublets and skirts of the late 18th Century working class. The arts, crafts and trades portrayed are colonial and a little bit into the 19th Century. The aforementioned potter explains, by the way, how an early ceramicist had to search for his own clay, stoke his own fire, and create all the plates, bowls and candlesticks for the village. The guide at the *Apothecary shop* explains the herbs, poisons and other "cures" peculiar to the pioneer. A jar of leeches and a dentist chair designed to hold you down while the dentist yanked out your tooth are two of the spellbinders here. There is a special room next door just for drying the herbs from the neighboring herb garden.

The speeches that guides give regularly to school and scout groups are often the most interesting thing about a restored village. The hostess in the *Canal House*, for instance, demonstrates the wooden-knobbed weasel that used to draw the wool yarn into a skein. Every time the weasel made a full skein it would go "pop," thus explaining the childhood song about thirty years too late for me. I found you are more likely to get these anecdote-filled speeches if you latch onto some group going through. If there are just two or three people around, the guides will often only answer questions. And I, for one, have never come up with a tremendously relevant question about candle-dipping or wool-dyeing.

A favorite for children is the gristmill where huge stones grind the corn which the guide upstairs pours between the stones. Then you troop downstairs where the waterwheel is creating a loud whoosh. Here you discover the cornmeal pouring out the spout, while another guide explains the process.

There's a lot of walking to do here — several homes, the *General Store* (where you can buy the clay candlesticks the potter makes), the *Canal Museum* (explaining the workings of Morris Canal), and all the various craft buildings. Bring good shoes. And if you're expecting a lovely luncheon at the *Stagecoach Inn and Tavern*, forget it. They stopped serving meals there one hundred years ago. Bring sandwiches, or you can order hamburgers, snacks and soft drinks at the Grill near the Apothecary Shop. Allow three to four hours to tour Waterloo. Concertgoers can take a quick tour at reduced prices if they arrive at 4 PM. And a recent innovation — a food pavillion near the concert area — allows music lovers a chance to grab a bite before the concert.

HOURS: April-Oct.:10-6, Nov. - Dec.: 10-5 Daily. Closed Mondays
ADMISSION: Adults: $5.00; Senior Citizens: $4.00; Children: $3.00
Under 6 free.
LOCATION: Byram Twp., Sussex County. Take I-80 to Route 206N.
Left at Waterloo Road.
TELEPHONE: 201-347-0900

THE VAN CORTLANDT MANOR

Ever wonder why they call it a "Bar and Grill"? Or why a small whiskey glass is referred to as a "shot glass"? You'll find the answer to these and other questions you may or may not have asked at Van Cortlandt Manor, an 18th Century restoration on the New York side of the Hudson, where guides combine anecdotes and demonstrations in their tours.

Set on a rise overlooking both the Hudson and Croton Rivers, Van Cortlandt Manor is a prime example of the strong influence of the Dutch in the New York-New Jersey area. At one time in the late 1700's, the estate extended from the Hudson River to Connecticut. The Manor House is now run by the non-profit Sleepy Hollow Restorations and is one of the better colonial restorations in the area.

During spring one spectacular feature of the Manor is the rows of tulips that line the red brick walk between the outbuildings and the Manor. A neatly spaced flower, vegetable and herb garden beyond the walk brought back childhood memories of Dutch "neatness".

Tours begin at the reception center where accurately costumed guides take groups of fifteen people through the various buildings. Our group stopped first at the *Ferry House*. The ferry once plied the Croton River and travelers would stop here for food, drink, and lodging. The building is not large, but travelers would sleep three or four to a bed so they all managed.

At the other end of the long brick walk, topping a spacious green lawn, is the *Manor House* itself. While not as elegant as the Southern Colonial mansions, it is impressive for this area — three stories high with a two-story porch wrapped around it. A heavy Dutch door opens to the main floor where the atmosphere is one of burnished wood and quiet elegance. Delft tiles line the fireplaces. Chippendale and Queen Anne furniture fill the rooms, and English china rests in the practical Dutch cupboards whose doors could be closed at night.

The ground floor kitchen was a magnet for our group. Here the guide, still flushed from baking two rhubarb pies in the massive hearth fireplace, answered endless questions. She showed us the original Dutch oven (a heavy iron kettle with a close lid), the beehive oven in the back of the fireplace and the gridiron for baking steaks. She did everything in fact but share the rhubarb pies with us — those, I assume, are eaten by the employees when the last tourist departs.

Van Cortlandt Manor also includes a smokehouse, ice house, and blacksmith forge. The tours are geared for adults and school-age children.

       HOURS: 10-5 Daily.
   ADMISSION: Adults: $4.00; Children and Seniors: $2.50
              Combination ticket for other Sleepy Hollow Restorations available.
    LOCATION: Tappan Zee Bridge to Route 9N to Croton Pond Ave. one block east to South Riverside Ave., turn right and go ¼ mile to entrance.
   TELEPHONE: 914-631-8200

PHILIPSBURG MANOR

A large farm and gristmill, a wood-planked bridge that spans a tranquil stream, an old stone manor-house and a huge modern reception center filled with exhibits are all part of this "Sleepy Hollow" restoration. Set up as it would have been in 1750, with authentic furnishings and authentically garbed guides. You begin with a movie about the Philipse family who once managed 90,000 acres and shipped flour and meal down the Hudson. Unfortunately, they backed the losing side during the Revolutionary War and lost their holdings as a result.

Guided tours of the manor, a demonstration of the gristmill, and a walk around the large property and through the barn are part of the outing. You can see sheep and lambs gamboling about as you traverse the property. Administered in a highly professional manner.

LOCATION: Upper Mills, North Tarrytown, N.Y. Take Tappen Zee Bridge, then Route 9N. Look for signs.

HOURS, ETC. Same as Van Cortlandt Manor

CLINTON HISTORICAL MUSEUM VILLAGE

An old red mill with a churning water-wheel sits by a 200-foot wide waterfall to create the picturesque environment for this museum village. In fact, the red mill is one of the most photographed structures in New Jersey. It is this mill, filled with four floors of Americana, that is the hub of the "village". The other buildings are smaller and scattered along the banks of the river — but the mill dominates all. You can find a log cabin, a little red schoolhouse, a general store/post office, a blacksmith shop, a stone-crusher and an information center in the small complex.

However, there are no live blacksmiths or grocers here, but mannequins in appropriate dress in all these buildings, including the main mill. If you happen to be a lover of Americana you could probably spend hours browsing the four floors of the huge mill. Different scenes set with mannequins seem to loom at you suddenly in the darkened atmosphere. Within these confines are a Victorian gentleman at his office, an ornate child's bedroom, some Indians preparing corn, a colonial hearthside and much, much more. The scenes cover a span of three centuries and every once in a while there is a small collection, such as a shelf full of stereopticans, to discover — lots of antique tools and gadgets also.

In the dark, the mannequins almost seem to move. At least that's what the four-year old who accompanied me insisted. She was rather scared of these bland models who rode bicycles and baked bread. It made me think that if they converted this place to the "Old Haunted Mill" they could quadruple their business.

The museum does run a series of specials to attract the crowds. These include summer concerts, craft days and a harvest jubilee. The place is run, by the way, by a private, non-profit educational organization. Guided tours for groups are given at no extra cost but must be arranged in advance.

Across the river, the large stone building facing the mill houses the **Hunterdon Art Center** (closed Mondays), which is certainly worth a visit. Exhibits of prints, painting and sculpture are always on hand and it's free. In the summer a theater group performs here also.

From the art center you can walk up the main street of the small country town of Clinton. Some nice boutiques and a fern-hung luncheon spot make for pleasant browsing.

HOURS: April - Oct. 31: Mon. - Fri.: 1-5; Weekends: 12-6.
ADMISSION: Adults: $2.00; Seniors: $1.50; Children: $1.00; Under 6 free.
LOCATION: 56 Main St., Clinton, Hunterdon County (Off Rte. 78).
TELEPHONE: 201-735-4101.

HISTORIC TOWNE OF SMITHVILLE

Only 12 miles from Atlantic City and experiencing a bonanza of its own, The Historic Towne of Smithville is half a reconstructed colonial village and half a boutiquey shopping center in colonial disguise.

On one side of a large lake there are two restaurants and a cluster of "shoppes". Cross the bridge to the other side and you find a barnyard zoo where the kids can pet a real cow (an animal often missing from other petting zoos), a miniature train ride and a cruising boat that for a fee will putter you around the lake. There is also a replica of an oyster boat in the lake that just sits there and does nothing.

This side of the lake is called "old village" and it is here you find whatever reconstructions there are. Small houses — with glass doors so that you can peer through — represent a barber shop, a tobacconist, a boot shop, a school house, etc. Wednesdays to Sundays, from 12 to 5, summertimes only, there are "craftspeople" who show up in colonial costume to weave, spin or just occupy the little houses.

But it is the shopping area, on the near side of the lake, that gets the action. Starting with the Smithville Inn and the Quail Hill Inn, this place is bustling. Both inns are set up colonial style, with anterooms, halls and dining areas chock full of antiques like hutches, bedwarmers, and farm implements.

The Quail Hill Inn gets the group business. They advertise for weddings, anniversaries, bar mitzvahs, what have you. The Smithville Inn has nine dining areas and is the only genuine historic site in the whole place. It started out as a stagecoach stop in 1787. Additions bloomed and in 1952 it was completely refurbished and turned into a working restaurant.

Both the Quail Hill Inn and the Smithville Inn are open year round although the kiddie rides and the craftspeople across the river fold their tents and disappear at summer's end. The shoppes keep going full blast until Christmas though; then they go to "winter hours."

Ah, the shops. "Everything you never needed" (as one friend summed it up) — all on a pleasant green with brick walkways lined with flower beds. Candles, plants, shells, gourmet foods, scented soaps, toys, chocolates, etc. If you've never been to Peddler's Village, Lahaska, or New Hope or Cape May, or even if you have — here is where you can find unique items and the latest fad. The Kliban cats, and Mr. Bill shirts, unusual gift paper from England, they all surface at these boutique villages first. Now that Smithville is building up as a housing community, the boutiques will probably be joined by everyday-type shops.

HOURS: Vary for shops. For old town: Wed. - Sun. 12-5 (summer) for craftspeople. Restaurants: Daily.
LOCATION: Smithville, Atlantic County. On Route 9
TELEPHONE: 609-652-7777

WHEATON VILLAGE

A Victorian Village set around a green with houses styled in 1888 gingerbread, Wheaton Village is a nice, clean spot in the middle of a small industrial town called Millville about 35 miles east of Atlantic City. The village is dedicated to the glass industry that still flourishes in this corner of New Jersey and its main attraction is the **Museum of Glass.** The museum is housed in an elegant Victorian building and includes glass items that go back as far as 300 B.C.

Glass collectors will probably enjoy this museum with its flower-embedded paperweights, medicine bottles, cut glass and door-knobs. The main foyer boasts the chandeliers from the old Traymore Hotel in Atlantic City and the original brass sconces from the Waldorf Astoria.

Another attraction is the glass factory where visitors can watch from a gallery above while gaffers plunge their gathering rods into the blazing furnaces and then shape them into wine glasses, bottles and paperweights. Twice a day, there are "shows" which means an announcer with a mike explains just what the gaffer is doing. This is hot work and even from the gallery you can feel the intensity of the furnace.

Other buildings in the Village include a craft arcade where you can see weavers, potters and printers going about their work (and selling the products when they can). A general outlet for their work and other craft items is the *West Jersey Crafts Company.* *The Brownstone Emporium*, the *Jewelry Store* and the *Arthur Gorham Paperweight Shop* (which offers a wide variety of handmade paperweights) are other shops to visit on the green.

For kids there's a small play area, an 1876 schoolhouse to peek at and an 1880 Train Station (with a miniature train ride for an extra fee). And twice a day, at least during summer, an old-fashioned medicine show takes place on the green.

The General Store sells penny candy from an old-fashioned glass jar and the drugstore features an ice cream parlor. A restaurant called the Village Lunch Kettle serves food, but despite its pretty facade it's just an ordinary luncheonette inside with very ordinary fare. All in all, Wheaton Village is not a bad place to visit, especially for glass fanciers, but I thought the admission price a little high considering that so many buildings on the village green are actually stores.

  HOURS: Daily, 10-5 (Reduced schedule Jan. - Mar.)
ADMISSION: Adults: $3.50; Children: $2.00; Seniors: $2.50. Under 6 free. Family Rate: $7.50. Reduced winter rates.
LOCATION: 10th & "G" Street, Millville, Cumberland County. Take Routes 47, 49 or 55.
TELEPHONE: 609-825-6800

EAST JERSEY OLDE TOWNE

A reconstructed colonial village has been growing in Johnson Park, Piscataway, for lo, these many years. A good number of houses are up, set on a pleasant village green meant to resemble an 18th Century settlement in the Raritan Valley. Several of the buildings have been moved from other sites. One can find a church, a farmhouse, a tavern, a blacksmith shop among others and there are picket fences and tiny garden plots and brick walkways.

The big problem is that there are still no set hours for viewing the village — and many of the houses still have no furnishings. Therefore, a family that stops by on the spur of the moment on the basis of a guidebook entry will be disappointed. (And East Jersey Olde Towne has been mentioned as far back as the 1975 edition of *Away We Go* which reported it was to open in 1976.)

However, all is not dead at Olde Towne. There are many special openings such as on Memorial Day weekend, the Fourth of July, etc., which are all heavily promoted in the newspapers. There are also group tours available on a pre-arranged basis which can include lunch at the Indian Queen Tavern for a reasonable $5 a head. Another popular activity is weddings at the quaint (but small) Three-Mile-Run Church, a structure that dates back to 1703.

The director of Olde Towne hopes to have some regular hours set up soon. Still in all, it's best to call first.

LOCATION: River Road (Route 18) at Hoes Lane, Piscataway, Middlesex County
TELEPHONE: 201-469-6786

BATSTO

What was once a self-contained community lies within The Wharton Tract (a huge State preserve within the section known as the Pine Barrens). Tall trees, open lowlands, lakes with clusters of campgrounds are all part of this unusual region which reminded me of the North Carolina tidelands.

As for Batsto Village itself, it was once the center of the bog iron industry in New Jersey. Later glass was manufactured here, then lumbering and cranberry farming were tried. As you approach you find a handsome farm surrounded by split rail fences with horses, chickens and ducks in view. The huge farmhouse has a late Victorian tower rising eight stories from its center giving the place a "haunted mansion" look. The room inside are filled with 19th and

Waterloo Village in northern Jersey (above) and Batsto Village in the Pine Barrens (below) both started out as iron mining towns.

Photos: Courtesy N.J. Div. of Tourism

20th Century furniture and antiques. But you cannot get inside to see them without a tour guide who is not always available.

First stop is the Visitor's Center where Park Rangers will tell you what is open. Besides the Mansion, there is a General Store, a barn and lots of barnyard animals. A lovely lake stands at the center of Batsto where fishing is permitted and a nature trail starts beyond. On the other side of the lake there is a sawmill and a village of sixteen old ironworkers' houses. One of the homes is a museum set up as an ironworker's home and four are craft houses. The craftsmen are supposed to demonstrate pottery, weaving, candlemaking and wood carving. The day I visited, only the potter was currently in residence and he didn't show up for work. The number of craftspeople available varies every year according to the budget from the State.

Batsto certainly has the potential to become a first-rate museum village. The farm with its unusual main house, surrounding barns and wide swept fields all in the middle of the untouched pine barrens has the true look of the haunting past. It also has the extra added attraction of a horse and carriage ride (available Wednesdays through Sundays in the summer season).

However, visitors should know that tour guides are not always available either to the mansion or the ironworkers' homes, and that there is a general air of apathy about the place. The directional signs leading to Batsto from the Garden State Parkway are not too helpful either. Free.

HOURS: Memorial Day - Labor Day: 10-6; rest of year: 11-5. (Park only) Closed major holidays.
DIRECTIONS: Route 9 to 542 west. Or Garden State Parkway New Gretna exit to 9S to 542.
TELEPHONE: 609-561-3262

ALLAIRE VILLAGE

Set inside the greenery of Allaire State Park, this complex is also known as the Deserted Village and the Howell Iron Works. The huge brick furnace is one left over from the bog iron days when James P. Allaire bought the ironworks in 1822 and sought to establish a sort of ideal self-contained community. Since this was the age of Oneida settlements and Utopian communities, such a worker's paradise did not seem unusual. In fact, as long as the ironworks transformed local bog into pig iron, everything prospered. But after twenty-five years, competition from the high grade iron ore brought economic ruin to the region. The village became deserted.

Nowadays it's populated with craftsmen. All during the summer, a tinsmith, carpenter, blacksmith and several hostesses inhabit the stores and shops here at the deserted village. There are several other things going on in this park — particularly a railroad museum with old time trains and an operating railroad — which bring in the families with the kids. Nature trail, picnic area and lots of special weekend summertime activities are contributing factors to the comparative popularity of Allaire.

   HOURS: Park: 3 AM - 8 PM. Village: 10-5, May 1 - Labor Day.
 ADMISSION: Weekends: $2.00, Weekdays: $1.00 (Parking)
  LOCATION: Allaire State Park, Monmouth County. Take Exit 98, Garden State Parkway, go 2 miles west.
TELEPHONE: 201-938-2371

HISTORIC COLD SPRING VILLAGE

A delightful little restored village has sprung up among the pine trees on a quiet stretch of road not far from the hubbub of the Wildwood motels. In operation only since 1981, Cold Spring Village (not to be confused with the village of Cold Spring near Boscobel or Cold Spring Harbor in New York) has much of the charm that other restored villages aspire to. It's not so large as to be exhausting, nor so small that it might disappoint.

This is not a village set in a particular time — all the buildings are pre-1900 but they range from an ancient colonial to the large Grange Hall which dates back to 1897. In between, you will find a tiny 1820 Octogonal house and various forms of American colonial. These houses are not empty, nor do they employ guides — but each building is rented to an authentic craftsman or entrepreneur. A genuine weaver, an old fashioned printer, and a furniture maker are some of the tenants here. Others are the expected ice cream, candy and bakery stores.

In between the houses, there are bits of country nostalgia such as a horseshoe pitching pit (yes, you can try your luck) an old fashioned water pump (the water is undoubtedly from the cold spring) and a small farm enclosure. Walkways are made of crushed clamshells, and a horse-drawn carriage, on hand the day I visited, was a big hit with the children. Weekends only, the

Grange offers reasonable lunches and dinners (e.g. Turkey and fixings for $6.95, complete dinner). Entrance to the village is free.

HOURS: Memorial Day - Labor Day: Daily. Call for exact hours.
LOCATION: 731 Seashore Road, Cold Spring, Cape May County. Take G.S.P. Exit 0 to Route 109 to Seashore Road.
TELEPHONE: 609-884-1810

LIBERTY VILLAGE

Although the signs are still up and the entries continue in guidebooks, Liberty Village as a separate entity does not really exist anymore. The Glass Manufactury house still stands, and several other craft houses are open, including one where a specialist creates custom-tailored guns. But the colonial houses have been taken over by outlet stores, and the special museums, the church and the stocks on the village green no longer exist. The article on Flemington outlet stores has further information. (See chapter on *Outlets and Flea Markets*).

LONGSTREET FARM

For those who want to recapture the sights and smells of an era not so long past, a visit to Longstreet Farm quite fills the bill. Although the farm is kept to the 1890 to 1900 era, the machinery here was used well into the 1920s and may bring back memories to those born on a farm. Old fashioned combines and tractors, an apple corer, a machine that de-kernelizes corn (but only the hard corn meant for animals) and other antique contraptions are kept in a series of barns and sheds. Of course, animals are present although not in profusion. There are lazy pigs lying in the mud, horses swatting flies, cows, chickens and flies, flies, flies. In fact, if your child has ever asked why horses have tails, you can discover why here — they make the most efficient fly-swatters.

Open-slatted corn cribs that allow the air to circulate are on view. The milking shed is fitted out in the old way — with slots for the cow's head and buckets for old-time hand milking. It's much different from today's mechanized milking. The carriage house contains a variety of buckboards. And they do have people here, too. Since Longstreet is a living historical farm, the workers dress in casual 1890s clothes as they go about their usual farm chores: feeding, seeding, plowing, milking — all in a day's work according to the season. And the eggs and milk are sold at market as are the hogs that are killed in the fall in traditional farm custom.

No guided tours are given to individuals but groups may call ahead and arrange them. The main farmhouse is not open at this time. But the farm is open all year and follows the seasonal activities of plowing, harvesting, threshing, blacksmithing, sheep-shearing and ice-cutting.

The farm is just one portion of the beautiful **Holmdel Park**, which provides much lovely scenery. Across the street, a sheltered picnic area offers tables and a snack bar. In a hollow below the shelter, a pond allows ducks to swim gracefully and accept breadcrusts from visitors. And beyond the pond, a cultivated arboretum presents a colorful view of flowering crabapples, rhododendrons and hundreds of shade trees. The park also provides a nature trail that winds among the beach, oak, and hickory trees. Wildflowers and blueberry bushes are other plusses at this abundant county park. Free.

HOURS: 10-4 daily, Sept. - May. 9-5 daily, June - Labor Day.
LOCATION: Longstreet Road, off Holmdel Road. Take Garden State Arts Center Exit off Garden State Parkway, follow Keyport Road and look for signs.
TELEPHONE: 201-946-2669

FOSTERFIELDS

Another old-fashioned farm that dates to the turn-of-the-century in American agriculture, Fosterfields is being slowly developed by the Morris County Park Commission. The large farmhouse is not open to the public at this time although there are barns, outbuildings and some displays of farm implements on the premises. Farm activity is limited to Saturdays from the spring season until the fall. On these days a real live farmer hitches up the horses, sows the seeds, and performs other seasonal chores. The Park Commission hopes to increase activities here in the future. Free.

LOCATION: Route 24 & Kahdena Rd., Morris Twp., Morris County.
TELEPHONE: 201-285-6689

ISRAEL CRANE HOUSE

A handsome house built in the Federal period and then re-modeled in the Greek Revival style, the Crane house was moved from its original site to the present location by the Montclair Historical Society. The group also trains the docents who give guided tours throughout the three-story building.

Furnishings in the Federal and Empire style are evident in the main house. Upstairs in the garret, a full schoolroom exists. (One of the Crane's did run a school here.) An authentic blackboard (which is, incidentally, a large board painted black), an old-fashioned dunce cap and the elongated desks that accommodated several children at a time are part of the set-up. Also in the garret are a full tool collection and a mass of dried herbs.

Behind the main house is a two-story kitchen building recon-structed to resemble the 1840 kitchen that once existed. One unique feature of the Crane House is that the docents do allow you to sample the cooking. Just a tiny piece, but you can taste bread from the beehive oven, while the chicken simmers over the open hearth. Docents are quite good at explaining all details of the cooking utensils (such as the lazy-back which eased cooking chores for post-Colonial wives).

Beyond the kitchen building is a pleasant backyard planted with flowers and herbs in the 18th Century fashion. And beyond that, the *Country Store Museum* is housed in a small building erected by Nathaniel Crane in 1820. Although the items in the store are just wooden models and not for sale, you do get the sense of an old-fashioned post-office/store as the social center for a town. A small gift shop here offers books and mementos for sale. And be sure to climb the stairs to check out the craft room above where there are quilts, looms, a spinning wheel and often a craftsperson in attendance. Quilting classes are also held here. Free. (Donations accepted.)

HOURS: Sept. - June: Sun. 2-5. Group tours available weekdays.
LOCATION: 110 Orange Road (off Bloomfield Ave.), Montclair, Essex County
TELEPHONE: 201-744-1796

MILLER-CORY HOUSE

Every Sunday during the school season, volunteers cook, churn butter and perform seasonal tasks in and around this 1740 farmhouse. The everyday, humdrum tasks of colonial life — from soap-making to herb-drying are emphasized here. The house, the adjacent Visitor Center, and a separate kitchen comprise a small enclave of colonial life. In pleasant weather wool spinners and other workers may be found outside and the separate kitchen is the scene of soup and bread making. Good idea, since there is often a line for a tour of the Miller-Cory house itself.

Guided tours of the house proper take about half-an-hour, with 15 people to each tour. Although three tours may go on simultaneously, there may be a wait on a busy fall afternoon. The tour is most thorough and includes everything from how to tighten the rope springs on a bed to how to make utensils from a cow's horn. School children and adults will find the house tour highly educational while pre-schoolers may be content to simply mose around. They can tour the herb garden, the tool collection in the Visitor Center, and watch the outdoor volunteers at work.

HOURS: Sept. - June, Sun. 2-5 (Jan. - Mar.: 2-4)
LOCATION: 614 Mountain Ave., Westfield, Union County
ADMISSION: Adults: $1.00; Children: $.50
TELEPHONE: 201-232-1776

OTHER HISTORIC HOUSES (N.J.)

The number of historic houses in New Jersey is so large it would take an entire volume just to list them. Here are a few:

COOPER MILL: An 1826 mill that grinds corn into meal before your eyes. Open summers only, 10-5, and weekends in fall. Guided tours. Located on Route 24 in Chester Twp., Morris County, one mile west of Route 24 and 206.

OSBORN CANNONBALL HOUSE: An 18th Century house with period furnishings. 1840 Front St., Scotch Plains, Union County. Sun.: 2-4, Sept. - June. Call 201-889-1928

FORCE HOUSE: Next to Memorial Field in Livingston, the 18th & 19th Century homestead of a local family. Open and 2nd and 4th Sundays of the month, except summer. 366 S. Livingston Ave., Livingston, Essex County.

OGDEN-BELCHER MANSION: A well-respected restoration on a historic street in Elizabeth and one that you can visit only by writing to: The Elizabeth Historical Foundation, Box 1, Elizabeth, N.J.

ALLEN HOUSE: Operated as a tavern in the 18th Century as well as a home. Centrally located on Route 35, Shrewsbury, Monmouth County. And **MARLPIT HALL:** A refurbished colonial that started life as a Dutch cottage in 1685 and was later enlarged in the English style. Located at 137 Kings Highway, Middletown, Monmouth County. Both houses are open from April to December, Tues. & Thurs.: 1-4 PM; Sat.: 10-4; Sun.: 1-4. Admission is $1.00 for adults; 50¢ for children and free to children under 6.

GREENFIELD HALL: Personal items belonging to Elizabeth Haddon, furnishings, doll collection. Open Tues. & Thurs., 2-4:40. Closed summer. Location: 343 King Highway, Haddonfield, Camden County. Telephone: 609-429-7375.

MARSHALL HOUSE: One-time home of James Marshall who discovered gold at Sutter's Mill, California but never made any money from the find. Built in 1816. Prize possession is an 1843 friendship quilt. Headquarters Lambertville Historical Society. Open mid-April to mid-Nov., Thurs., Sat.: 2-4 PM. Adults 50¢, Children 25¢. Location: 60 Bridge St., Lambertville, Hunterdon County. Telephone: 609-397-0770 or 609-397-2531.

VAN RIPER-HOPPER HOUSE: Dutch colonial farmhouse with period furnishings, local history, herb garden. Open Fri. - Tues.: 1-5. Free. Location: 533 Berdan Ave., Wayne, Passaic County. Telephone: 201-696-1776.

SOMERS MANSION: Oldest house in Atlantic County has unusual roof shaped like an upside-down ship's hull. Headquarters of Historical Society. Local memorabilia. Hours: Wed. - Fri.: 9-12 & 1-6; Sat.: 10-12 & 1-6; Sun.: 1-6. Location: Route 52 to Shore Rd., Somers Point. Telephone: 609-927-2212.

ACORN HALL: Mid-Victorian home in the Italianate style with many original furnishings in its two parlours. Children's toys and gadgets. Well-kept lawn with huge oak and Victorian garden with gazebo. Open Thurs. 11-3; Sun.: 1:30-4, Spring through Fall only. Adults $1.00, Children 50¢. 68 Morris Ave., Morristown, Morris County. Telephone: 201-267-3465.

WINTERTHUR

The *creme de la creme* when it comes to American decorative arts, Winterthur is Henri DuPont's version of hundreds of restored homes rolled into one. The main mansion contains 175 rooms, each one decorated in a pre-1840 style. In many cases the rooms are more than merely decorated — whole dining rooms, kitchens, etc. (including walls, ceilings and fireplaces) were transported panel by panel and placed inside the mansion. Six style periods are shown: Seventeenth Century, William and Mary, Queen Anne, Chippendale, Federal and Empire.

Each piece here is documented, so that the Duncan Phyfe room, for instance, had its architectural elements removed from a specific house in New York where Phyfe furniture was used. You can find a striking plantation dining room removed in its entirety from a South Carolina home, a New England kitchen, a Shaker bedroom, a New York parlour, and a flying staircase copied from the Montmorenci estate in North Carolina. One oft-photographed room features authentic 18th Century Chinese wallpaper that covers both the walls and the ceilings.

There are more than rooms at Winterthur. The Cobblestone Court, right inside the building, looks like a movie set for an 18th Century film. This courtyard features the facades of four different buildings, including The Red Lion Inn and a typical Connecticut home.

The mansion at Winterthur can be seen by tour only. However, the *George and Martha Washington Wing* (18 rooms, many of them very early, but not on the same level as the main house), the DuPont House, the Visitor Center, and the gardens are open for individual perusal.

The Pavillion is the main visitor's center. Here you can enjoy a view of the gardens while you purchase breakfast, lunch or snacks, all buffet style. A large book and gift shop, restrooms and brochures are available here also. It is here that you can board the trams that take you around the gardens. The price is $1.00.

The gardens, by the way, are almost as famous as the mansion. The grounds are large, though, with pockets of flowering displays at dispersed areas; so it is best to take the tram. Particularly popular in the spring when the azaleas, rhododendrons and dogwoods are in bloom, the gardens also include a reflecting pool, a magnolia copse and a sundial garden. Sixty acres altogether are under intense cultivation here.

House tours vary. During the open season (Spring and Yuletide) you see fewer rooms because larger groups are taken through.

Otherwise reservations are necessary and you go in smaller groups. Needless to say, you never get to see all the rooms on one tour, so many people go back several times. For lovers of 18th Century architecture and furnishings this is the premier place to visit. Only a multi-millionaire could lavish this attention to detail on his "collection."

HOURS: Tues. - Sat.: 10-4; Sun, holiday Mondays & July 4: 12-4. Closed other Mondays and major holidays.

ADMISSION: Reserved Tour: Adults $6.00; Children 12-16: $3.00. Not offered during spring or Yuletide season. For spring & autumn tours: Adults: $5.00. American Sampler Tour: $2.00; Gardens: $2.00 25% discount for seniors, students under 12 and groups of 25 or more. Children under 12, free.

LOCATION: NJ Turnpike to 295 & Delaware Memorial Bridge then north on I95 to Route 52 (Exit 7). Left on 52 to Winterthur.

TELEPHONE: 302-654-1548

HAGLEY MUSEUM

Another DuPont complex but this one is suitable for children. Basically, this is a recreation of the original black-powder mill that began the DuPont fortune. The "museum" section offers exhibits that trace industrial development throughout the 19th Century. At the powder yards beyond, you can see the water still flow through the mill races.

The residence here is called Eleutherian Mills and was the home of the original E. I. DuPont. The handsome Georgian structure is surrounded by gardens, a barn full of carriages and a cooper's workshop. There is a picnic area and snack vending machines on the grounds also.

HOURS: Tues. - Sat.: 9:30-4:30; Sun.: 1-5.

ADMISSION: Adults: $2.50; Seniors: $1.25; Students: $1.00; Children under 14, free with adult

LOCATION: Greenville, Delaware, off Route 141

TELEPHONE: 302-658-2400

See Also: *Pennsbury Manor* and *Speedwell Village* ("Homes of the Rich and Famous"), *Jockey Hollow/Wick Farm* ("Where Washington Slept, Ate and Fought), *New Jersey Historical Museums* ("Museums of All Kinds") and such tours as *Bordentown* and *Mt. Holly* in the "Walking Tours" chapter.

MUSEUMS OF ALL KINDS

Photo: Courtesy N.Y. Convention & Visitors Bureau

In This Chapter You Will Find:

New Jersey — Art and Science Museums

New Jersey State Museum, Newark Museum, Montclair Art Museum, Morris Museum of Arts and Science, Bergen Community Museum, Monmouth Museum, Other Museums of Art and Science (Paterson, Jersey City, Rutgers, Princeton, Drew).

New Jersey — Specialty Museums

Franklin Mineral Museum, The Golf House, Bell Labs Exhibit, Squibb Headquarters, National Broadcasters Hall of Fame, Windmill Museum, Raggedy Ann Doll Museum, Aviation Hall of Fame, Campbell Museum, Salem Generating Station, Edison Memorial Tower and Museum.

New Jersey — Historical Museums

Museum of Early Trades and Crafts, Schoolhouse Museum, Ocean County Historical Museum, Hopewell Museum, Ocean City Historical Museum, Spy House Museum, Cape May Historical Museum, New Jersey Historical Society, Monmouth County Historical Society, Camden County Historical Society, Rogers Exhibit.

New York Museums

Metropolitan Museum of Art, American Museum of Natural History, The Cloisters, The Frick Collection, Museum of Modern Art, Guggenheim Museum.

Pennsylvania Museums

Franklin Institute, Philadelphia Museum of Art, Pennsylvania Academy of Art, Rosenbach Museum and Library, University of Pennsylvania Archeology Museum, Barnes Foundation, Buten Museum, The Mercer Mile, Brandywine Museum, Phillip's Mushroom Museum.

←

Across the river and through the trees — the Cloisters offers a view of New Jersey.

NEW JERSEY STATE MUSEUM

It stands in Trenton, pristine and white against the backdrop of the Delaware River, the very model of a modern, well-kept museum. There is no admission charge. The separate Museum Theater, just adjacent, offers a well-proportioned stage and comfortable seating for movies and live performances. The Planetarium, housed in its own section, seats 150 people and offers two weekend shows. There is a large lunchroom ringed by vending machines that is perfect for school children and families who bring their own lunches. The restrooms are clean, well maintained and plentiful. The State Museum at Trenton seems to have everything — except customers.

Although parking is plentiful on weekends, the Saturday I visited there must have been less than fifty people in the whole museum complex. Even the Walt Disney movie — an adventure film entitled "Candleshoe" that was showing absolutely free in the 416 seat auditorium — played to a crowd one-fifth of capacity.

Set up as a family museum, with exhibits to interest both children and adults, the museum offers a balance between the art and science sections. The addition of several new galleries of paintings and decorative arts, which range from 17th century urns to 20th century cubist canvasses, brings a new dimension to the Jersey collection. The natural science section offers an excellent collection of stuffed animals posed within their natural habitats. Another large display is devoted to life around the seashore with relief dioramas depicting the chain of tidal life from worms to higher life. There are also full exhibits on insects, minerals and the solar system. The first floor is devoted to changing exhibits of art and sculpture and special items.

As for the **planetarium**, shows are given two or three times on weekends and during the week also during summer. Children under seven are not admitted, although there are special "Stars for Tots" shows once in a while. The seats are comfortable and the simulated sky has great depth once the stars get moving around. There is a gift shop outside the planetarium with lots of science items. Another gift shop upstairs has a larger selection.

The short weekend hours do not leave much time for dallying. If you want to see the exhibits, the planetarium show and the free movie, visit the gift shop and have a bite to eat you really have to hustle. On weekdays, parking is a problem.

For people living within easy driving distance of the New Jersey State Museum, it is a bargain not to be missed. For those of us further away, it is a worthwhile stop when you are down in the Princeton-Trenton area. Free.

HOURS: Daily 9 am - 4:45 pm. Weekends: 1-4:45 pm
LOCATION: 205 West State Street, Trenton. Use Route 29 along Delaware River or Route 1 into State Street.
TELEPHONE: 609-292-6464

THE NEWARK MUSEUM

The Newark Museum has long acted as both a citadel of culture and a hub for cultural activity in a city not noted for its tourist attractions. Let's face it — Newark has image problems. In fact, the first question anyone asks about the Newark Museum is if there is a parking lot nearby. Yes, there is. The ParkFast Lot is directly behind the museum and you can enter the sculpture garden from there.

While the museum's garden looks forlorn in the winter, in spring and summer it is alive with the chatter of office workers who use this serene walled-in courtyard as a picnic area. Along with benches and shade trees there are several pieces of sculpture — the most striking is George Segal's Tollhouse which features a man in a turnpike tollhouse. He guards the entrance from the parking lot and is most effective. A tiny one-room schoolhouse and a small fire museum are also part of the garden scene.

The Newark Museum has long been noted for its oriental collection, and a recent Tibetan Exhibit was widely publicized. One part of this exhibit — the intricate and colorful altar — is on permanent display. Aside from the major changing exhibits, there are many permanent galleries in this medium-sized museum. Among them are:

An African room on the first floor which shows the clothing, money, headdresses and culture of certain West African tribes; an American Indian exhibit on the second floor which is included in the museum's school tours and features New Jersey as well as other Indian groups; and a newly opened 1820 house which is made up of several rooms from a typical well-to-do family home of the Federal period. Handsome, well-balanced rooms include a parlor with its Federal eagle mirror and a kitchen with open hearth fireplace.

The third floor is devoted to science and is popular with students. Here the displays are both permanent and changing. You might find volcanoes, fossils, a bird exhibit, and sections devoted to the metric system and soft energy. There are some hands-on exhibits up here of the type that are so popular with children.

The museum also offers a Junior Museum, which is in one corner of the first floor. Down here you will find a mini-zoo with ferrets, rabbits, snakes and turtles in peculiar, funnel-like cages. The **Dreyfuss Planetarium**, a 50-seat facility is also here. Sky shows are available on weekends only during the school year and cost 50¢. In summer, however, the sky shows are offered on Monday and Wednesday as well.

The planetarium, the Junior Museum and school-related sections of the adult museum may be booked at off hours by school groups. In fact, the Newark Museum is unusual in that it seems to run the bulk of its school tours in the morning, before the building officially opens. Whether the administration does this for the happiness of the staff or in order to keep the school groups away from the general public, I do not know. It results in one convenience: the public is less likely to get trampled by a troop of school kids; and one inconvenience: parents of pre-schoolers, who favor morning excursions, will never find the museum open before twelve. Free.

The Ballantine House (which has a separate listing in this book) is next door. You enter through the museum.

HOURS: 12-5 Daily, except major holidays.
LOCATION: 49 Washington St., Newark (facing Washington Park)
TELEPHONE: 201-733-6600

THE MONTCLAIR ART MUSEUM

A true art museum nestled in a town that was once an artists' center, the Montclair Museum reflects a high level of community support. Built in 1912, this is not somebody's leftover mansion but a solid, stone neo-Classical edifice dedicated to the showing of painting and sculpture. The major collection is of American paintings covering a period of three centuries. Many a familiar name — Edward Hopper, Mary Cassatt, Benjamin West — is represented here, along with a host of other American artists. Two large rooms are reserved for the special exhibits which are often of important American painters of various schools.

Additional collections include prints, tapestries and needlepoint, the Whitney silver collection, Chinese snuff bottles, and American costumes and accessories. And upstairs, a permanent Indian collection is of interest to the kids. Costumes and artifacts go beyond New Jersey's Lenni Lenape — the Plains and Southwest Indians are given equal treatment here with good displays of Sioux and Navajo dress.

This is quite an active museum what with lecture series, morning coffee hours, gallery talks, Saturday night movies and an ongoing art school downstairs. Unfortunately, it closes down in the summer. Free (donations accepted).

> **HOURS:** Tues. - Sat. 10-5; Sun. 2-5. Closed July and August.
> **LOCATION:** Bloomfield Ave. & South Mountain Ave., Montclair, Essex County.
> **TELEPHONE:** 201-746-5555

MORRIS MUSEUM OF ARTS AND SCIENCES

On rainy days, empty weekends or just any day, there's nothing like a quick trip to a local bastion of culture to uplift the spirit, educate, and get the kids out of the house all in one fell swoop. The Morris Museum of Arts and Sciences is one of these dependable bastions. Housed in a lovely old mansion surrounded by great trees, it is small enough not to be to exhausting to young children. It is also varied enough to appeal to children of all ages, plus their parents.

Of its many exhibits one of the most popular is the first floor room devoted to the Story of Sound. Here you can pull telephone receivers from the wall and listen to voices as they would sound in different periods of time. I've seen children as young as two years old listen with rapt attention to the incomprehensible voice on the other end. A new computer exhibit is always crowded also.

Next door, the Focus on Fibers exhibit is a graphic, colorful presentation of the different materials and dyes used by mankind throughout the ages. A technological game is here — one of matching up textures and fibers. Neither I nor my children have ever figured out how to win this game, but it's fun pressing the buttons and turning the dials just the same.

Science and Technology is also represented by a rock and mineral exhibit as well. (This one comes complete with a dark room for viewing fluorescent rocks.) The natural sciences are represented by glass-encased exhibits of stuffed animals in their natural environments, plus a live zoo downstairs. The children usually trek down to this room with its lazy alligator and turtles safely behind glass cases. And since it is called a museum of arts and sciences, there is always at least one major art exhibit on display that is changed every few months.

Social Sciences are found on the second floor. Here, 3rd, 4th and 5th graders can see graphic examples of their studies of both North American Indian and colonial life. Besides the colonial kitchen and everything you'd ever want to know about the Lenni Lenape Indians, the second floor also offers a special "touch and feel" room for two-to-seven year olds.

Other popular exhibits are the model railroad in the basement and the tiny dinosaur room, also downstairs. And last, but not least, is the Museum Gift Shop where my son has bought at least thirty rocket erasers at 35 cents each, only to lose them mysteriously as soon as we get home. The museum also includes a comfortable 300 seat theater which is the scene of many special events and shows.

HOURS: Daily, 10-5; Sun., 2-5; Summer: Tues. - Sat. 10-4
ADMISSION: Adults, $1.00; Children, 25¢
DIRECTIONS: Route 24 to Normandy Parkway, Morris Twp., Morris County
TELEPHONE: 201-538-0454

BERGEN COMMUNITY MUSEUM

Here is another local museum that offers both the arts and sciences, with a nice balance between the adult and children's exhibits. Although much of the gallery area in this 25-year-old private institution is given over to changing exhibits, the permanent collection includes the Hackensack Mastodon and the newer Dwarskill Mastodon and several other natural history displays.

For children there is the Discovery Room with touch and feel exhibits and a small "shadow" room a la Franklin Institute. Another room displays snakes, frogs and fishtanks and of course the inevitable Indian collection is placed about. Changing exhibits include photographs, invitational paintings and technological displays. And there is always some family activity offered at 2 P.M. on Saturdays. The museum is located (or should I say, hidden) in the right wing of the Bergen County Community Services Building, a huge brick building in the typically bureaucratic style of architecture.

HOURS: Tues. - Sat.: 10-5: Sun.: 1-5.
ADMISSION: Adults: $1.00; Children: $.50
LOCATION: Corner of E. Ridgewood and Fairview Aves. Paramus, Bergen County
TELEPHONE: 201-265-1248

THE MONMOUTH MUSEUM

What makes this museum a cut above the others for children is that it has the largest hands-on exhibit in New Jersey. Actually, this handsome modern building has both adult and children's sections in its limited area but the children's museum is by far the more interesting.

In this section you find one complete exhibit that runs at least a year. The one I saw was called "Habitat" and it showed great imagination by using fairly simple materials to mount a first-rate display. Unlike the dazzling machinery and computers you find at The Franklin Institute in Philadelphia or Sesame Place Park, the display at Monmouth Museum relied on wood, fabric, paint and lighting. Put your hand inside a hole to feel fur or smooth surface and guess what it is — sometimes it's a walrus tusk. Walk under a roof of strings that depicts roots growing underground. An animal's burrow turns into a metal tunnel slide which transports the child from the second to the first floor. (Obviously popular!)

The Habitat exhibit included live snakes in a desert panorama, a green forest glade, a cityscape and such, all done at minimal cost and with maximum ingenuity. When Habitat ends, in the spring of 1982, a complete new theme exhibit will be installed.

The adult section of the museum is also changed completely every so often. The exhibit I saw depicted seaside life in the late Victorian era, complete with wooden carousel and turn of the century costumes — very well done also. But the adult section is only the size of a large room, so exhibits are limited.

Although the Monmouth Museum is located inside the campus of a community college, it is a private institution and is not free, so

be warned beforehand. During school season, the children's exhibit
is very popular.

> HOURS: Tues. - Sat. 10-4:30. Sun. 1-5.
> ADMISSION: Adults: $1.50; Children, Seniors, Students: $.75
> DIRECTIONS: Exit 109, Garden State Parkway, then west on Newman
> Springs Road (Route 520) to entrance of Brookdale Community College.
> TELEPHONE: 201-747-2266.

OTHER N.J. MUSEUMS OF ART AND SCIENCE

THE PATERSON MUSEUM: Established in 1927, the Paterson
Museum is known particularly for its mineral exhibit. Every child
visiting the museum can play the mineral game and win a mineral
of his own. There is also a large exhibit on the Lenni Lenape
Indians here and one on the history of Paterson. Free. **Hours:**
Mon. - Fri.: 1-5; Sat.: 10-12 & 1-5. Closed Saturdays in summer.
Closed major holidays. **Location:** 268 Summer St., Paterson,
Passaic County. **Telephone:** 201-742-4820.

JERSEY CITY MUSEUM: Located on the top floor of the Jersey
City main library, the museum is a combination of rotating
exhibits of contemporary art (usually one-person shows) and a
permanent gallery of 19th Century paintings and furnishings.
Free. **Hours:** Wed.: 11:30-8, Thurs. - Sat.: 11:30-4:30. Closed
Saturdays in summer. **Location:** Jersey & Montgomery Ave.,
Jersey City. **Telephone:** 201-547-4514.

RUTGERS GEOLOGY MUSEUM: A super-large room ringed
by a balcony comprises this science museum located on the second
floor of the Geology building on the Rutgers campus. A reconstructed mastodon, charts of geological periods, small fossils,
mineral display, etc. Interesting lectures and demonstrations for
school groups. The small gift shop has small rocks and minerals
for sale at very reasonable prices. Free. **Hours:** 9-4, Mon. - Fri.,
Sept. -June. **Location:** College Ave., Queens College, Rutgers,
New Brunswick. **Telephone:** 201-932-7243.

RUTGERS UNIVERSITY ART GALLERY: Housed in modern
Voorhees Hall, the art gallery includes a permanent collection of
American artists with many well-known names, such as Winslow

Homer, among the exhibits. Prints, sculpture and changing displays. Free. **Hours:** Summer: Weekdays, 10-4:30; Sun., 1-4; Winter: Weekdays, 10:30-4:30; Weekends: 12-5. **Location:** Voorhees Hall, Hamilton St., Queens Campus, Rutgers Univ., New Brunswick. **Telephone:** 201-932-7237.

PRINCETON ART MUSEUM: Mentioned in the section on Princeton but worth another mention here since it is one of the nicest art museums in New Jersey. Not overly big, but modern, well-lit, and with a collection that encompasses European and Oriental art as well as American. Free. **Location:** Princeton Campus, Nassau St. & Washington Road, Princeton, Mercer County. **Hours:** Tues. - Sat.: 10-4; Sun.: 1-5. Summer Hours: Tues. - Sun.: 2-4. **Telephone:** 609-452-3783.

DREW UNIVERSITY ARCHAEOLOGY MUSEUM: Not much space in this new museum to display all the artifacts, but there is a mummified bird, a model of a temple, pottery shards and lots of information on excavations. However, as with other small, specialized museums, the interest is not only in the displays but in the lectures and slide shows given to groups. Call first for reservations to these. Free. **Hours:** Wed.: 1-4; Weekends: 1:30-4:30. Closed school holidays. **Location:** Embury Hall, Drew Univ., Route 24 (Main St.) Madison, Morris County. **Telephone:** 201-377-3000, Ext. 305.

New Jersey: Specialty Museums

FRANKLIN MINERAL MUSEUM

New Jersey is both the zinc mining and fluorescent rock capital of the world. While this may not be on the same level as a financial or entertainment capital, it does provide one mecca for rockhounds — Franklin Borough in Sussex County. Here, in a small building nestled in the green-clad mountains you will find the Franklin Mineral Museum.

Children seem to have a fascination with rocks — as any mother who has ever dumped odd-sized stones out of her darling's pockets can attest. At the Franklin Mineral Museum you can dig for rocks with pick and shovel at the adjacent Buckwheat Dump. The

Museum itself is divided into three sections: a fluorescent rock display, a general exhibit on zinc and other minerals, and a replica of an actual mine.

Once you enter the unprepossessing building and pay the reasonable entrance fee, you are ushered into a long, narrow room by the genial guide. There you face a row of gray, ordinary rocks of varying sizes behind a glass case. The guide flicks off the lights, and lo and behold — the rocks turn into an extraordinary array of shining colors. Green, purple, blue luminous rocks, many with unusual patterns, glow behind the glass while the guide explains their names and properties. The guide flicks on the light and it's all over. The rocks are back to their old pedestrian form.

Next on the agenda is a tour of the mine replica by a retired miner who is in himself a mine of information about working conditions. Zinc mines, it seems, were much safer than coal mines, and the plaster labyrinth we entered was not so much scary as claustrophobic. The replica is actually above ground, but the walls and ladders and narrow passages are so authentic I could have sworn I was underground. We passed ore cars and plaster miners while our guide assured us that the walls were friendly and that miners only fear the large excavations.

Once the tours are over, you are free to examine the exhibits in the third room which include a number of unusual rocks and zinc mining materials. A gift shop in the main lobby also sells a very good selection of rocks, gemstones and necklaces at non-inflated prices.

But for many, the highlight of the trip is the chance to go prospecting in the rock dump at the back of the museum. You must bring your own equipment — pickaxes, hammers, shovels (or just your own hands since many of the rocks are loose) plus a bag to carry your specimens. Those who hope to find a fluorescent rock need a special lamp to determine whether they have a genuine article. School age children love the dumphunting, but they must be accompanied by an adult until they are fourteen.

HOURS: April - Nov. Wed. - Sat.: 10-4:30; Sunday: 12:30-4:30
Tours take about one hour.
ADMISSION: Adults: $1.50; Teenagers: 75¢; Children: 50¢ Same rate applies for dump
DIRECTIONS: Route 80 to Route 15 Sparta, then Route 517 to Franklin then one mile north on 23. Museum is on Evans St.
TELEPHONE: 201-827-3481

THE GOLF HOUSE

Set among the posh country estates of Somerset Hills, the Golf House is a combination of museum, stately house and working headquarters of the United States Golf Association. It is truly a mansion in the grand manner with well-placed spruce, pine and dogwood framing the landscape. A circular driveway leads you up to the white portico where you almost expect a butler to take your bags. However, you simply park in the adjoining lot and enter the massive doors. A receptionist will give you some literature and tell you it's a self-guided tour. Originally built by John Russell Pope back in 1919, (Pope was one of America's leading architects and also designed the Jefferson Memorial among others), the home was bought by the Golf Association in 1972 and has been open to the public ever since.

The tour generally starts in the old dining room which now houses paintings, pictures and golf clubs of the famous. The clubs of Franklin Roosevelt, Woodrow Wilson and of course, Dwight D. Eisenhower are displayed here. Also on view, over the marble fireplace, is the Moon Club used by Alan Shepard to play a shot on the lunar surface in 1971. Clubs such as those used by trick-shot artist Joe Kirkwood and those donated by USGA champions are also on view.

Further on, an exhibit of golf balls shows their evolution from feathery to gutta percha to the rubber ball of today. Clubs also evolved from rather primitive curved instruments to the sleek metal irons used nowadays. The exhibits are well mounted and explicit enough to interest even such a nonaficionado as myself.

A huge panelled family room with a magnificent fieldstone fireplace is the setting for masses of championship medals, trophies, photographs and cartoons all relating to you-know-what. On the other side of the house a lovely library, containing 6,000 volumes, is housed in what was once the ballroom of the mansion.

Those more interested in architecture and art than golf can view the magnificent flying staircase with its handsome grandfather clock on the stairwell. A bust of Eisenhower by Jo Davidson, a painting by Eisenhower of the 18th hole of the Augusta National Golf Course and some colorful costumes of early golfers are all here for inspection. One of New Jersey's nicest freebies.

HOURS: Mon. - Fri. 9-5; Weekends: 10-4. Closed holidays.
LOCATION: Route 512, east of Route 202, Far Hills, Somerset County
TELEPHONE: 201-234-2300

THE BELL LABS EXHIBIT

Tucked quietly in the lobby wings of the giant Bell Labs complex is a first rate science museum. It 's the sort of thing the state could do if they had the money and technological expertise. Bell Labs — where the transistor and magnetic bubble were born — has plenty of both.

At the exhibit, the medium is the message. The message — which is that AT&T works day and night repairing trunk lines and thinking up faster ways of speeding our phone bills to us — is frankly, boring. But the medium! That giant map of the United States with its rows of tiny colored lights that blink across the country. Those banks of phone receivers that tell you of the marvels of Ma Bell. A talking computer! (All it said was, "The number you have reached is not a working number." But at least now I know why I can't get a straight answer from the phone company).

The exhibit is geared to the 12-year-old and up, but a smart 10-year-old or a dumb 40-year-old can enjoy it too. Push a button and round marble "molecules" cascade down a changing series of steps. Push a button and the lights go up on the Loop Theater (the script unfortunately was too technical for me). Push a button and you see yourself, rather faintly, on TV.

Over at the other wing (the right hand side of the lobby) the exhibit is devoted to history. On this side you can see the original receiver and hear Alexander Graham Bell shouting "Mr. Watson, come here, I need you!" You can also hear a 1933 stereophonic recording of Leopold Stokowski conducting symphonic music (kids love this — I don't think they ever hear good orchestra music nowadays). Another recording you can hear is the original soundtrack of the first talking picture, "The Jazz Singer," with Al Jolson coming over rather tinnily through the receiver. There is also a display of phone service of the future but the much-vaunted "picturephone" is not here and will not be ready for years.

If you visit, you might feel more comfortable going on a weekend when there are no employees milling around the lobby. Free.

HOURS: Weekdays: 8:15-5:30. Weekends: 1-5:30. Some exhibits closed Mondays.
LOCATION: South St. & Mountain Ave., Murray Hill, (New Providence) Union County.
TELEPHONE: 201-582-3000.

SQUIBB HEADQUARTERS

There are really two museums here. One is a small pharmaceutical exhibit that traces the history of Squibb products from their humble beginning and includes old-fashioned microscopes, old patent medicine bottles, etc. The other is the adjacent art gallery which rotates its shows. Because new artists are often shown here and reviewed by art critics, the Squibb galleries have achieved a certain importance in the New Jersey art world. Another "show" you get at Squibb is the spectacular gathering of waterfowl that come by the hundreds in fall and winter to stay at the pond that fronts the complex. Free.

HOURS: 9-5 Mon. - Fri. Weekends: 1-5
LOCATION: Route 206 between Princeton and Lawrenceville, Mercer County

NATIONAL BROADCASTERS HALL OF FAME

This is one of those interesting museums that are basically one man's baby. In this case, Arthur Schreiber began and now directs this monument to the radio and highlights of its past. The basic displays are of old microphones, old radios, earphones, props and tributes to those inducted into the Hall of Fame such as Bing Crosby and Bob Hope.

You begin your tour with a short slide presentation of the history of radio — or rather a history of radio's social impact. The early music broadcasts, the beginning of network radio (which led to network television), the voices of world leaders whose rhetorical styles were so suited to the medium are included. Whether it was the big bands broadcasting from downtown Cincinnati, the Orson Welles program that panicked America or the soap operas (so called because the sponsors of those dramas were soap companies), radio helped to shape the 20s, 30s and 40s. Alas, during the 50s it looked like radio was a goner until Rock and Roll saved the medium (if not the eardrums of the nation's teenagers).

After the slide show, you may peruse the exhibits and listen to tape recordings of old programs. There is also a well-stocked gift counter that offers books and interesting souvenirs. Unfortunately, when The National Broadcasters Hall of Fame moved from its original address (a reconverted bank building) to its present location, they lost some space; so not all the original displays are up. Hopefully, they will get a new location. The collection here has much nostalgia to offer those who remember when the radio was the most important piece of furniture in the house.

HOURS: Mon. - Fri.: 10-3; Sun.: 12-3. Closed Sat. Winter Hours: Sun. - Thurs.: 12-3
ADMISSION: Adults: $2; Children: $1.
LOCATION: 22 Throckmorton St., (off W. Main St.), Freehold, Monmouth County
TELEPHONE: 201-431-4656

THE WINDMILL MUSEUM

Designed and built by Poul Jorgenson and his wife, the sixty foot Volendam mill is a seven story structure with sail arms that measure 68 feet from end to end. Although the sail arms can turn, the windmill is not used as such but as a museum. Old milling tools, ancient millstones, and wooden shoes are on display as Mr. Jorgenson gives a guided tour to explain the workings of windmills. The tour lasts 45 minutes to an hour (depending on the age of the children).

HOURS: April - Labor Day: Daily 10-12 & 1-6; Sept. - Nov.: Daily except Tues.: 10-12 & 1-4
ADMISSION: Adults: 75¢; Children: 25¢
LOCATION: Adamic Hill Road, near Milford, off Route 519, Hunterdon County
TELEPHONE: 201-995-4365

RAGGEDY ANN DOLL MUSEUM

Another one of those one-man museums you find scattered about New Jersey, but in this case it is a woman who has amassed the collection. Hundreds of dolls of all types are here, plus dollhouses, carriages, trains and other toys. Figures include 19th century bisque and wooden dolls and 20th century plastic ones. There is particular emphasis on character dolls — Winston Churchill, Elizabeth Taylor, Elvis Presley and other personalities over the ages peer from behind the glass. The museum dolls are for perusal only, but there are two rooms devoted to items for sale. Jean Bach, the owner and collector, also does antique doll appraisals (for a small fee). The museum is housed in a rambling Victorian house that is not far from the outlet and specialty shops of Flemington.

HOURS: April - Dec.: Wed. - Sun.: 10-5. Weekends only Jan., Feb., March.
ADMISSION: Adults: 75¢; Children: 50¢; Under 5, free.
LOCATION: 171 Main St., Flemington, Hunterdon County.
TELEPHONE: 201-782-1243

AVIATION HALL OF FAME

Aviation achievements from balloon voyages in 1850 Perth Amboy to modern day flights are commemorated by this fairly new hall of fame. This small aeronautical museum, opened in 1976, is located on top of the old Teterboro Airport control tower. Views of the runway, and a short film on aviation history await. Most of all you can listen in to pilot-control tower conversation over the radio. For those who remember when a Sunday afternoon outing with the kids was a jaunt to the airport, this one sounds interesting.

HOURS: 10-4 Daily
ADMISSION: Adults: $1.25; Children: $1.00
LOCATION: Atlantic Aviation Hangar, Teterboro Airport, off Route 46, Bergen County
TELEPHONE: 201-288-6344

CAMPBELL MUSEUM

For America's biggest soup company, what else but a collection of soup tureens and ladles? However, since the decoration of tureens was considered high art in the 17th and 18th centuries, the collection here is quite dazzling. Porcelain, silver, pewter — the most extensive collection in the world is found here and includes pieces used by European royalty as well as some highly historical artifacts. Free.

HOURS: Mon. - Fri. 9:30-4:30. Closed holidays.
LOCATION: Campbell Place, Camden. Off Route 30 near Ben Franklin Bridge
TELEPHONE: 609-964-4000.

SALEM GENERATING STATION

Despite all the bad publicity nuclear energy has gotten lately, this museum tries to show the bright side of the atom. A refurbished ferryboat, now anchored and dubbed "The Second Sun," serves as an information center for nuclear energy at the Public Service Electric & Gas Company's generating station in a corner of Salem County. Hands-on exhibits include a neutron gun which you can fire to start your own chain reaction and a model nuclear reactor. Exhibits on the history of energy, a 25-minute film on Edison and the "Century of Light" and several walk-through mini-movies are on hand. Groups by reservation. Free.

HOURS: Wed. - Fri.: 9-4; Sat.: 10-4; Sun.: 12-6
LOCATION: Lower Alloways Creek, Salem County. Take Exit 1 from N.J. Turnpike to Route 49 through Salem to Hancock's Bridge, then follow signs.
TELEPHONE: 609-935-2660

EDISON MEMORIAL TOWER AND MUSEUM

The tower is shaped like an electric light with a bulb on top and commemorates the site of Edison's Menlo Park laboratory, birthplace of the incandescent bulb. The original laboratory was moved to Greenfield, Michigan, by Henry Ford for his Americana Museum, but there is a small museum here with mementos of Edison's achievement. Free.

HOURS: Wed. - Fri.: 10-12 & 1-6; Sat.: 10-12 & 1-6; Sun.: 1-6.
LOCATION: Christie St., Menlo Park, in Edison State Park, Middlesex County.
TELEPHONE: 201-549-3299

New Jersey: Historical Museums

MUSEUM OF EARLY TRADES AND CRAFTS

Created in 1970 to preserve the life and times of early settlers, this small museum shows the labor of love of its creator and curator. Thirty-eight years of collecting and research went into the exhibits. Diaries, ledgers, advertisements, broadsides, and newspapers were scoured for details of everyday life in the Colonies — most particularly life in the New Jersey colony. The exhibit on brooms, for instance, is based on the business of one particular broommaker in Florham Park. He started out with one broommaking machine, used local cattails for the brush, and did business as a sideline to farming. Later, as times prospered, the broommaker had several employees and a full time business. This information and much, much more is imparted by the curator and docents who greet each visitor at the door.

For the first generation of settlers, home meant a one-room shack with a dirt floor. Furniture was crudely made from the wood of surrounding trees. You ate what you grew or what you bartered. Mother was the family doctor and every household had an herb garden that was used for medicine as well as flavoring.

Major exhibits of the museum change every few months but each one takes a particular trade or craft and follows it through three generations. The exhibit I encountered emphasized shoes. Shoes were made by the father of the family in the first generation. Cobblers came in later. Leather was taken from the hides of cows that were slaughtered for food. Shoes which were made at night by candlelight had neither right nor left feet. Both halves of the pair were exactly the same. Just imagine — a colonial mother didn't have to stand there in the morning and repeat, "No, the left shoe goes on the left foot," as I do.

Besides the changing exhibits, there is a permanent room set up as a colonial kitchen. This one is of a typical household and is poorer and sparser than those you would find in the homes of wealthy landowners such as the Ford Mansion. The museum also contains a complete set of tools for the 34 trades that existed in New Jersey at the time of the Revolution. Although the museum is not very large, the lectures are so comprehensive that you should plan to spend at least an hour here.

HOURS: 10 AM - 5 PM Daily. 2-5 PM Sunday. Closed major holidays.
ADMISSION: Free (one dollar donation suggested)
LOCATION: Main Street (Route 24) and Green Village Road, Madison, Morris County
TELEPHONE: 201-377-2982

SCHOOLHOUSE MUSEUM

Although this historical museum is set inside an 1873 school-house, only one section of the vast paraphenalia collected here is devoted to the little old schoolroom. Besides the teacher's platform, desks, maps and schoolbooks, there is also a colonial and Victorian kitchen and sections set up as typical rooms of the 19th Century. Over 3,000 items are jammed into the one huge room — everything from bobbin lace to beaver hats. Upstairs, the attic has even more with lots of 19th Century dresses, firemen's uniforms, etc. Memorabilia of the church, early Dutch settlers and local celebrities (including a well-known actor), tools and harness and more are all to be found in this well-stocked museum. Free. (Donations accepted).

HOURS: Mid-April - Mid-Dec.: Sun. 2:30-4:30. Wed. by appt.
LOCATION: 650 East Glen Ave. right off Route 17, Ridgewood, Bergen County.
TELEPHONE: 201-445-1778 (Director): 201-447-3243 (Museum).

OCEAN COUNTY HISTORICAL MUSEUM

Basically a historic house with rooms set up in comfortable 19th Century fashion. A music-library room, and a well-set dining room set the tone. The Victorian kitchen is of particular interest since it is chock full of useful gadgets that have since been deemed non-essential. A gizmo for softening corks had the curators mystified until a tourist told them what it was.

Upstairs a child's bedroom is all set up and a small schoolhouse impresses the youngsters. Downstairs, in the basement there is a museum-type memorabilia including a machine for harvesting cranberries and pictures of Lakehurst during the age of dirigibles.

HOURS: Tues. - Thurs.: 1-3; Sat.: 10-12
ADMISSION: $1.00 per person
LOCATION: 26 Hadley Ave., Toms River, Ocean County
TELEPHONE: 201-341-1880

HOPEWELL MUSEUM

Again, a combination historic house/museum with rooms done up in particular periods. The house itself is Victorian, but the rooms display colonial, Empire and Victorian furnishings. An 1880 organ and a Joseph Bonaparte sideboard are prized possessions here. In the back of the mansion, an addition houses a large Indian collection and a great many costumed mannequins. The costumes include ballgowns, wedding dresses and other finery worn in the 19th Century. Free. (Donations accepted).

HOURS: Mon., Wed., Sat.: 2-5
LOCATION: 28 East Broad St. (Route 518) Hopewell, Mercer County
TELEPHONE: 609-466-0103

OCEAN CITY HISTORICAL MUSEUM

Life in the 1890's is graphically depicted in this historical museum which harks back to the heyday of the Jersey shore. Ocean City, the quiet and sober neighbor of Atlantic City, has attracted families to its beaches since 1879. Costumes, furnishings, Indian artifacts and mementos of the wreck of the Sindia are all here. Free.

HOURS: June - Aug.: Mon. - Sat.: 10-4; Sept. - May: Tues. - Sat.: 1-4. Closed holidays.
LOCATION: 409 Wesley Ave., Ocean City, Cape May County.
TELEPHONE: 609-399-1801.

SPY HOUSE MUSEUM

A combination of historic site and two museums make up this unusual complex by the seashore. One section is a cottage erected in 1663 and called "The Spy House" because it was a favorite meeting place of Revolutionary War spies. The Shoal Harbor Marine Museum and the Penelope Stout Museum of Crafts of Man comprise the rest of the complex. You can find lobster pots, eeling equipment, a variety of furniture in this tripart museum.

HOURS: Mon., Sat.: 1-3; Sun.: 2:30-5.
ADMISSION: Adults: 50¢; Children, Seniors: 25¢; Under 5 free.
LOCATION: 119 Port Monmouth Rd., Port Monmouth. (Take Exit 117 off Garden State Parkway to Route 36E to Port Monmouth.)
TELEPHONE: 201-787-1807

CAPE MAY COUNTY HISTORICAL MUSEUM

Housed in a well-preserved 18th Century home, the museum includes an 1820 dining room all set up, a children's room with antique toys, and much glassware and china. Across the yard the well stocked barn features harpoons from Cape May's whaling past, Indian artifacts and farm implements. Here also is the huge glass prism top to the old Cape May lighthouse. Visits are by guided tour and take about an hour. The adjacent Genealogy Room is of interest to many historians because of the number of Mayflower descendents in the Cape May area. There is also a small gift shop in the museum proper.

HOURS: Summer: Mon. - Sat., 10-4; Winter: Tues. - Sat., 10-4. Closed Jan. and Feb.
ADMISSION: Adults $1.50; Children $.50
LOCATION: Route 9 at Cape May Court House, Cape May County
TELEPHONE: 609-465-3535

NEW JERSEY HISTORICAL SOCIETY

One of the most extensive collections of books, manuscripts and other material about the Garden State is found in the library of this 4-story building. The museum section consists of rooms set up with colonial, federal and Victorian furnishings, and smaller rooms relating to specific interests such as music and printing. Artifacts of everyday life, plus rotating exhibits on quiltmaking, shipbuilding, etc. are featured here. Free.

HOURS: Mon. - Sat.: 12-4:15.
LOCATION: 20 Broadway, Newark.
TELEPHONE: 201-483-3939

MONMOUTH COUNTY HISTORICAL ASSOCIATION

Another combination of museum and society headquarters is housed in a handsome, 3-story Georgian colonial not far from the scene of the battle of Monmouth. Impressive collections of mahogany furniture, old china, glassware and paintings furnish the historical rooms of the "mansion" (it was actually built in 1931). You can also find specialty rooms devoted to dolls, old boxes, and so forth, plus an attic filled with bicycles, pony carts, and other leftovers from the 18th and 19th centuries.

HOURS: Tues. - Sat.: 10-4; Sun.: 1-4.
ADMISSION: Adults: $1.00; Children: $.50; Seniors: $.75.
LOCATION: 70 Court St., Freehold.
TELEPHONE: 201-462-1466

CAMDEN COUNTY HISTORICAL SOCIETY

Three sections include: a museum with early American glass, fire-fighting equipment, military artifacts and the tools of early handicrafts set up in "shops" of cobblers, carpenters, coopers, etc.; a library with 18,000 books and pamphlets, manuscripts and newspapers; and Pomona Hall, an excellent example of early Georgian architecture furnished in both 18th and 19th Century fashion. Free.

HOURS: Mon. - Thurs.: 12:30-4:30; Sun.: 2-4:30.
LOCATION: Park Blvd. & Euclid Ave., Camden.
TELEPHONE: 609-964-3333.

THE ROGERS EXHIBIT

Located a block and a half from Paterson's Great Falls, this interesting exhibit is not quite a permanent museum but rather a long-standing display housed in a huge glassed-in room that was once the Rogers Locomotive Factory. It contains a fascinating compilation of photographs, factory machines, old posters and early inventions.

Paterson seems to be the only community in New Jersey that does not equate the historical with the quaint. The great silk spinning machines, the pictures of grim, immigrant workers, the metal shell of the first submarine all testify to the fact that the dominant thrust of the 19th Century was the Industrial Revolution. The Rogers locomotive that stands outside the building was the Iron Horse that opened up the plains. Free.

HOURS: Contact Great Falls Park, 201-881-3848 or Great Falls Tour, 201-881-3896.
LOCATION: Spruce Street, off McBride, Paterson.

OTHER NEW JERSEY HISTORICAL MUSEUMS

There are dozens of other small historical museums dotted about the state. These reflect the past highlights of a particular region, as do many of the ones mentioned in this chapter, and are no less important. However limitations of time and space make it impossible to visit or even list the many historical museums available. Since these museums are usually of local interest they are often mentioned in local newspapers and special events are always written up. Readers interested in history should also check the listings of historic houses in this book. They are very similar in scope and content to the historical museums and may be found in such chapters as *"Where Washington Ate, Fought and Slept"*, *"Homes of the Rich and Famous"*, *"Walking Tours"* and *"Restored Villages, Mills, Farms and Homes"*.

New York Museums

METROPOLITAN MUSEUM OF ART

This huge Palladian building that covers several blocks of New York's Fifth Avenue is still the Grande Dame of museums this side of the Atlantic. It is the repository of a European culture wafted to our shores by millionaires whose art collections were donated for reasons of either generosity or tax exemptions. At one time the museum was so old-Europe centered that it admitted neither American nor "Modern" art. However, all that has changed.

With the addition of the American Wing you now get a museum and a half at the Met. The "wing" is, in fact, equal to most medium-sized museums. The three floors encompass American furniture and decorative arts, recreated 17th and 18th Century rooms, paintings and sculpture. To view it chronologically you must take an elevator and start at the top with the William and Mary chairs, descend through the restored rooms, the many paintings of George Washington (including the original "Crossing the Delaware"), pass the Frederic Remington sculptures and end up on the first floor with large well-lit canvasses by Whistler and John Singer Sargeant. To get back to the main museum you cross the piece de resistance: the Englehard Garden Court. This immense courtyard contains purple willowed Tiffany sceens, Louis Sullivan stairs and a complete bank facade. The glass-in courtyard offers potted palms, garden chairs, ashtrays for smokes and a wonderful 1900s ambience.

But to begin at the beginning — when you first enter the Metropolitan's huge marble lobby you may feel as if you've entered Grand Central Station by mistake. Milling crowds, a central information booth, several ticket booths, coat-check areas, signs for the restaurant and rest-rooms, a bookshop and a jewelry counter doing booming business — this is a museum? Well, one traditional feature of the museum is that from the front lobby it's Greeks to the left, Egyptians to the right and Europeans upstairs.

If you are with young children you might as well go for the mummies and the Temple of Dendur. Great stone sarcophagi and ancient sphinxes have a fascination for children that roomfuls of paintings simply don't. The Medieval armor on the first floor is another child's favorite.

The second floor houses the European paintings which start with the Medieval period. From there you wander through Italian and Northern Renaissance, Dutch Masters, English portraits and French landscapes.

There are so many rooms to wander through — a Renaissance patio and a medieval tapestry hall, rooms devoted to gilded musical instruments and, of course, the whole American wing. There's no time to see it all.

For the exhausted, there's always lunch at the Fountain restaurant where you can enjoy cafeteria-style food around the statued pool of an atrium. Don't expect too much from the food, and the din of two hundred people and clanking silver can become a bit much. But it's a unique place and both children and little old ladies like it.

HOURS: Tues.: 10-8:45; Wed. - Sat.: 10-4:45; Sunday: 11-4:45.
ADMISSION: Suggested donation: $3.50 Adults; less for children and seniors. Children under 12, free.
LOCATION: 5th Ave. between 81sth and 84th Sts., N.Y.C.
TELEPHONE: 212-879-5500

AMERICAN MUSEUM OF NATURAL HISTORY

Best known for its dinosaur collection — the bones have been carefully reconstructed to form the skeletons of Tyrannosaurus Rex and other favorite prehistoric animals — but there is plenty else here. The museum is huge and its collection totals more than 34 million artifacts and specimens.

First established in 1869, the museum has long been one of New York's greatest, although it began to look quite rundown a few years ago. However, renovations and a paint job have spiffed it up recently. Some of the spiffiest sections are:

The new Hall of Asian People is a full wing filled with exhibits, mannequins, costumes and music that take you from Samarkand to the islands of Japan. You could spend half a day in this hall alone.

The Gem and Mineral collection has a sparkling new setting. Huge sections of quartz and amethysts glow behind modernistic lucite cases in a darkened room. As for the famous jewels such as the "Star of India" — what I saw was a replica. Apparently the museum is not going to chance another robbery of its prize collection.

With all the different wings, halls and galleries, it's easy to get lost here. Luckily there are not only floor-plan maps available at the Information Desk but tours which leave about six times a day. The guides take you on an excursion of museum highlights. Check at the Information Desk for scheduled times, or just latch onto a group when they pass you.

Everyone has a favorite section in this museum. For the 4th graders I accompanied on a school trip it was the giant blue whale, the stuffed penguins and seals in the Ocean Life Hall. Of course, the dinosaurs on the 4th Floor rated high, as did the early mammals. Also in the vast building there are great stone heads from Central America and three floors of cheetahs and elk and elephants but who can see the complete Museum of Natural History in one day?

The **Hayden Planetarium** is right next door but you can gain entrance through the museum proper — although you must pay a separate fee. The planetarium is one of the largest in the country and runs both regular star shows and specials for children on Saturday morning. There are also Laserium concerts here, a lunar landscape, and a nice big meteor chunk to inspect.

As for eating, there is a cafeteria in the basement (although you practically have to belong to the Explorer's Club to find it) which serves typical institutional food with plastic everything. Or you can try the one or two bistros that have sprung up behind the museum on Amsterdam Avenue.

HOURS: Mon., Tues., Thurs., Fri.: 10-4:45. Wed.: 10 AM-0 PM.
Weekends: 10-5.
ADMISSION: (Suggested) Adults: $2; Children: $1.
LOCATION: Central Park West and 79th St., New York.
TELEPHONE: 212-873-1300

HAYDEN PLANETARIUM ADMISSION:
$2.35 Adults; $1.35 under 12.
Telephone: 212-873-8828 for planetarium schedule.

THE CLOISTERS

High on a tree-covered bluff just minutes from the bustling streets of Manhattan's Washington Heights, there stands a world apart. The Cloisters, a museum built in the style of a 14th Century monastery, displays the art and architecture of the Middle Ages in a setting completely devoted to that single age. Unlike its mother museum (for the Cloisters is a part of the Metropolitan Museum of Art) which tries to cover the span of art from antiquity to the 20th Century, this monastic replica covers only the 12th to 15th Centuries in Europe. But the Cloisters includes both religious and secular art and geographical variety. The red tile roof and campanile of the building reflect the style of a Southern European monastery. But inside you will find the actual stones, colonades and worn steps of a Romanesque Chapel, a Spanish apse and a Gothic hall complete with arched ceilings and flying buttresses.

The Cloisters gets its name from the covered walkway surrounding an enclosed garden that was typical of the Medieval monastery. The main cloister at the museum is the large central one on the first floor. Completed before 1206 and taken stone by stone from a Benedictine abbey in southern France, this cloister with its rounded arches and peaceful interior garden sets a tone of otherworldliness for the entire museum.

There are several other cloisters downstairs which one can walk through. Of particular interest to gardeners is the herb garden here. Two hundred species of plants grown in the Middle Ages sprout among the espalier trees and arcades of a Cistercian cloister. Here you will find not only the Physick herbs, but quite a few poisonous plants as well. Deadly Nightshade among others was routinely grown by monks who were the only apothecaries of their time.

Every museum has its star attractions and certainly one of the stellar crowd-pleasers at the Cloisters is the Hall of the Unicorn Tapestries. Remarkable in their color, preservation and realism, these several panels of tapestries tell a story which you read by moving from one to the other (they are not hung in consecutive order). The story of the hunt, killing and resurrection of the Unicorn was commissioned by a lord and shows the life of the Medieval aristocracy as well as the symbolism of the age. The "Belle Heures of the Duc de Berry" and the Chalice of Antioch are two other attractions in the downstairs treasury.

Of course no visit to a museum is complete without a stop at the gift shop. At the Cloisters you can find books, records of medieval music, posters, jewelry and replicas of statues and artworks. You can even find a do-it-yourself needlework kit for the famous unicorn in the garden.

Since the Cloisters is built on a bluff overlooking the Hudson, be sure to drink in the view of Fort Tryon Park and the wild Palisades across the river in New Jersey. John D. Rockefeller Jr. paid for it all — the Cloisters, the park and the view, when he donated the whole shebang in 1938.

    HOURS: Tues. - Sat. 10-4:45. Sunday 1-4:45
    ADMISSION: $2.50 suggested donation
    DIRECTIONS: George Washington Bridge to Henry Hudson Parkway
        North. Take first exit off Parkway to Fort Tryon Park.
        Follow signs.
    TELEPHONE: 212-923-3700

THE FRICK COLLECTION

This little jewel of a museum, housed in the former mansion of the coke and steel magnate, is a must for art lovers. The European paintings and furniture display a heavy emphasis on both the Renaissance and Eighteenth Century. The Fragonard Room with panels painted for Madame Du Barry and the Boucher Room with panels commissioned by Madame de Pompadour have the appropriate French furniture and ambience to take you back to the reigns of the various Louises. Medieval paintings, enamels, Rembrandts and lots of 18th Century British portraits and landscapes abound.

Since this was once a home, the paintings are hung much as they would have been in the days of opulence. Gainsborough ladies and Turner landscapes decorate the comfortable halls, and a lovely inner courtyard provides the sort of atrium for rest and contemplation cultured people once thought necessary. There is also a lecture hall for the free talks which are given at eleven o'clock certain weekdays.

Only the first floor is open, but this is a formidable collection, so allow at least an hour to browse through. Children under ten are not admitted and those under 16 must be accompanied by adults — they are serious about art in this place.

HOURS: Sept. - May: Tues. - Sat. 10-6; Sun. 1-6. June - Aug.: Wed. - Sat. 10-6; Sun. 1-6. Closed major holidays.
ADMISSION: Adults — $1.00 (except Sunday — $2.00). Students and Senior Citizens: $.50.
LOCATION: One East 70th St. (At Fifth Ave.) N.Y.C.
TELEPHONE: 212-288-0700

MUSEUM OF MODERN ART

The arbiter of taste for the modern world, the MOMA should be seen by everyone at least once. The collection ranges from Henri Rousseau and early Impressionists to the latest works. A leader in the collecting of photographs and films as art, the museum has also a section on industrial design which lets us all know what is good design and what isn't. An ice cream scoop featured here becomes *the* ice cream scoop to use. Outside there's the sculpture garden and outdoor cafe (lousy food!) that have been copied by everyone. Downstairs, the movies. Special exhibits honor the heroes of modern art. Ongoing renovations may change the layout.

HOURS: Fri. - Tues.: 11-6; Thurs.: 11-9; closed Wed.
ADMISSION: Adults: $3.00; students: $2.00; children and seniors: 75¢.
LOCATION: 11 West 53rd St. (between 5th & 6th Aves.), N.Y.C.
TELEPHONE: 212-956-7070.

GUGGENHEIM MUSEUM

New York's other modern museum is known as much for its Frank Lloyd Wright architecture (which resembles an inverted

Tower of Babel and clashes with the rest of Fifth Avenue) as for its interior. The masters of modern art are part of the permanent collection and there are plenty of special exhibits in the realm of paintings, sculpture and what-have-you.

HOURS: Tues: 11-8; Wed. - Sun.: 11-5.
ADMISSION: Adults: $2.00; students, seniors: $1.25
LOCATION: 1071 Fifth Ave. (at 88th St.), N.Y.C.
TELEPHONE: 212-860-1313.

Pennsylvania Museums

THE FRANKLIN INSTITUTE

If you go to Philadelphia to see Independence Hall and the Liberty Bell, don't leave without taking the kids to the Franklin Institute. It's one of the best hands-on museums ever, and is a fitting tribute to America's great Renaissance Man. You really can't miss it. The Institute covers almost a square block and is the only Classical building in Philadelphia with a Boeing 707 sticking out of its side. Actually, the 707 rests in the adjacent Science Park (open spring and summer) but is attached to the museum in umbilical cord fashion.

Once you enter the museum you find that the plane offers "flights" every twenty minutes. Naturally, you never take off, but sound effects duplicate the feeling. For those jaded kids who have been on a real plane, there is always the full-size steam locomotive down in the basement. This train travels only ten feet and leaves only once an hour. But here again, the sound effects, movements and real steam give you the feel of an old-fashioned train ride.

Other daily events include a man-made lightning show which runs once an hour, and a demonstration of the printmaking process on an old-fashioned machine. There is also a **planetarium** (separate tickets needed for this) which holds a special younger children's show on Saturday mornings. Regular shows, for kids over seven and adults, are run several times on weekends. And then there is the Discovery Theater wherein such popular shows as the freeze-the-hot-dog-and-then-break-it extravaganza keep the kids fascinated.

But the special events are just part of what the Institute has to offer. The permanent exhibits are almost all made for touching, jumping on or walking through. On the second floor, for instance, there is a large plaster model of the human heart which you walk into. Walk up and down, more exactly, for you go up the stairs to the ventricles, peer through the aorta, make a few turns then go down the stairs. The passageways are narrow as these stairs are made for children and thin adults. Fat grownups may be caught between the Devil and deep red ventricle.

Most popular of all with kids is the Energy Room with its giant lever. There are ropes hanging from the lever which the kids climb up, Tarzan style. With each rope they are moving 250, 500 or 1000 pounds of weight respectively. Of course the kids have plenty of fun whether they are absorbing any science or not.

There are four floors to the museum with special rooms devoted to mathematics, physics, nuclear fission, time, aviation and such. Among the most fascinating of the exhibits are: an area where you can take pictures of your own shadow; a chain reaction you can start with ball bearings; a Rube Goldberg-type machine that does absolutely nothing useful when you set it in motion; a small two-seater "plane" ride; and a real ham radio. There are also exhibits on ships, the electro-magnetic spectrum and holography.

For those who becomed famished from all the scientific work of pushing and pulling gadgets, there is the duly scientific Mac-Donald's with its computer-timed French fries right there in the basement. Outside, you can also find a vendor of Pennsylvania soft pretzels and American soft drinks doing big business.

HOURS: Mon. - Sat.: 10-5; Sun.: 12-5
ADMISSION: Adults: $2.50; Children: $1.50
LOCATION: 20th St. and Benjamin Franklin Parkway, Philadelphia
TELEPHONE: 215-448-1000

PHILADELPHIA MUSEUM OF ART

It is a Greek temple that surveys the town and the river from an imposing height, with a magnificent flight of steps leading up to its classical columns. The steps, in fact, are as famous as the museum ever since Sylvester Stallone ran up them in the movie, "Rocky".

But inside the pillared entrance (you can avoid most of the steps by parking in the back parking lot), an eclectic collection awaits. Galleries of European art include the Johnson Collection on the first floor, which is heavy in Renaissance paintings. Twentieth Century art comes next and includes Marcel DuChamps' famous "Nude Descending A Staircase." The variety of the museum is evidenced by the fact that there is a medieval cloister, an Indian temple, a Chinese palace hall and a Japanese teahouse all within these portals. And one whole section, devoted to Americana, includes period rooms filled with Philadelphia style bonnet-and-scroll top bureaus, secretaries and chests. There is plenty of early silverware, also.

Tours are offered by volunteer guides at no extra cost. They leave on the hour, from 10 AM to 3 PM and originate in the West Entrance Hall.

HOURS: Wed. - Sun.: 10-5. Closed legal holidays.
ADMISSION: Adults: $1.50; Children, students, seniors: $.75. Free on Sunday until 1 PM.
LOCATION: Benjamin Franklin Parkway & 26th St., Philadelphia
TELEPHONE: 215-763-8100

PENNSYLVANIA ACADEMY OF FINE ARTS

An ornate Victorian building created by architect Frank Furness, it is as striking an edifice as you will find anywhere. Inside, a domed ceiling of deep blue with twinkling stars, ornamental bronze railings and marble floors recreate the atmosphere of 1876 when this structure went up in time for the Philadelphia Centennial. A teaching institute as well as a museum, the Academy was originally founded by Charles Willson Peale and was home to Thomas Eakins and Mary Cassatt.

The permanent collection is dominated by American artists — Peale and Gilbert Stuart and others. Benjamin West's well-known "William Penn's Treaty with the Indians" hangs in the rotunda. A number of portraits of George Washington (it was not unusual for an artist to copy the same work over and over again in those days) hang in the rotunda also. However the collection also emphasizes more recent artists on the American scene.

The Academy is situated in Philadelphia's Center City, close to the grandiose City Hall. From September to July, an hour tour leaves the Grand Stairhall on weekdays at 11 & 2. Special tours can be arranged for groups, of course.

HOURS: Tues. - Sat.: 10-5; Sun.: 1-5. Closed major holidays.
ADMISSION: Adults: $1.00; Seniors, students: 50¢
LOCATION: Broad and Cherry Streets, Philadelphia
TELEPHONE: 215-972-7600

ROSENBACH MUSEUM AND LIBRARY

Located two blocks south of Rittenhouse Square in a lovely section of Philadelphia, this townhouse was once the home of rare book collectors. The books and furnishings of the Rosenbach brothers are at once a paeon to the good life and a paradise for collectors. Since one brother searched for antiques while the other concentrated on books, the home is a treasure trove of decorative arts at the same time it is an important research library.

There are 130,000 manuscripts and 30,000 rare books which range from medieval illuminated manuscripts to letters written by George Washington and Abraham Lincoln stored here. Lewis Carroll's own edition of *Alice in Wonderland* and the manuscript of James Joyce's *Ulysses* together with hundreds of first editions are shelved in what is essentially still a home with beautiful and delicate furniture.

The dining room where the brothers entertained wealthy guests features an Empire style table, Venetian Grand Canal scenes, Chippendale chairs and a delicate glass chandelier. A painting of Fanny Kemble by Thomas Sully and a scrolled fireplace adorn the cozy parlor. Some of the upstairs rooms are more museum-like with displays of special exhibits in glass cases and there is a room devoted to the illustrations of Maurice Sendak. Up here you will also find the personal library of Dr. Rosenbach. The Doctor made a career of finding rare books for wealthy clients, but when he made a particularly good discovery he often kept it for himself. Hence this collection of thousands of first editions and gold-bound tomes.

The tour guides sprinkle many personal anecdotes in with the recital of facts. Loves, hates, mistresses, fallings out — you learn it all.

Although the Rosenbach brothers lived in this house only from 1950 to 1952, when they were both old, the house and collection seem to come out of some turn-of-the-century novel by Henry James. It seems incredible that this cultured, even dandified atmosphere existed in the post-World War II period. Yet it's all here — oriental carpets and Herman Melville's bookcase (stacked with first editions of "The White Whale"), 17th Century gold chests and delicate French parlors. The museum is a must for collectors, librarians, art historians and anyone who wants pointers on how to live with class. Not for children, but senior high school and college students are welcome.

HOURS: Tues. - Sun.: 11-4. Closed holidays. Closed August.
ADMISSION: Adults: $1.50. Students, Seniors: 75¢
LOCATION: 2010 Delancey Place, Philadelphia
TELEPHONE: 215-732-1600

UNIVERSITY OF PENNSYLVANIA ARCHAEOLOGY MUSEUM

A full-blown museum, three stories high and a must for lovers of archaeology, antiquities and mummies, the University Museum is set amidst the congestion of the U of P campus in Philadelphia. But once inside, the halls echo of timeless antiquities even though modern pollution is slowly leeching the limestone from an ancient temple.

The Egyptian section is particularly good. A towering lotus-leaf pillar and one of the world's twelve remaining sphinxes (a small one but complete except for the eroded nose) are some of the many artifacts here. And upstairs one room is devoted to the art and science of mummy making. Statues of pharoahs, cats and gods are all part of this first-rate Egyptian room.

Another gallery is devoted to Chinese statues and miniatures, many of them acquired in the 1920s from money hungry Warlords. Some excellent pieces, including Buddhas, horses and ancient vases are to be found here. A full tour of the museum also brings to light rooms devoted to the Near East, Polynesian and African cultures.

Since this is a working museum, don't be surprised if you stumble over art students doing sketches of masks and statues. The archaeology students are dispersed around the world, digging up even more treasures. Volunteer guides conduct gallery tours on Wednesday and Sunday at 1 P.M. and a small cafeteria offers small lunches and hamburgers.

HOURS: Tues. - Sat.: 10-4:30; Sun.: 1-5. Closed Holidays. Closed Sunday from Mem. Day to Labor Day.
ADMISSION: Adults: $2.00; Children: $1.00
LOCATION: Univ. of Pennsylvania, 33 & Spruce Sts., Philadelphia
TELEPHONE: 215-898-4000

111

THE BARNES FOUNDATION

Eccentric millionaires may be lovable from a distance but just let one leave a museum behind and you realize all the problems inherent in eccentricity. Actually, the Barnes Foundation is a museum by accident. Its true function is to serve as an art school and research center. It is open to the public on a limited bases and probably only for tax reasons.

The handsome Renaissance building is located in the lovely Philadelphia Main Line suburb of Merion, next to St. Joseph's College. The landscaped grounds seem to invite inspection. But wait! You can't put a foot on the grass without writing ahead for permission. In fact, you need permission for just about everything in this place. The rules and regulations are formidable. Groups are not allowed to bring in more than twenty-five persons at a time. Since most bus groups number about 48, there is a problem right off the bat. Second problem is that only half the museum is open at any given time (due to the shortage of guards). That means the open portion is shifted every hour and three-quarters, and if your group shows up just at the changing of the guards that's too bad. All pocketbooks, by the way, must be checked downstairs before people enter the museum. No spike heels for ladies, no photographs inside or out. One gets the feeling that the ghost of Mr. Barnes (who invented argyrol and collected this outstanding collection) does not want strangers staring at his paintings.

Is all this worth it? If you like Impressionist painters, the answer is "yes". The largest collection of Impressionists in the United States resides here along with Cubists, and 17th century masters. El Greco's "St. Jerome and the Angel" is here along with Cezanne's "The Card Players". At least I think that's what the paintings are called — another peculiarity of the Barnes Foundation is that there are no titles, no dates, and no information about any of the paintings except for the artist's name at the bottom of the frame. No brochures, no floor plans, no nothing. So you may see dozens of Renoirs — dozens of plump, rosy nudes and children holding flowers — but you have no idea when each was painted.

This can cause considerable consternation among people who are used to having it all spelled out for them. I passed a couple from my bus tour who were puzzling about the creator of an African wood-carved sculpture housed on the second floor balcony.

"I think his name is Cote d'Ivoire," the husband said.

Helpfully, I summoned up my high school foreign language skills. "That's French for The Ivory Coast," I said. "It's undoubtedly a carving from West Africa's Ivory Coast, circa 1800."

The couple smiled and slunk away. It made my day.

If you go to the Barnes Foundation, for Heaven's sake make reservations first. And be prepared for bad lighting, eccentric hanging of pictures (you can miss a Picasso because it's up there over the transom) and a host of rules and regulations. But in spite of all the obstacles, this is a first-rate collection which every art lover should see.

> **HOURS:** Fri., Sat.: 9:30-4:30. Sun.: 1-4:30. Closed July & Aug.
> **ADMISSION:** $1.00
> **LOCATION:** Latch's Lane, Merion, Pennsylvania
> **TELEPHONE:** 215-667-0290

BUTEN MUSEUM OF WEDGWOOD

Run by a family of Wedgwood collectors, the museum is housed in a beautiful, Main Line mansion that was once the home of pianist Josef Hoffman. The 10,000 examples of Wedgwood include Jaspar, Parian, black basalt, busts, etc. Lectures for groups. Talks also given at certain times during the day for individuals. The talk explains some of the techniques used by the Wedgwood Company to create their distinctive china.

There are several rooms of displays, with one large room set aside as a sales shop. If you want to buy Wedgwood this is the place. Although the prices did not seem different from those any place else, the selection is wide.

> **HOURS:** Tues. - Fri.: 2-5; Sat.: 10-1
> **ADMISSION:** Adults: $1.50; Seniors, students: $1.00; Children: 50¢
> **LOCATION:** 246 North Bowman Ave., Merion, Pa.
> **TELEPHONE:** 215-664-6601

THE MERCER MILE

Three unusual museums in Doylestown are the legacy of Henry Chapman Mercer (1856-1930) a businessman, ceramicist, archaeologist, and according to many, an eccentric. The highly individual creations are known collectively as the Mercer Mile since they are within close distance of one another. They consist of:

THE MERCER MUSEUM: A sprawling, turreted structure of reinforced concrete, the museum houses a vast collection of America's pre-Industrial tools and crafts. Mercer was one of the first to collect early Americana (although everyone seems to be doing it now). He collected with the eye of an archaeologist, and all the minutae of everday life — from kitchen utensils to hatmaking machines — are revealed here. Small objects are exhibited in rooms by craft (e.g., the evolution of buttermaking) while larger objects are left free-standing or are suspended. Visitors often gasp when they step into the main section of the museum and find Conestoga wagons, harpoons and whaling skiffs suspended from the ceiling. Six floors of exhibits surround the central hall. Gallows, hearses, prisoners docks and the kitchen sink — it's all here. A library of early Americana is also on the premises.

> **HOURS:** March - Dec.: Mon. - Sat., 10-5; Sun.: 1-4:30
> **ADMISSION:** Adults: $2.00; Seniors: $1.50; Students: $1.00
> **LOCATION:** Green & Ashland Sts., Doylestown (Take Rte. 202 or Rte. 611 to Ashland St.)
> **TELEPHONE:** 215-345-0210

FONTHILL MUSEUM: The home of Mercer, it looks like a Spanish fantasy set on the quiet Pennsylvania landscape. Filled with the colorful Moravian tiles from his factory, the home has arches and winding stairways and uneven rooms and beautiful views. Guided tours only. Reservations suggested. **Hours:** March - Dec.: 10-3:30. **Admission:** Adults: $2.00, Seniors: $1.50, Students: $1.00 **Location:** E. Court St. off Rte. 313, Doylestown. **Telephone:** 215-348-9461

MORAVIAN POTTERY AND TILE WORKS: A short walk from Fonthill, the Tile Works shows the machinery and raw materials of the tile making process (workers are not always present) and also houses a gift shop where these unusual tiles may be bought. **Hours:** March - Dec. 10-4. **Admission:** Adults: $1.75, Seniors: $1.00, Students: $1.00, Family: $3.50. **Location:** E. Court St. off Rte. 313. **Telephone:** 215-345-6722.

THE BRANDYWINE RIVER MUSEUM

From the front it's a century old grist mill; from the back it's a strikingly modern glass tower overlooking the Brandywine River, and altogether it is a most pleasant museum where the setting and structure are almost as interesting as the paintings within.

Inside the stone and glass structure, the atmosphere belongs to the Brandywine River artists (a group that formed around Howard Pyle and N.C. Wyeth) and to Wyeth's talented progeny, particularly Andrew and his son Jamie. Both Pyle and N.C. Wyeth were famous illustrators and many an older edition of "Treasure Island" or "King Arthur" contain their realistic action pictures. Although storybook illustrators have never reached the heights of adulation that "purer" artists enjoy, nevertheless they are among the most respected painters in America.

Howard Pyle began a summer teaching center in the Brandywine Valley in 1898. The artists from this regional center include Maxfield Parrish, Peter Hurd, Frank Schoonover, George Weymouth, and, of course, N.C. Wyeth. But it is Andrew Wyeth, whose painting "Christina's World" is world famous, who holds the compelling interests for viewers in this museum. The strong emotional impact of his many canvasses dominates the collection here. You can also find a small number of Jamie's paintings in the permanent collection and of course there are always special exhibits which emphasize one or the other of the Brandywine artists.

After viewing the exhibits, you can sit back and enjoy a snack in the Tea Room (open 11:30-2:30 weekdays and 12-3:30 on weekends). Here you can look down on the leafy trails, the meandering river and the wildflower garden below. This lovely preserve is part of the Brandywine Conservancy, which keeps 5,000 acres in a state of nature — a most poetic place that seems to attract strollers, readers and young romantics.

As for children, there is a special Christmas display intended for them which runs throughout the month of December. It includes model trains, porcelain dolls and decorated Christmas trees.

HOURS: Daily except major holidays, 9:30-4:30
ADMISSION: Adults: $1.75; Senior Citizens: $1.00; Children: 75¢; under 6 free
LOCATION: On Route U.S. 1, Chads Ford, Pa.
TELEPHONE: 215-388-7601

PHILLIP'S MUSHROOM MUSEUM

Actually, there's not much to the museum — it's one large room that depicts the growing, picking, packing and cooking of the edible fungi. Exhibits and dioramas give the history and strange growing habits of the button-capped vegetable. A short movie explains the spore and spawn of mushrooms and, more importantly, gives some helpful cooking hints. Did you know you can slice them with an egg slicer? And should cook them only three minutes?

The museum is really just an excuse to browse in the gift shop which is stocked with towels, stationery, ceramics, etc. all with a mushroom motif. What's more, you can buy fresh mushrooms at $1.25 a pound here in the mushroom capital of the world. Since this "museum" is only half a mile from Longwood Gardens and close to the Brandywine Museum, it makes an easy stop for tourists either coming or going. Free.

> **HOURS:** 7 days a week.
> **LOCATION:** Route 1, Kennett Square, Pa. ½ mile south of Longwood Gardens.
> **TELEPHONE:** 215-388-6082

See Also: Museums that are part of a larger entity are mentioned under the title of the larger attraction — e.g., *The Glass Museum* (Wheaton Village), *West Point Museum* (West Point), *American Museum of Immigration* (The Statue of Liberty). New Jersey planetariums that are not part of a museum are listed in a separate chapter entitled, *"Other Outings."*

THE CLASSICS

Photo: Courtesy N.Y. Convention & Visitors Bureau

In This Chapter You Will Find:

United Nations Headquarters
The Statue of Liberty
Ellis Island
World Trade Center
Empire State Building
RCA Building
Circle Line Tour
West Point
Independence Mall, Philadelphia

←

The Statue of Liberty — you can visit from the Jersey side, too.

UNITED NATIONS HEADQUARTERS

The first thing you notice as you approach the United Nations complex is the line of colorful flags half-circling the entrance. All member nation flags are flown at the same height — only the UN flag is unfurled higher. The next thing you notice as you step through the iron gates is that this place is clean! No old newspapers, candy wrappers or soda cans litter the area. The United Nations may not police the world, but they sure know how to police the grounds!

Outside sculpture includes a gigantic abstract object next to the circular fountain, a Japanese Peace Bell ensconced in a pagoda, a Soviet "heroic" style sculpture of a man beating his sword into a plowshare (if only their politics imitated their art) and more. If you visit in the spring be sure to check out the gardens which are in back of the buildings. Daffodils and cherry trees bloom in early spring while the rose garden with its twenty varieties of tea roses blossoms later. There are also 52 dwarf fruit trees, sycamores and wisteria on the well-landscaped grounds.

Nearly a million people a year visit the UN Headquarters, and naturally most of them take the guided tour. Guides from 24 different nations conduct these tours which are open to the public seven days a week. The tours combine a short history of the aims, structure and activities of the United Nations itself with a description of the art and architecture you pass along the tour route. Here you will find out about the behind the scenes work of UNESCO, WHO and other specialized agencies. Many photographs of their work decorate the walls.

The number of chambers you enter during the tour depends on whether the various Councils are meeting or not. The General Assembly, which is usually open, is a huge hall with high domed ceiling and more than 2,000 seats. The slatted back walls are interspersed with banks of windowed booths where translators, photographers and TV people sit. This is the hall most often seen on television when a world-shaking meeting takes place.

The other chambers — the Security Council, the Economic and Social Council and the Trusteeship Council — were designed by a Norwegian, Swedish and Danish architect respectively, and their furnishings were donated by those countries. They all display the vertical and horizontal lines and rich wood grains we associate with "Danish Modern." In fact the whole complex has a definite Scandinavian look. A human thirst for color and representational art is seen in the gifts of other countries: a colorful tapestry from Senegal, the blue stained glass windows of Chagall, the stark reds of Roualt's "Christ Crucified," and a crimson Peruvian cermonial mantle.

The tour ends in the Public Concourse where you can proceed to the bookstore, gift shops and postal counter (a mecca for stamp collectors). Handicraft items from around the world, flags, dolls of all nations are priced reasonably, but no better than anywhere else. The bargain is the fact that there is no sales tax anywhere in the UN complex! For hamburgers and french fries there's a good coffee shop here.

> **HOURS:** 9-4:45 daily
> **ADMISSION:** Free. For tours — Adults: $2, Children: $1.
> Children under 5 not admitted on tours.
> **LOCATION:** 1st Ave. between 45th & 46th St., N.Y.C.
> **TELEPHONE:** 212-754-7713

THE STATUE OF LIBERTY

It has only been a few years since Liberty State Park opened and what a blessing it is for New Jersey residents who want to see the Statue of Liberty. No longer do we have to take the long ride to New York, pay a toll for the tunnel and then wait at Battery Park for the ferry. Now, from late April until late October, New Jerseyans can zip right over to Jersey City and take the ferry to either the Statue of Liberty or Ellis Island.

The statue seems just a stone's throw away. Actually it is only a half mile away and lies in New Jersey waters. However, Miss Liberty has always been considered New York's statue because she faces the New York Harbor where the ships, passing with their loads of immigrants, could see her lifting her lighted torch. As for New Jersey — let's face it — the Lady has her back turned on us.

No matter, once aboard the *Circle Line Ferry* (which is a pleasure in itself on a nice, breezy day) you get a view from all angles as the boat turns to make port. Liberty Island, where the statue stands, is larger than one would expect. On its 12½ acres there are several administration buildings, a large open park, and a souvenir building, with a pleasant, tree-shaded picnic area behind it. Also, you'll find esplanades rimming the island. From here you can savor the view of Manhattan's towers — although you'll need a telescopic lense to get a decent picture — plus the wide expanse of the harbor with its bustling boats.

When you enter the Statue proper, you first find the **American Museum of Immigration** which occupies the bottom floor of the pedestal. Dedicated to the millions who entered the United States during its peak immigration years, the museum includes photographs and descriptions of the major ethnic groups who make up the "melting pot." The famous, from Steinmetz to Einstein, are highlighted here as examples of the contributions of various groups.

Now for the climb. You can take an elevator to get to the top of the pedestal, (although the wait is long during peak seasons) or the stairs if you're up to it. But once you get to the pedestal you have no choice. Either walk twelve stories' worth of narrow, winding stairs to the crown, or forget it and enjoy the view from where you are. There are repeated warnings that once you begin the upward ascent to the crown there is no turning back. The space is so narrow that two people cannot pass at one time . . . therefore you must go up the up staircase and down the down staircase. No change of heart halfway up is allowed here. For those who achieve the crown, there is a great view. Kids enjoy the hike just to prove they can do it.

Both as a visit to a national shrine and as a pleasant day's outing on the water between two great ports, a trip to the Statue of Liberty is a must — at least once in a lifetime.

LOCATION: To reach Liberty State Park take the N.J. Turnpike to exit 14B. The ferry is now a short distance from the Park.

FERRY SCHEDULE: Three to four sailings daily, last week in April until last week in October. Otherwise use ferry from Battery Park, N.Y.C.

FARE: Adults $1.50, Children $.50

TELEPHONE: (Liberty State Park) 201-435-8509

ELLIS ISLAND

Something unusual indeed. The buildings are decaying, the great halls echo with dust and jackhammers, some wooden structures are literally falling into the sea — and yet it's fascinating. A ferry trip from Liberty State Park or the Battery takes you past the Statue of Liberty to this other island, where twelve million immigrants passed inspection to enter the New World.

Ellis Island was abandoned as an immigration station in 1954 (it had been used briefly both as a Coast Guard Station during World War II and as an enemy alien detention center after that). It was put up for sale but no offer was taken, and so for 25 years it simply went to pot. Vandals took whatever was worth taking, while the buildings and seawall began to crumble. In 1971 the effort to save Ellis Island began and by 1976 the Main Building was sturdy enough to accommodate visitors. But even the Main Building is not really renovated — the work being done is simply to stop further deterioration.

The tour begins as you step off the ferry and are met by a Parks Department guide who accompanies you into the large red and white brick building with its fancy 1900ish turrets. After a briefing in the main hall, groups are divided up and the tour begins. But the tour is more a description of what it was like than an explanation of what you see. Because you don't see very much — empty rooms, empty halls — a table set up with some chairs.

The millions of human beings who went through these halls in the old days were steerage passengers. Those who travelled first and second class were hastily inspected aboard their ships. But third-class passengers had to stop at Ellis Island to get clearance. If a doctor marked an "E" on your back, you were deported. If you were a young woman with no family, husband or fiance to meet you, back you went. In one case, romance or at least marriage, bloomed at Ellis Island. The guide related how once a man stepped out of line and offered to marry a girl who was about to be deported. They were married that day on the island. In fact, all fiances who came to call for their intended found they could not leave Ellis Island with the girl and without a marriage certificate. Talk about shotgun weddings!

Besides your health and marital status, you were asked questions about your money and possible criminal record. If you passed all these "tests," you were allowed to leave the island. Sometimes the inspectors fooled the immigrants and gave them cigar wrappers instead of American money.

Probably the most interesting thing about Ellis Island is the people in your tour group who have their own stories, which the guides are always eager to hear. In our group, there was an elderly Italian who had been detained on the island for two weeks in 1920 because someone in his family was sick. It was a common practice for those who had communicable diseases to be sent to the infirmary while the rest of the family waited in the dormitories. Those with incurable diseases, such as tuberculosis, were sent back.

Since the tour includes considerable walking and climbing the guide cautions the elderly to stay behind and rest. Yet it is the elderly who remember what Ellis Island meant — that it was an "Island of Tears" for some, and a place of fear, confusion and sometimes chicanery for others — who are most anxious to take the full tour. It was the old Italian with a limp and a cane who outpaced us all.

Younger children will probably not appreciate this tour, although there are special school tours for fourth grade and above. But for the descendants of all those Italians, Greeks, Germans, Jews, Turks, Scandinavians and others who once passed through these halls, the Ellis Island tour is an interesting and strangely emotional experience. Living history indeed.

HOURS: Ellis Island Ferry departs Liberty State Park area from Late April to Late October. Call for departure times.
FARE: Adults $1.50, Children $.50.
TELEPHONE: 201-435-9499 or 201-435-8509

WORLD TRADE CENTER

The highest skyscraper in New York offers the best view of the metropolis, the river, New Jersey and Brooklyn. On a clear day the 360 degree view is terrific. You buy tickets on the mezzanine floor and then take a special elevator that whisks you up to the 100th floor in a few seconds. Once there, you can sit at the various windows and drink in the panorama of the bay, the city and the provinces beyond. Conveniently, the outlines and names of landmarks are traced on the glass at every viewpoint, so you know what you are looking at.

There are also exhibits on the inner walls, a souvenir shop and a snack bar (featuring the world's most indifferent employees). For those who like to go outside, there's a rooftop promenade several flights up which is open when the wind is not too strong.

HOURS: 9:30 AM - 9:30 PM
ADMISSION: Adults: $2.50; Children & Senior Citizens: $1.25; Under 6, free.
LOCATION: 2 World Trade Center Plaza, N.Y.C. Take PATH direct from Hoboken or Jersey City.
TELEPHONE: 212-466-7377

Photo: *Courtesy N.Y. Convention and Visitors Bureau*

The view from below is good, but the view from the top of the World Trade Center is even better.

THE EMPIRE STATE BUILDING

The 86th floor observatory has both an enclosed area and an open promenade. High powered binoculars are available for a fee. Here you will also find the snack bars, vending machine and souvenir counter. The view to the West offers New Jersey and the Hudson, to the North you get Central Park and beyond, while the East gives you the UN building and Queens. While the observation windows here may not be as wide as the World Trade Center, nor the tower as spiffy as it once was, you are closer to the heart of Manhattan from this vantage point. There's an observatory on the 102nd floor included in the same ticket. This one is enclosed. And you can find the *"Guinnes World Book of Records" Museum* in the basement of the Empire State Building where, for a separate fee, you can see all sorts of oddities.

HOURS: 9:30 AM — Midnight daily
ADMISSION: Adults: $2.50, Children: $1.35
LOCATION: 34th Street & 5th Avenue, N.Y.C.
TELEPHONE: 212-736-3100

RCA BUILDING

Not so high, but there's plenty of outdoor space here (although the indoor space is limited). You can see small gardens and urns set high above the city and get a bird's eye view of St. Patrick's Cathedral. Since the price is high and the view less exciting than the other skyscrapers, many people prefer to take the Rockefeller Center Tour which costs just a little bit more and ends up here anyway. Kids, though, may find the tour boring.

HOURS: April - Sept.: 10:00-9:00; Oct. - March: 10:30-7:00
ADMISSION: Adults: $2.50; Children: $1.15, Students: $1.85
LOCATION: 30 Rockefeller Plaza, N.Y.C.
TELEPHONE: 212-489-2947

THE CIRCLE LINE TOUR

A standard tourist attraction since it started in the post World War II era, this boat ride takes three hours and covers 35 miles.

Basically, you circle Manhattan island in a three-floor "yacht" (which doesn't look much different than a three-floor ferry) which has both open and closed areas and long benches for seating. From the 42nd Street pier the boat heads southward on the Hudson, gaining views of both New York and New Jersey. Passing the Statue of Liberty, the ride continues around the tip of Manhattan then up the East River, around the Harlem River as far as Spuyten Duyvil and then back to home base. An announcer points out the monuments, skyscrapers, bridges and churches, offering anecdotes on the more interesting ones and lots of facts and figures. High point for the kids is the Little Red Lighthouse underneath the George Washington Bridge.

You can get a nice river breeze on this one and Manhattan never looks better than from a distance.

> HOURS: March 31 to Mid-November. From two to seven sailings a day depending on season.
> ADMISSION: Adults: $6.00; Children under 12: $3.00
> LOCATION: Pier 83, Foot of West 42nd St., N.Y.C.
> TELEPHONE: 212-563-3200

WEST POINT

West Point has a beautiful view of the Hudson, grey Collegiate Gothic buildings that rise from rocky inclines, parades of cadets on Saturday mornings and football games in the fall. But what I liked best about it was the museum.

The **West Point Museum** contains two floors of exhibits, models, mock-ups and memorabilia. But there is more here than Napoleon's sword or Mussolini's hat. There is a point of view that is uniquely military. "Power lies in the barrel of a gun," said Mao-Tse-Tung. And at the West Point Museum you see history from the view of that gunsight.

The decisive battles of the world are recreated by tiny toy figures set in position against each other behind glass. A full explanation of each battle and its significance is printed below the display. The Dark Ages began because the Roman infantry could not hold out against the Goth's cavalry in the 4th Century. The Feudal Ages ended because the overencumbered knights were no match for the English longbow at Agincourt. The Modern Age began when guns replaced swords somewhere in the 16th Century, and technology replaced physical prowess. And ever more so with each succeeding age.

In other museums the American Indians are shown as teaching the white man how to plant corn. In this museum we see them teaching us guerilla warfare. In other museums the caveman's artifacts change from primitive to cultured. In this museum the caveman's club is transformed into the bushman's boomerang, the feudal knight's mace and on and on. Since much of the museum is chronological, you end up with the casing of the atom bomb and the spacesuit of an astronaut, and the technological superiority of you know who.

There are other things at the museum also-mannequins dressed as Roman infantrymen with bearskin headdresses and a 12th Century Zouave outfit that would delight any costume designer. There's a set of hundreds of toy soldiers that duplicate every facet of Napoleon's army down to the last supply wagon. There's a room devoted to the history of West Point itself from the beginning when it was a military outpost commanded by a man named Benedict Arnold. And of course there are the mementos of war — Napoleon's golden sword (donated by General Eisenhower, who received it after the liberation of Paris) and Mussolini's hat (rescued by an American general after Il Duce was unceremoniously strung up in the street).

Outside the museum there are lots of lovely walks and benches where you can picnic anywhere. The terrain is very hilly here but there are buses which take you up to Mitchie stadium if you've come for a football game. The Thayer Hotel is practically on campus and has a restaurant that is open to visitors. And the West Point Chapel is quite striking if you don't mind all those steps you have to climb to get up there. Free.

HOURS: Daily. For Museum: 10:30-4:15
LOCATION: Route 218, West Point, N.Y.
TELEPHONE: 914-938-3507

INDEPENDENCE MALL, PHILADELPHIA

If the Bicentennial did nothing else, at least it got the city of Philadelphia to spruce up its historic area, to revamp or rebuild everything and turn Independence Mall into a first-class tourist attraction. The National Park Service administers many of the historic buildings, although the city and private organizations operate quite a few also.

First stop should be the great big, brick **Visitor Center** at Chestnut and 3rd Street. Here you can pick up a clearly marked map of the historic areas. A thirty-minute film is shown here about once an hour, which will give you the necessary background for your tour. Because of recent Federal cuts, the Center may not be open at all times unfortunately.

If you have children with you, certainly stop to see **Franklin Court** (at Chestnut and 4th Street). This complex includes a very interesting underground museum. As you descend a winding ramp you pass many displays of Benjamin Franklin's inventions, furniture, etc. At the bottom area there is an unusual show. A miniature model of the 1776 Continental Congress rises up, and taped voices discuss the adoption of the Declaration of Independence. Then the model sinks down again. Over to one side a bank of telephone receivers stands. Here you dial a particular number to hear what various famous people such as Mark Twain or John Adams had to say about Franklin—a lively way to impart history.

Next, it's on to the grassy mall (bounded by Chestnut, Walnut, 5th and 6th Streets) where **Independence Hall** and the **Liberty Bell** await. The bell is in its own glass pavilion. The line is usually not too long since it doesn't take that long to get a look and take a picture. The bell is huge, of course, and looks just like you would expect it to.

Independence Hall is shown by a Department of Interior guide, so there may be a wait, but there's a separate room where you can sit down and hear a preliminary talk. The Hall is most impressive, although not very large by today's standards. You can see the inkstand used by the signers of the Declaration of Independence, benches, etc. The guide gives a very full explanation of the events surrounding the adoption of the Declaration.

HOURS: Some buildings may be closed in winter. 9-5 Daily.
ADMISSION: Free
TELEPHONE: (Visitor Center) 215-597-8975.

THEME PARKS,
AMUSEMENT PARKS,
BOARDWALK AMUSEMENTS

Photo: Courtesy Great Adventure

In This Chapter You Will Find:

Great Adventure
Hersheypark
Vernon Valley Action Park
Sesame Place
Magic Valley
Land of Make Believe
Wild West City
Boardwalk Amusements

Keansburg
Long Branch
Asbury Park
Point Pleasant
Seaside Heights
Atlantic City Area
Wildwood

Small Amusement Parks

Bowcraft
Bertrand's Island
Clementon Lake Park

←
Some like it steep — Rolling Thunder roller coaster at Great Adventure.

GREAT ADVENTURE

Great Adventure is a theme park without any discernable theme. It is more like a giant amusement park with a drive-through Safari tacked on. However, it is colorful and popular, although its huge acreage often tires young visitors. Like many other parks, its recent emphasis has been on teenage attractions.

When Great Adventure first opened, the decor of the attractions spread over 1100 wooded and landscaped acres might have been called eclectic mishmash. Now, it looks more like a turn-of-the-century amusement park. The original Yum-Yum Palace — a fanciful ice cream and snack emporium — echoes of England's Brighton. The bandstand by the lake is pretty enough to host an 1890 picnic party. And the great carousel with its glinting mirrors is a true Nineteenth Century import. It gives a rather creaky ride, but it looks impressive. The entrance area looks like Disney World's Liberty Square and is filled with snack bars and souvenir shops.

If you turn to the right from the entrance plaza, you will find the largest concentration of rides, especially those designed to test the stomachs of teenagers and young adults. "Lightning Loops", the big roller coaster that turns you upside down is in this area and "Ride the Rapids" (for those who find the Log Flume too tame), plus Trabants, Himalayas and other whirling devices. For parents who opt for song and dance routines, the *Americana Music Hall* seats a large crowd and is a great comfort in that it is cool and covered. The two other showplaces in the park — the *Great Arena* and the *Aqua Stadium* — are both open to the elements (which have always been either blazing sun or drizzling rain whenever I visited). At the Haunted Castle, actors dressed as Dracula, Frankenstein and assorted ghouls try to scare you out of your wits (or at least they try to scare customers away from the heavily advertised Haunted Mansion in nearby Long Branch and into Great Adventure.)

On the extreme left side of the park is the *Best of the West* section. The Great Teepee offers gifts; the Western fort houses both the Runaway Train and the Sky Ride; the Great Arena and the flume ride splashes along. Across the river, a double track roller coaster called Rolling Thunder appeases the mounting roller coaster mania that has gripped this nation's teenagers.

For parents with young children there is a *Kiddie Kingdom* with its Red Baron, Lady Bug and such. The bumper car ride has only a few working bumper cars so the line around it can be interminable. There is also a petting zoo and a small Ferris Wheel but not enough rides for the six-to-ten year old crowd. However for both parents and young children there are plenty of shows. The revue in the Music Hall featured some very talented young people who danced, sang and pranced to Broadway melodies. If only the kids liked this stuff as much as their parents do.

Younger children will more likely enjoy the mini-circus in the Great Arena. Another top family show is "High Divers" at the Aqua Stadium. There's more than thrilling dives to this one. Buffoonery, clown diving and audience involvement make it enjoyable for all. But since these shows are in open arenas, wear a hat or go late in the afternoon. There are hardly any shaded areas at all.

Great Adventure seems clean and fairly well managed. But games like Fascination, Skee Ball and miniature golf (at $1.50 a person) aim to extract ever more money from your pockets. You can get better Skee Ball at any Boardwalk, and when the park admission is this high, I prefer to go for the "free" rides and shows. There's plenty of them and you can go on as often as you like.

As for food — Great Adventure will never win any culinary prizes for its roast beef or fried chicken. Picnic areas are outside the park — plenty of hot dogs and pizza stands inside. It's best not to eat heavily before using any of the rapid rides.

> **HOURS:** Early April - Late June, call first. Last week of June - Labor Day: 10 AM - Midnight. Safari opens 9 AM. Open weekends, Sept., Oct.
> **ADMISSION:** Adults: $14.95; Children: $13.50. (Combination Park-Safari ticket). Under 3, free.
> **LOCATION:** Jackson Twp., Ocean County. Take N.J. Turnpike to exit 7A, then I-95 to exit 16.
> **TELEPHONE:** 201-928-3500

HERSHEYPARK

When the urge to get away for a two or three-day vacation (complete with amusement park for the kiddies) combines with an urge to avoid the crowds at the seashore and the snailpace on the Garden State Parkway, one place to consider is Hershey, Pennsylvania. Set in the green and rolling hills of the Pennsylvania Dutch dairy country, the town that gave birth to the great American chocolate bar now offers a theme park, a zoo and several resorts for an overnight stay. Since it is situated a bit of a drive over the New Jersey border, most travelers find it more convenient to sleep over and spend one day at Hersheypark, one day exploring the countryside.

As for Hersheypark, itself; it's a theme park very much like Great Adventure, perhaps a little smaller. There are several open theaters where parents can rest their feet and enjoy Broadway-style entertainment while the kids try the Fender Bender for the fourth time. A single admission price pays for all the rides and shows although of course they get you for the extras. The crowds here are well behaved and there is little problem of anyone ducking ahead in line. Of course the number of people in the park varies from time to time, but since Hersheypark is a little out of the way, it does not seem to get flooded with humanity. It is green and clean, as they advertise.

You enter Hersheypark through *Tudor Square*, a small Elizabethan enclave of shops and restaurants. Then it's on to the *Rhineland* with its many rides. Here you will find the kiddie rides, a giant carousel, a two-armed Ferris Wheel and some in-betweeners. The next area, *Der Deutschplatz*, is dedicated to Hershey's Pennsylvania Dutch milieu. A crafts barn featuring local talent and a Dutch Restaurant featuring a chicken noodle dish are here. The dish featured a lot more noodles than chicken but it was a welcome diversion from the standard hamburger-hot dog-pizza places that dominate theme parks.

An aquatheater featuring dolphin and human diving acts, an ampitheater for the song-and-dance shows and two small theaters for puppet shows and children's comic shows all offer alternatives to rides. For the strong stomachs there are three roller coasters including the Sooper Dooper Looper (wherein you are turned upside down at the rate of 66 feet a second). The Coal Cracker is an extended flume ride for those who like to make a big splash.

There is a good, medium-sized zoo covering ten acres off to one side of the park. It seemed an unnecessary addition to me, but it does give something to those who hate rides. The Kissing Tower, a gentle space needle, offers a nice view and is something different for mothers with young children. Monorails, skyrides, and antique auto rides make this park well suited to families with kids under ten, although there are enough scary rides to please the teenagers and young adults.

Outside the park, and absolutely free, is Hershey's **"Chocolate World,"** a simulated factory tour in the Disney style. There you ride in automated cars past scenes of dairy farms, African cocoa tree plantations, and assembly belts full of kisses and chocolate bars. The whole time you are wafted past rivers of milk and glowing red roasters, the smell of chocolate assails your nostrils.

For those who like flowers there are the well-known **Hershey Rose Gardens** near the hotel which would be of interest during the blooming season. The **Museum of American Life** is nearby and depicts the Indian heritage plus the Conestoga wagons and implements of the farmers. The town of Hershey itself has a well-known drug store and street lights that are shaped like candy kisses. The Hershey Corporation also runs three facilities — a hotel that is built in the grand tradition with cavernous lobbies and beautiful dining room, a motel that includes a movie house and conference center, and a nearby campground.

> **HOURS:** June - Labor Day: 10:30 AM-10 PM. Some Sundays after. (Also open certain weekends in May)
> **ADMISSION:** $12.95. 4 and under: Free.
> **LOCATION:** Route 322, Pennsylvania, approachable from either 283 off The Pennsylvania Turnpike or Route 83 off 81.
> **TELEPHONE:** Hersheypark: 717-534-3916;
> Visitor Center: 717-534-3005

VERNON VALLEY ACTION PARK

In the last few years, Vernon Valley has burgeoned from a summer stop that offered go-kart rides into a multi-million dollar action park. They now have an Alpine Slide (that's a low, wheeled cart you maneuver down a fiberglass chute), water slides, speed boats, paddle boats, swimming pool, tidal wave pool, disco skating, scenic sky ride (that's the ski lift left over from winter), kayak rides, bumper boats and a complete children's section. The only problem is that the administration has not grown as fast as the park. It's as if Disneyland were operated by the local PTA Fun Fair Committee. The logistics of feeding and processing the hordes of people that arrive on weekends requires an expertise that seems to be missing at Vernon Valley.

The attractions here are sparkling new and at the same time familiar. The water slides you see all along the Jersey shore are present but somehow the lines do not move as smoothly. The tidal wave pool is a Japanese attraction. It was terribly overcrowded the day I was there, and Americans, unlike the sedate Japanese, jump in the waves, float on rafts and generally create a dangerous situation.

As for the race cars and speedboats — driver's licenses are required for these. Here you are allowed 2 rides for a single ticket which means the waiting lines move at the pace of a turtle. And at the water slide each person gets twenty minutes to "slide" so the rest of the line must wait for each twenty-minute period to end.

Luckily, there are rides at which the lines move more smoothly. The Alpine ride, for instance, where everyone gets one turn at a time, the sky-ride, and the miniature golf course had no long lines of frustrated amusement seekers. The children's play park with its Sesame Place type of cargo netting and colorful punching bags is an open area.

As for food — the policy here is ridiculous. No food is allowed to brought into the park. (You can picnic in the parking area.) This is not unusual for theme parks. But other parks have a hot dog or pizza or grape cooler stand every few feet to compensate. At Vernon Valley the cafeteria service was wholly inadequate for the crowds that were there — and the upper Pavillion was cordoned off for a private group that particular day, so it could provide no solace. It is also unusual for a park that solicits group visits not to have a separate booth that handles group tickets and a special area where buses can pull up.

Action Park has just installed Cobblestone Village, where parents can browse and buy things. And according to their brochure, they are planning to install a whole new Fantasy Isle with more children's action rides. I would suggest that rather than constantly expanding with more rides, Vernon Valley put some of its money into good management team and make better use of what is already available. With the variety of rides and the beautiful mountains, the park has much to offer the "action" generation.

At the moment the park appeals primarily to teenagers and young adults. These repeat customers have apparently figured out the ticket policy and know how to get their money's worth. Obviously, the time to visit here is during the week when access to the rides is easier. The rides themselves, by the way, seem to be in perfectly good condition and there are plenty of lifeguards around. However, this is an action park where people operate the rides themselves, so accidents do happen. The First Aid Squad was called out three times the day I visited.

Lockers and changing rooms are available for those who bring swimming gear. Liquor is served, also.

HOURS: Memorial Day to Labor Day — Daily. Call for Spring & Fall hours.

ADMISSION: $3 entrance fee (no rides). Various ride packages range from $3 for kids to $14 for everything.

DIRECTIONS: Route 80 to Route 23N to 94E for 3 miles

TELEPHONE: 201-827-2000

SESAME PLACE PLAYPARK

Big Bird to the rescue! At least that's what many parents hoped when they heard of the new Sesame Place Park that opened in 1980 in Langhorne, Pennsylvania. Here at last was a park that catered to the younger child (3 to 13) and certainly that group (or at least the under 10 set) have been neglected by other theme parks. In many ways Sesame Place has lived up to its promise. But let's clear up some misconceptions first.

Sesame Place is not an amusement park. No roller coasters or train rides. Neither is it some sort of futuristic educational area where your child enters at one end and comes out the other a veritable Einstein. Unless your 4-year old has looked at a see-saw and remarked "What a marvelous example of the fulcrum principle" his mind will be no more stretched here than at any other new and exciting place.

What does get stretched is the muscles. In this very active park, two-thirds of the child's time will be spent on outdoor activities. Although the park covers only 2½ acres, there is enough action to fill 4 to 6 hours depending on the child's age. Cargo netting to climb on, tunnels to slide down, a rope pulley, a plank bridge to wobble over and the *Count's Ballroom* (a large trough where kids can bounce and slide among thousands of plastic balls) are just some of the activities. Due to parent "feedback" in 1980 (complaints?) these activities have been expanded to allow grownups to accompany their kids. For the many parents who simply sit and watch there are now giant sun umbrellas. However, there is no tent covering the major outdoor section and if it rains the park suggests you stay home. If it's hot be prepared to sizzle. A change of clothes for the kiddies is suggested since two activities here have water spouting through tunnels. A bathing suit is an even better idea on warm days.

Indoors, the *Science Building* houses all those push-pull gadgets gleaned from a host of hands-on-museums. The Screening Room offers a chance to pose against a screen, then see a picture of your shadow. A microphone turns you voice to light waves, and pedalling a bicycle does the same thing. The cartoon-making Zeotrope was so popular I never got to it. Most of these exhibits allow only two people at a time. The Sesame Street set is also housed in this building and frankly I was disappointed. I had somehow expected a real miniature TV studio with cameras, cables, lights and a real Mr. Hooper or Big Bird. Instead I found a stage set of the famous stoop complete with Oscar's garbage can. Good for picture-taking or watching yourself on a hoisted TV, but that's it.

The *Computer Gallery* in a separate building, houses 70 computer game machines. Many of these require an ability to spell (and certainly an ability to read), yet the games were simplistic. I guess parents are meant to help out, here. The games take tokens (3 for $1) and frankly, are no match for Space Invaders.

The two other buildings are a fast food restaurant where you watch your lunch being prepared (just like Burger King only everything here is healthy!) and *Mr. Hoopers Store* — a gift shop that offers every Sesame Street toy and game ever produced. Nice, but on the expensive side.

Summing up: On the plus side Sesame Place is safe! Carpeting, plastic mats, double netting — you don't have to worry about major mishaps. You can picnic here — there are plenty of tables scattered around. Or bring your own Cokes and Fritos to supplement the health food at the restaurant. Water fountains and toilets come in all sizes.

On the minus side: The games themselves are fine — but the lines! There's no policing of the queues. There are not enough indoor activities and not enough signs explaining how to work things. And on sunny days, the heat beating down on the concrete becomes fierce. Still in all, most children enjoy it thoroughly. Bring hats, sun-tan lotion.

HOURS: 10 AM to dusk, Mid-April to Mid-Nov.
ADMISSION: $6.50 tax included.
DIRECTIONS: Route 1 South through Trenton to Oxford Valley Mall, Langhorne, Pa. Turn right at New Oxford Valley Road just before Mall.
TELEPHONE: 215-757-1100

MAGIC VALLEY AMUSEMENT PARK

Several years ago, Magic Valley started out as a small, reasonably priced amusement park in the resort area of the Poconos just the other side of the Delaware Water Gap. Right now its biggest attraction to New Jerseyans is the fact that traveling west on Route 80 — even on a Saturday — is a darn sight easier than traveling south on the Garden State or New Jersey Turnpikes.

The park itself seemed disappointing at first. The road there, once you got off Route 209, was narrow and bumpy, and the park site is on a hill. In fact, my husband kept asking, "Why did they build it here?" Well, they built it there because **Winona Five**

Photo: Courtesy Magic Valley Park.

Many theme parks offer live entertainment in addition to mechanical rides. Here, a country singer at Magic Valley.

Falls, a series of small cascading waterfalls was already established there. And the attraction is supposed to be the lure of beautiful nature plus the excitement of mechanical rides. Actually, both the waterfalls and the working "craftsman" (a broom maker, a chair caner, etc.) were practically ignored by the crowd in favor of the rides, the food and the arcade.

The rides seem skimpy at first, but that's because they are spaced fairly close together. Actually there are nine adult rides, although they are not as large as those in the superparks. Because there were no long lines the day we visited, (a Saturday, mind you) the thirteen-year-olds were able to go back innumerable times to the Screaming Demon (a moderate roller coaster), the Tilt-A-Whirl, and the Yo-Yo (separate swings which revolve). There are also two ferris wheels (one of the caged, upside-down variety), several scrambler type wheels, and a scary paratrooper ride. For little ones there is one each of kiddie cars, kiddie boats and kiddie motorcycles plus a small carousel. The Red Baron serves the 5 to 7 age group while the Antique Cars, popular with everyone, had the only long line.

Most of the rides were moderate enough for family groups to have fun. For parents with weak stomachs, however, there is less divertisement than you find in the major parks. However, the Pepsi Players do put on a song and dance revue twice a day in the pavilion area There is also a small outdoor theater where kiddie shows are offered several times a day. A small arcade allows you to lose your money faster than in Atlantic City. And of course there are the waterfalls which are somewhat like a smaller version of Bushkill Falls with the same rustic pathways and up-and-down trails.

For shopping there is a large gift shop near the falls. For food, hot dogs and pizza stands dot the landscape and there are restaurants for heartier fare. The park does provide a picnic area for those cagey enough to bring their own food, but it's over on the other side of the parking lot.

All in all, Magic Valley offers about one-third the attractions of Great Adventure at about one-half the price. However, it is clean, the attendants are well mannered and the selection of rides is geared more to the whole family. The oft-neglected 8 to 11 age group can find rides here that are thrilling but not death-defying. And you don't have to hike for miles to get from one ride to the other. As with many other single-admission amusement parks, your enjoyment depends completely on how crowded it is on the day that you visit.

ADMISSION: Adults: $7.50. Under 4, free.
HOURS: Summer: 10-9. Weekends: 10-10. Spring and Fall:
Weekends: 11-6
DIRECTIONS: Route 80 west to Exit 52. Route 209 North to Bushkill,
PA.
TELEPHONE: 717-588-9411

LAND OF MAKE BELIEVE

Compared to the super-slick, multi-million dollar theme parks, Land of Make Believe looks amateurish — yet there is something very charming about the place. It is definitely designed for younger children (3 to 9 approximately) and has none of that nervous-making razzmatazz usually associated with amusement areas.

A simple maze, a candy cane "forest" (which kids try to climb), a high balance beam, a talking scarecrow (my eight-year-old never figured out how this was done) are a few of the staples here. *Santa's Barn* is where you creep through a magic chimney to the darkened room where Santa sits. (Some young children might find this frightening, so parents must accompany them).

Other low-key entertainments are the *Punch and Judy* shows (a chicken and a rabbit perform) and a darkened *Halloween House* that didn't have too much in it except the dark. The mechanical rides (which cost extra) include a miniature 1863 train and several standard little kiddies rides. The hayride for 50¢ is the best bet, if you have no allergies. Although the wagon is pulled by a tractor rather than horses, this excursion into rustic yesteryear is fun for both kids and adults.

The scenery, the wide-open blue sky, the picnic area in a country field and the closeness to Jenny Jump Mountain all add up to a pleasant excursion. It's way out in the country and everything about it — including the gravel and grass parking lot is bucolic, but I liked the simple pleasures it provided and the low entrance price. It's not completely unsophisticated by the way — the snack bar serves the usual greasy hamburgers and the gift shop sells standard tourist items.

HOURS: Weekends from Memorial Day. Late June to Labor
Day: 10-5; Sundays: 11-5. Certain weekends after Labor
Day.
ADMISSION: $1.50
LOCATION: Route 80 to Exit 12. 2 miles to Hope, N.J. Follow signs.
TELEPHONE: 201-459-4220

WILD WEST CITY

Take a plot of land in the hills of Sussex County, line it with small, rustic buildings, one large saloon, and a hitching post, add some horses and some young men dressed as cowboys and what do you have? You have New Jersey's version of a one-street western town that serves as center stage for Wild West City.

The action at Wild West City consists of a series of "shows" held in the middle of Main Street while the audience lines up behind the hitching posts to watch. The shows may last for either five minutes or half-an-hour and two of them involve audience participation. There is a demonstration of cowboy rope twirling and bullwhips, but most of the shows are recreations of Hollywood-style legends — shootouts at high noon, saloon fights and holdups. Each little drama is accompanied by narration over the loudspeaker — which, unfortunately, is often garbled.

"The stranger rode into town. He was looking for just one man — the old gunslinger. Now the Marshal comes out to face him — face the young gunslinger who must test his skill." While this narration goes on, two actors face each other until one guns the other down. I was there on a rather hot, humid, and the poor actors were wearing flannel shirts, leather vests, heavy boots and other cowboy accoutrements. When one of them bit the dust, he certainly earned his day's pay on that hot dusty street.

The neckerchief that cowboys wear comes in quite handy for another staple of Wild West City. That is the regular hold-up of the stagecoach and train. The stagecoach ride, which costs extra, gets held up every time it makes its run through town. (Since younger children may get frightened by the robbers, an adult should accompany children under six on this ride). If riding on an authentic, non-cushioned stagecoach is not your cup of tea, you can watch the holdup from the pleasant picnic area behind the "town". One advange of Wild West City is that there are plenty of picnic tables so you are not doomed to eat the hamburgers at the Golden Nugget.

You can also see the stage hold-up enacted on Main Street at 12:45 PM when a whole gang (well, three men) rob the coach and make off with a sack of gold. At this point the Sheriff rounds up a posse — all the children may join — and hands out some plastic Deputy badges. It seems to take forever, but finally they all march off to find the bad guys.

Once the villains are caught they are put on trial. (The crowd, by the way, always votes for hanging.) The villains however, manage to escape justice. The had better, the same six cowboys seem to do everything here.

One other way you get held up at Wild West City is by your own children who will absolutely insist on buying a gun. If you're planning a visit, let your child take his own toy gun along — joining the action is part of the fun here. And don't wear your best clothes — it does get dusty here.

HOURS: 10:30-6:00 Daily, Mid-June - Labor Day. May & Oct.: weekends only.
ADMISSION: Adults: $4.00; Children: $3.50
LOCATION: Netcong, Sussex County. Take Route 80 to 206N. Follow signs.
TELEPHONE: 201-347-8900

BOARDWALK AMUSEMENTS

There are small arcades, video game rooms and water slides at any number of Jersey shore resorts. However, you can find the larger amusement centers at the following towns. They are located on the beach so just keep driving until you hit the ocean. Don't expect cleanliness or good restroom facilities at these places — they are often dirty, sweaty, greasy and carny. However, they are a tradition associated with summer (the season lasts from Memorial Day to Labor Day) and they are cheaper than theme parks. They also offer certain advantages which theme parks do not: rainchecks on tickets, easy availability from any shore point, no waiting lines and no need for parents to pay for tickets if they don't like the rides.

All directions are for the Garden State Parkway (G.S.P.) exits.

KEANSBURG: An older area that had its heyday back in the 1940s. This is where Ralph Kramden was always going to take Alice in "The Honeymooners." The boardwalk runs about 4 or 5 blocks long and includes 30 kiddie rides, 15 adult rides and a pool. A new water slide appeared in 1982. Concessions and arcade. **Directions:** G.S.P. to Exit 117, then Route 36E.

LONG BRANCH: The **Haunted Mansion** is the largest and goriest of the many haunted houses you find at seaside piers. This one uses live actors who grab at you. The rest of the pier consists of arcade games and food concessions. Across the street a waterslide offers eight chutes at once, plus bumper boats. There are several souvenir shops alongside the pier. **Directions:** Take G.S.P. to Exit 105, follow signs.

ASBURY PARK: The long boardwalk on Ocean Avenue is dotted with miniature golf games, adult rides and several indoor arcades, which offer a variety of machines, pokerino, etc. Palace Amusements, another large indoor arcade complete with carousel is not on the boardwalk but around the corner from it. The town may seem forlorn but the amusements are still popular. **Directions:** G.S.P. Exit 100A-N or 102S.

POINT PLEASANT: A smaller amusement center with rides geared more for children although there are a number of adult rides present. Indoor arcade and miniature golf. Less variety than some of the larger amusement areas and the prices are slightly higher, but the atmosphere is not as honky-tonk and I found it rather pleasant. **Directions:** G.S.P. Exit 98-S or 90N.

SEASIDE HEIGHTS: New Jersey's version of Coney Island. The largest of the boardwalk amusement centers, with solid amusements and concessions along the boardwalk and on the piers. Some larger rides are here such as a big Ferris Wheel and the Pirate Ship besides the usual assortment of Trabants and Red Barons. The indoor arcade includes a carousel, air hockey games and food stands along with the usual Skeeball and machine games. Rides active even during the day. A popular teenage hangout. **Directions:** G.S.P. Exit 82 to Highway 37E. Go through Toms River to bridge, follow signs.

ATLANTIC CITY AREA: Only one full amusement pier still runs at Atlantic City at this time although there are arcades and pizza joints dotted along the changing boardwalk. Nearby **Brigantine** hosts a horror castle and amusement pier. **Ocean City**, fifteen minutes to the south, offers a long boardwalk devoted primarily to stores and eateries with a small amusement center at the northern end. **Directions:** G.S.P. Exits 40/38S, 36/38N (Atlantic City and Brigantine); 30/25S, 25/29N (Ocean City).

WILDWOOD: The amusement section of the boardwalk goes on for miles and I counted seven separate fun piers. The piers vary in solidity of their wood planking (one is actually concrete) and their prices, but the rides are very similar. The usual lineup is a haunted house, a crazy house, a few kiddie rides and the popular adult rides such as Flying Bobsleds, Tilt-A-Whirl, Trabant, etc.

Water slides and sack slides are specials at several piers. And both the boardwalk and the piers boast an endless number of concessions, games and food stands. **Directions:** G.S.P. Exit 4.

SMALL AMUSEMENT PARKS

BOWCRAFT AMUSEMENT PARK: A small park set down plunk amidst the hurly-burly of Route 22, it is open all year round although many rides are not available in winter. Paddle boats, a train ride, miniature golf and several kiddie rides make this a popular place for the under-ten set. Go-karts, baseball batting, Tilt-A-Whirl, Scrambler and auto-cars bring out the teenagers and the dating groups. The usual dirty, carny atmosphere here at the rides and the tent arcade, but it's very convenient for people in the area and you don't have to battle the beach traffic to get there. **Season:** Winter: Arcade only. Warm weather: full park. **Location:** Route 22, Scotch Plains, Union County **Telephone: 201-233-0675**

BERTRAND ISLAND PARK: For those who swim and boat on Lake Hopatcong or use the free state park beach there, this amusement park has been around for a long time and some of the concessions look it. Some new rides have been added to satisfy the increasing crowds. The island is approachable by either land or water. Bertrand Island Park includes a swimming lake, beach and bathhouse — for a fee. Sightseeing boats, a petting zoo and kiddie rides amuse the young ones. Adults and older kids will find the Enterprise, Scrambler, Ferris Wheel, Flume Ride and others available plus arcades and miniature golf. And although some rides look rickety there is a beautiful old carousel from Coney Island here, too. **Season:** Memorial Day - Labor Day. **Location:** Lake Hopatcong, Morris County. Take Route 80 to Mt. Arlington exit. **Telephone:** 201-398-2000.

CLEMENTON LAKE PARK: Set on 40 acres about eight miles east of Camden, this amusement park has been operating for 75 years now. Five kiddie rides and 18 adult rides include an old-fashioned carousel and a roller-coaster called the Jackrabbit. A small size showboat offers rides around the lake. Prices vary according to the rides, although there are group rates. A new single price entry may go into effect in 1982. **Hours:** Mid-April - Late June: Weekends only, 12-8. July - Labor Day: Daily, except Monday, 12-10 PM. **Location:** Route 534 off Routes 30 or 42, Clementon, Camden County **Telephone:** 609-783-0263

ZOOS, AQUARIUMS,
NATURE CENTERS,
WILDLIFE REFUGES

Photo: *Courtesy Great Adventure.*

In This Chapter You Will Find:

The Bronx Zoo
Great Adventure Safari
Turtle Back Zoo
Staten Island Zoo
Terry-Lou Zoo
Space Farms Zoo
Other Small Zoos (N.J.)
New York Aquarium
Wildlife Refuges
   The Great Swamp
   Brigantine National Wildlife Refuge
Nature Centers

← Kangaroos in New Jersey? Yes at Great Adventure's Safari.

THE BRONX ZOO

While the smaller zoos of New Jersey are fine for younger children, once the kids have reached third grade it's time to take them to the largest urban zoo in America. Not necessarily the best (that honor belongs to the San Diego Zoo according to most experts) but the largest. Actually, the Bronx Zoo is in a period of transition. One section is devoted to the older concept of caging animals for inspection. Structures built like Greek temples house the lions, tigers and monkeys. Victorian-style esplanades allow room for throngs of visitors, while the animals are cramped into small, concrete spaces. On the other hand, the open sections allow the animals to roam free while visitors watch them from across moats, from skyrides, and in summer, from the monorail.

While you can see the animals up close in the old zoo houses, the open environments present a more realistic view of animal behavior. And since there are over 5 miles of terrain to cover and over 3,600 animals to see, it's a lot easier to take either the skyride or the monorail (or both) when they are in season. These cost extra on Free Days but are part of the summer Friday through Monday Combination Ticket. The open sections are divided geographically as follows:

Wild Asia: Open only in summer. A 40 acre habitat where elephants, rhinos, deer and antelope roam free. Visitors view them from the glassed-in monorail, "The Bengali Express". **Africa:** Lions, gazelles, antelopes, zebras and gnus roam the grassy slopes. You can view them from surrounding walkways and bridges or from the slow-moving Skyfari ride. **South America:** A smaller section devoted to anteaters and such. There is a wildfowl pond nearby where you can enjoy the aquatic birds at their colorful best. **North America:** An extensive section that includes a walk-in Wolf Wood (no, they don't bite you), polar bears (how do they take the New York summers?), and lots of bison and bull elk.

Certain special houses, open all year round, offer the best this zoo or any other can come up with. First is *"The World of Darkness."* A top-notch display of bats, owls, and other nocturnal animals, it costs 25¢ and is worth every penny. Special lights allow you to watch the racoons, porcupines and bush babies cavort on the forest floor. They think it's night because the zoo has reversed the light cycles. It's a world of strange creatures with glittering eyes, unique and thrilling; and to top it all, there are special bat-flying demonstrations twice a day.

The *"World of Birds"* is free and is housed in an ultra-modern concrete cylindrical building. Here you will find three floors of birds in a unique setting. Trees vault up the three stories while a variety of birds perch on the first, second and third story branches. Other special houses include the Penguin, Aquatic Bird and extensive Reptile House.

The newly refurbished *Children's Zoo* offers a host of fun things especially for kids under ten. Giant rope "spider webs" to climb, snail "shells" to ride in, and prairie dog burrows to explore practically turn this into an educational amusement park. The cost is extra (80¢ for kids, 70¢ for adults) but well worth it. You could spend almost an hour here alone. Another kids' favorite is the elephant and camel ride section (open warm weather only), and of course the *Bengali Express* with its narrated safari ride is always popular.

If you don't bring a sandwich (and there are plenty of tables if you do), there is a cafeteria open all year round. Warm weather opens the snack stands, the Pub and the zoobar.

> **HOURS:** Daily, 10-5, Sun. 10-5:30 PM. (Winter: 10 AM - 4:30 PM.)
>
> **ADMISSION:** Free Tues. - Thurs. Friday - Monday: Adults: $2.50 Children 2-12: $.75. Combination admission/ride ticket available.
>
> **LOCATION:** George Washington Bridge to Cross Country Expressway east to exit 4B, Bronx River Parkway North. Take exit marked "Bronx Zoo" then left to Bronxdale parking field.
>
> **TELEPHONE:** 212-933-1759

THE SAFARI AT GREAT ADVENTURE

The largest safari outside of Africa takes about an hour to drive through and covers six miles and six continents. And although you do not get to see certain animals (such as tigers, panthers and lions) close up, you do get to see scads of them. Other animals, such as camels, elk in heat, jealous giraffes and short-tempered rhinos get almost too close for comfort. The brochure warns that you should keep car windows closed at all times so take an air-conditioned car if you're visiting on a 90-degree day. As for vinyl-topped cars, the baboons will strip them, so you must bypass the baboon territory.

The road through the Safari is three lanes wide and you may travel at your own speed. Each area is separated from the other by wire fences so you must wait for the guards to open the gates between one habitat and another. Surprisingly, the warning signs to keep windows closed are apparent only in the dangerous cat sections. I noticed a number of cars with open windows and people who nuzzled deer and fed popcorn to camels. Camels, in fact, seem like the beggars of Great Adventure — they sidle up to the cars in the motheaten rags of their summer skin and seem to be looking for handouts.

In the African Plains section you can watch herds of elephants eat and socialize. And nothing can make you feel smaller than to sit knee-high to a giraffe as he nudges up against your car — unless it's sitting between two giraffes who are having a love-triangle spat and using your car as a barrier zone. The animals have right-of-way here, and if you get in real trouble honk for a Safari guard. One rhino did take particular exception to our baby blue station wagon. He looked suspiciously as if he were going to charge and sure enough a guard did wave us on quickly. I don't know what statistics there are on car bumping at Great Adventure, but the modern light-weight compact car is no match for a two-ton rhino.

The Australian section is new and unique. No other safari has animals from this side of the world. Great Adventure has gone to some pains to re-create a familiar habitat for these shy creatures. Kangaroos, wallabies, wallaroos and the flightless emu strut, waddle and bound on the hilly terrain. The kangaroos are much smaller than I had imagined and do not spend their time standing up, ready to punch. They move about on all fours and since their front legs are so much shorter than those powerful hind-quarters, they look for all the world like lopsided dogs with giant tails.

For those with metal-topped cars the ride through baboon territory is always of interest. These curious apes will scamper all over you car, check on the occupants, pull on the hood ornament, knock your grillwork and then pass on to the next car. They will also strip off anything they can — hence the restrictions against vinyl tops and sides. An air-conditioned bus ride through the whole park is an alternative for baboon viewers, but it costs $1.50 extra for each rider.

> **HOURS:** 9-6 Daily, late June - mid-Sept. Weekends April, May, Oct.
> **ADMISSION:** $5.25. Combination with amusement park: $14.95
> **LOCATION, ETC.:** See Great Adventure entry.

THE TURTLE BACK ZOO

The Turtle Back Zoo is the largest zoo in New Jersey and now houses about seven hundred animals. It is by no means big or exhausting, however, and its convenient size plus its well-designed children's areas make it a favorite with tots, pre-teens and parents.

Run by the Essex County Park Commission, the zoo began life in 1963 but has grown steadily since then. Since it began as a children's zoo, there were many fanciful settings — a wedge of cheese housed rodents; the three pigs had their own house. It is now more than fifty percent an adult zoo, and the administration is moving away from the "cute" settings into more natural environments for the animals.

The zoo is built in a circular pattern on hilly terrain, so you get a hike as well as an education when you visit. From the castle-like main entraince you may head right to the children's zoo or straight ahead to the main section. A petting area over to the left is a favorite of young children. (Not too young — a very small child may become terrified of a nibbling goat). But lambs, goats and other small animals love to eat the special food that youngsters hand them (you buy the food at special machines nearby) and do not seem to mind human contact at all. You may also buy a special key which turns on a tape-recorded description of the animal's habitat and habits at special lockboxes throughout the park.

Although there are no elephants or lions here, you can find Siberian tigers, panthers and leopards at the zoo. When I say you can find them, I mean they are resident there. The last time I visited, only the cubs were out in the open cages. There are plenty of hooved animals out in the open, however. Camels, midget deer, yaks and buffalo are there aplenty. Even the ugly wildebeest, which my daughter missed on her fourth grade class trip to the Bronx Zoo, is available for viewing here. There is also a very large collection of birds and of course, turtles (although the name of the zoo derives from a hill shaped like a turtle's shell).

The bat cave, where you enter a dark tunnel to view the night creatures, and the seal pond, where the daily feedings bring appreciative crowds, are two star attractions. The peacocks, which roam about at will, are always good for a picture when they spread their tails.

Of course there is more to a zoo than the animals. There is the pony ride for children under 60 pounds of weight. And there is the train ride — a rather good one at that. A midget steam railroad takes you through the wood past the reservoir, through a tunnel and back again. For fifty cents a person it is a good buy. There is also an educational center where lectures on animals are given at designated times. Picnicking is allowed and a small cafeteria is available.

HOURS: Mon. - Sat.: 10-5; Sunday: 11-6. Winter: 10-4 Daily.
ADMISSION: Adults: $2.00; Children, Seniors: 75¢
LOCATION: 560 Northfield Rd., West Orange (behind South Mountain Arena), Essex County.
TELEPHONE: 201-731-5800

STATEN ISLAND ZOO

This square-block, city zoo is of interest for two reasons: 1) it is convenient to those within easy driving distance of the Goethals Bridge, and 2) it is primarily an indoor zoo, so it is available during the winter.

The big collection here is the snakes. Since snakes take up little room (experts assure us that snakes like those little glass cubicles where zoo-keepers put them), it is possible to crowd an amazing variety of them into one large zoo-house. The biggest rattlesnake collection in the world resides here, along with cobras, pythons, cottonmouths, a krait, an asp — you ask for it, they got it. Since reptiles are not very active you may find two — or is it three, or one? — pythons curled around one another with head and tail indistinguishable. At the end of the room a family of alligators remind you there's more to the reptile class than just snakes.

In the *Mammal House*, there resides one panther, one lion, one leopard and one Siberian tiger, but these animals pace the traditional city zoo cage and seem unhappy at the prospect of a lifelong jail sentence. The monkeys, on the other hand, seem to have a fine time.

The zoo is unusual in that it also sports a small aquarium. Coral fish, sea anemones; and piranhas are among the colorful and dangerous fish floating behind glass. Invertebrates, including spiders, scorpions and centipedes, are also displayed in lighted niches.

Outside, in warm weather, there are flamingoes and Galapagos tortoises on display. A pleasant children's center includes a farm and petting zoo. Altogether, a pretty place with trees, benches, picnic tables and snack bar, the Staten Island Zoo is marred only by those old-fashioned cages for the big cats. There are no hooved animals here, by the way — they don't have the space.

Whenever my son watches one of those disaster movies on TV wherein the local population is being devoured by overactive tarantulas or man-eating fish, he turns to me and says: "Where was that zoo where we saw the piranhas and the spiders and the poisonous lizards?" It was the Staten Island Zoo.

HOURS: 10-4:45 Daily.
ADMISSION: Adults: 75¢; Children 50¢; Under 5 free.
LOCATION: 614 Broadway, Staten Island.
TELEPHONE: 212-442-3100

TERRY LOU ZOO

A privately owned zoo and therefore more expensive to enter than a tax-subsidized one, Terry-Lou has been a New Jersey fixture for many years. It doesn't look like much from the outside — a small barn-like structure across from a corner of the Ash Brook Golf Course serves as the main entrance. It does, however, contain an interesting variety of animals in its collection.

For instance, two elephants, a pygmy hippo, lions and tigers, giraffes, bison and llamas all reside here. Some of them are stars. The tiger has appeared in Exxon commercials and the two giraffes have had a stint in show business also. As for the monkeys, well, they're always the stars of a zoo anyway. They are housed indoors where you will find several chimpanzees, two mandrills, some ringtail lemurs and a few frisky types.

Because cages at the Terry-Lou are mesh (a heavy Cyclone fence type) you can get a closer look at these animals than at many other zoos. In fact, if it weren't for the smell that is an inherent part of a monkey house, I would have continued an eyeball-to-eyeball confrontation with an intelligent chimpanzee for an hour.

The main outside area features mammals with an adjacent section for birds and alligators. Large animal crackers are available (at the rather high price of 75¢ a handful), and the mesh cages allow you to feed llamas, deer, etc. without fear of fingerbite.

The complete area of the Terry-Lou Zoo runs about one square city block. The area is flat and easy for young children and older folk to navigate. It should take about one hour to see it all, depending on the attention span of your children. A few animals may be petted, but by no means all. Pony rides are often available.

HOURS: Daily 10-dark. Check during winter.
ADMISSION: Adults: $3.00; Children: $1.50
LOCATION: 1451 Raritan Road (corner of Terrill) Scotch Plains, Union County
TELEPHONE: 201-322-7180

SPACE FARMS ZOO

Another private zoo, this one in a completely rural area that closely approximates the natural surroundings of many of the animals housed there. The trip takes you well into the mountains of northern Sussex County, past farms of Herefords and horses grazing peacefully among the green hills.

The zoo is set up for family outings with many picnic tables, swing sets and slides for the youngsters. There is plenty of space at Space Farms (although the name derives from the family that runs it.) One hundred acres are devoted to rather simple cages of grizzly bears, lions, tigers, hyenas, monkeys, etc. plus several buildings filled with antique cars, sleighs and other collections. A large pond at the center of the acreage allows ducks and geese to paddle about, while pens of yak, llamas, buffalo and goats dot the surrounding hill.

Bears include Goliath, the largest brown bear in captivity, grizzlies, polar bears and the rare Hokkaido bear from Japan. Although the bear cages seemed smaller than those at public zoos, Mr. Space assured me the bears inside were happy. At any rate, Space Farms has the highest reproduction rate for animals in captivity of any zoo in America, according to Mr. Space. Maybe it's the fresh air, or the diet of fresh meat, or the natural smell that emanates from the bear cages — but there were plenty of cubs rollicking around on the day I visited.

The entrance building to the property includes a *Museum of Americana* (everything from Indian arrowheads to old clocks), a snack shop and a gift shop. And though the entrance fee is relatively high here, between the animals, the "museums", the swings and slides you can make a day of it. Picnic lunches allowed.

HOURS: Daily 9-5, May 1 - Oct. 31.
ADMISSION: Adults: $4.50; Children 3-12: $1.50

OTHER SMALL ZOOS (NEW JERSEY)

There are a number of small zoos tucked away in local city and county parks that are pleasant to visit when you are in the vicinity. Among them are:

VAN SAUN PARK ZOO: A charming children's zoo with a birdhouse and a few cages of animals, an adjacent 1860s farm and a miniature train ride. All this is set in a large county park with lots of picnic tables and a duck pond. Located off Route 4 in River Edge, Bergen County at Forest Ave. Telephone: 201-265-1028.

COHANSIC ZOO: Located in the City Park, Bridgeton, Cumberland County (at Routes 49 and 77). The park also includes picnic areas and nature trails. Telephone: 609-451-4802.

CAPE MAY ZOO: Chickens, ducks, goats, a lion, a ferret, a monkey and deer inhabit this small county zoo which also offers a barn. Located off Route 9 at Cresthaven Road in Cape May Court House, Cape May County. Telephone: 609-465-5271.

THE NEW YORK AQUARIUM

It's in Brooklyn, of course and you can get there easily (since getting lost in Brooklyn is an even more traumatic event to New Jerseyans than getting lost in Manhattan). Since the aquarium is right smack in the middle of Coney Island, many people prefer visiting in the spring or fall to avoid getting caught up in the hurly burly of boardwalk amusements. Unfortunately, the dolphins who perform in the "training" show leave for Miami in mid-September and don't return until May so you'll miss them if you venture forth in winter. I suppose the right time to go is early June.

This concrete aquarium is home to whales, sharks, seals, penguins and a variety of tropical fish. One star attraction is the electric eel which lights up every once in a while. The whales swim around lazily in the big tank — what you see is mostly their underbellies, and the sharks, most of which are rather small, have a building all to themselves. For many, it's the yellow tangs and sturgeon fish and other strange and beautiful denizens of the deep that make a trip to the aquarium worthwhile.

In good weather the training show takes place in an outside arena. A dolphin or whale jumps up and learns to take a fish from the trainer. Since they are just learning this can sometimes look more like amateur night than Broadway. In fact, many people are disappointed in the New York Aquarium, partly because of this and partly because it is not large. It certainly does not compare favorably with the Miami Seaquarium where there is lush acreage, separate islands full of turtles and crocodiles, and a show featuring dolphins who wear football helmets and push footballs with their snouts. It's not Marineland and it's not Sea World — but of course, those places are profit-making enterainment centers.

This is the only decent-sized aquarium within easy driving distance. And it does have real whales and real sharks and penguins and an area where children can handle starfish and other creatures of the sea. So if your children have never been to an aquarium, if they have never seen fish that look like rocks and fish that look like dragons, or sharks at feeding time, it is certainly worth a visit. There is a nice souvenir stand by the way and a nice view of the beach and ocean.

> **HOURS:** 10-5 daily.
> **ADMISSION:** Adults: $2; children: 75¢
> **LOCATION:** 8th Street and Surf Avenue. Take the Verrazano Bridge to the Belt Parkway (direction of JFK Airport) and stay on until 8th Street exit. There is a sign for the Aquarium.
> **TELEPHONE:** 212-266-8500

Wildlife Refuges

THE GREAT SWAMP

The remains of a glacial pocket, the Swamp serves as both a refuge for animals and a 5,800-acre barrier to suburban development. It was saved some years ago from the fate of airport development by a group of conservationists and donated to the Federal Government which now administers it. The area is a combination of marshes, grassland, swamp woodland and hardwood ridges. There are some stands of mountain laurel and rhododendron but a botanical wonderland it's not.

Actually, there are sections that look like a great locale for a movie called "The Creature From the Black Lagoon." Tall, leafless trees, crackling twigs, swampy underbrush . . . well, it's a swamp

Photo: by Bill Mawhinney

Waterfowl and small animal life can be observed at the many wildlife refuges and nature centers in New Jersey.

after all. Not smelly like the Okefenokee, and not deep, but still a swamp. Wooden boardwalks have been built in several observation areas so that families can traverse the wetlands and observe whatever wildlife is around. Mostly it's small — woodchucks, muskrats, frogs — and there are deer and foxes, too, though they tend to stay in the interior away from humans. There are blinds for picture taking which most often will turn out to be of birds and insects. Swamp officials recommend visits in the early morning or late afternoon. Sunday afternoon the wildlife won't come out because there are too many people around.

The Swamp consists of two-thirds wilderness and one-third management area. There are several hiking trails in dry areas but picnicking is verboten. Observation centers are at Long Hill Road in New Vernon and at 247 Southern Boulevard in Chatham Township (this one run by Morris County). Old sneakers or waterproof shoes are recommended. Insect repellent in the evening. Free.

> **HOURS:** Dawn until dusk.
> **LOCATION:** Morris and Somerset Counties. Headquarters at Point Pleasant Road, Basking Ridge. Also Nature Centers run by Morris and Somerset Counties have interpretive centers. Read Nature Center section.
> **TELEPHONE:** 201-647-1222

BRIGANTINE NATIONAL WILDLIFE REFUGE

Only eleven miles from Atlantic City but a world of immense quiet and peace. There are over 20,000 acres of grassy tidal marsh interspersed with tidal bays and channels with some brush upland area that support deer, fox and other small animals here. But the main area of the refuge is for the protection of waterfowl that use the Atlantic Flyway in their travels from Canada to Florida. Many birds (up to 150,000) winter completely in New Jersey now.

The snow goose, Canada goose, brant and black duck are among the many birds who stop here. The refuge offers a calendar of wildlife events — e.g., November 1-10: concentration of 100,000 ducks, geese and brant; June 20th: Canada goose round-up.

A self-guided tour of eight miles by car or foot circuits the waterfowl impoundments. Lunch areas en route. Headquarters provide leaflets, restrooms, displays and wildlife films at specific times. Free.

HOURS: Daylight except during hazardous conditions.
LOCATION: U.S. 9, one mile east of Oceanville, Atlantic County.
TELEPHONE: 609-652-1665

NATURE CENTERS

So what's a nature center? Not knowing, I expected to find a little log cabin in the woods where a grizzled old codger showed his bird nest collection and talked about owls. Actually the centers are a lot more sophisticated than that. What I found, at the few I visited, were modern buildings filled with classrooms, auditoriums, displays, professional staff and a host of activities, particularly on weekends. Of course the buildings are just the center of the nature area, which also has trails, wildflowers, birds, and small animals. Some Centers include cross-country ski trails. And weekend programs may cover such diverse activities as maple-sugaring, ski instruction, movies, lectures on backpacking, bird walks, trail walks, etc. Lectures for school groups and movies for families are staple fare. Courses usually cost a small fee while guided walks and rambles are free. And naturally, one may visit these centers and walk the trails without participating in the structured programs at all.

Not all the centers are big and beautiful but they all serve their communities well. In many cases, the displays are equal to what you would find in a small museum of natural history. Here are some of New Jersey's nature centers:

LORIMAR NATURE CENTER — 790 Ewing Ave., Franklin Lakes, Bergen County. Telephone 201-891-1211. Run by the Audubon Society. There is a Living Museum and a demonstration farm besides the nature program and field trips. Nature trails open every day while the Visitor's Center is available Tues. - Sat. 10-4 and Sun. 1-5.

FLAT ROCK BROOK NATURE CENTER — 443 Van Nostrand Ave., Englewood, Bergen County. Telephone: 201-567-1265. Solar-heated building, 150 acres of forest with trails, brook. Various weekend activities, tree identification, classes for school-children, local artists' show. Run by self-supporting environmental organization.

BERGEN COUNTY WILDLIFE CENTER — Crescent Ave., Wyckoff. Telephone: 201-891-5571. A little of everything here — wildlife, daffodil preserve, waterfowl pond, nature trail, garden. At the Center, museum programs and films. Open daily except for legal holidays.

HARTSHORN ARBORETUM AND BIRD SANCTUARY — Forest Drive, Short Hills, Essex County. Telephone: 201-376-3587. Plant and wildlife museum. Classes in basket-weaving, plant propogation, dyeing, etc. Live animals, such as rabbits, ferrets, snake museum. 16½ acres of oak, maple, rhododendrons. Open daily. Museum: Tues. - Thurs.: 2:30-5. Sat.: 9:30-12. Sun.: 3-5 in fall and spring.

CENTER FOR ENVIRONMENTAL STUDIES — 621 Eagle Rock Ave., Roseland, Essex County. Telephone: 201-228-2210. Nature walks, slide lectures, classes for both children and adults. Center is also embarkation point for many daytrips — preregistration required.

RIKER HILL PARK GEOLOGICAL MUSEUM — Livingston, Essex County. Telephone: 201-992-8806. Administered by Center for Environmental Studies. Reconverted army barracks now houses fossil museum with skeletal reproductions. Quarry with fossil digs open for tours in good weather. Museum open Tues., Thurs., Sat. all day.

TRAILSIDE NATURE CENTER — Coles Ave. & New Providence Road, Mountainside, Union County. Telephone: 201-232-5930. Part of *Watchung Reservation*. New building includes auditorium and displays. Old nature museum has displays of beehives, eggshells, etc. Weekend programs, nature walks. Planetarium also.

GREAT SWAMP OUTDOOR EDUCATION CENTER — 247 Southern Blvd., Chatham Twp., Morris County. Telephone: 201-635-6629. On one edge of the swamp and run by the county. Wooden building contains exhibits, library, classrooms. Nature trails, guided walks, wooden walkways into swamps, special programs such as maple-sugaring. Closed July and August, when nature center moves to Schooley's Mountain Park, Route 24, Long Valley.

SOMERSET COUNTY PARK ENVIRONMENTAL EDUCATION CENTER — 190 Lord Stirling Park, Basking Ridge. Telephone: 201-766-2489. At the other edge of the Great Swamp. Modern building with classrooms, displays, separate solar-heated house. 8½ miles of trails and wooden walkways. Bird-watching, guided hikes, winter sleigh rides.

PORICY PARK NATURE CENTER — Oak Hill Road, Middletown Twp., Monmouth County. Telephone: 201-842-5966. 250 acres of land with trails. Fossil bed in park, fossil walks. Museum has art and nature displays, art programs, school programs. Building open Mon. - Fri. 9-4. Sun. 12:30-3:30.

SANDY HOOK VISITORS CENTER — Gateway National Recreation Area, Highlands, Monmouth County, off Route 36. Telephone: 201-872-0092. Summer activities include canoe trips and dune walk. Center has slide show, exhibits. Winter and spring weekend activities: holly forest walks and passes for lighthouse tours and Fort Hancock batteries. Classes by reservation.

Note: Parents of young children should also check out the mini-zoos in such places as *The Newark Museum, The Morris Museum* and the *Bergen Community Museum.*

THE OUTDOOR LIFE

Photos: Courtesy N.J. Div. of Travel & Tourism

In This Chapter You Will Find:

Ski Areas
New Jersey Ski Areas
New Jersey County Operated
The Poconos Ski Areas
New York State Ski Areas

The Jersey Shore
The Upper Shore
Long Beach Island
The Cape

Hiking
Fishing
Camping
State Parks and Forests

←——

Sea and Ski: The Jersey shore above and the Sussex County mountains below provide opportunities for both.

SKI AREAS

New Jersey Ski Areas

GREAT GORGE — VERNON VALLEY: One ticket buys access to the whole complex. By far the largest ski area in New Jersey, this place can get awfully crowded on weekends with lines at both the lifts and the cafeteria. The most persistent complaint is that on weekends busloads of amateur hotshots take over the slopes here. However, they do have night-skiing at a slightly lower rate from 6 p.m. to 10:45 p.m. Altogether GG/VV has 14 double chairlifts, one triple chairlife, complete snowmaking equipment, 3 mountains, ski rentals, lessons, cafeteria and nursery. Vertical drop of 1033 feet. Lift tickets are up to $18 ($15 for Juniors) but that price remains the same for weekends and holidays.

> **LOCATION:** Route 94 near McAfee in Sussex County.
> **TELEPHONE:** 201-827-2000 - for general information. 201-827-3000 -for ski report.

HIDDEN VALLEY: A particularly lovely area which becomes a private hideaway for lot owners on weekends until 5:30 p.m. However, it is open to the public five weekdays and seven evenings. One double chairlift for beginners and one triple chairlift for those who go to the top of the mountain. Only five trails but they limit access to Hidden Valley (mostly by limiting school groups when necessary — usually Friday nights during the height of the season) so overcrowding is not a problem. Cafeteria, ski school, classier atmosphere than Vernon Valley. Weekdays: $15; Night: $10.

> **LOCATION:** Breakneck Road, Vernon Twp., Sussex County
> **TELEPHONE:** 201-764-6161

CRAIGMEUR: One chairlift, one T-bar, two rope tows. A popular family area which caters to intermediates and beginners. Four slopes, cross-country program, night lighting. It's conveniently located to the northern suburbs and can get quite crowded on weekends (actually it's the cafeteria that's crowded with mothers who sit and watch the clothing while Dad teaches the kids a few pointers). No difficult slopes here which is why it's so popular with the beginners. Various rates for adults, juniors, ranging from $13 down. Weekdays it's $10.

> **LOCATION:** Route 80 to Green Pond Road (Route 513) Newfound-land, Morris County
> **TELEPHONE:** 201-697-4501

PEAPACK SKI AREA: One rope tow, no lifts and natural snow only. This is a place for those who like their sports natural. Nice for beginners and families who don't believe in going into bankruptcy for a day's skiing. A few warnings, however. Wear leather mittens for the rope tow — plastic mittens can't take it. And the place is open only on weekends and Monday through Thursday nights. (The man who runs it has to work weekdays to support it.) Rentals of ski equipment and ski instruction available. Snack shop on weekends. Cost is $7 for the day.

> LOCATION: Route 206 just two miles north of the 202-206 intersection, near Peapack, Somerset County.
> TELEPHONE: 201-543-4589 weekends.

SKI MOUNTAIN: This one is for the Philadelphia and suburban crowd since it's only 15 minutes from the city. Three ski slopes, one trail, 100% snowmaking equipment, 7,000 skiers-per-hour capacity, one double chair lift, one T-bar, two super-pony and one pony lift. Night skiing. Restaurant at base lodge. Large ski school.

> LOCATION: De Cou Road & Branch Ave., Pine Hill, Camden County
> TELEPHONE: 609-783-8484

HOLLY MOUNTAIN: One chair lift, one tow, five trails (one novice, two intermediate, two advanced intermediate). Vertical drop 150 feet. Instruction, night skiing, snack bar.

> LOCATION: Lower Alloways Creek, Salem County (Route 49 to Jericho Road).
> TELEPHONE: 609-935-9888

ARROWHEAD SKI AREA: For YMCA members, although non-members may ski at a higher rate weekdays. No lifts, four rope tows, four trails, some snowmaking equipment, snack bar, instruction.

> LOCATION: Marlboro, Monmouth County on Route 520 opposite State Hospital
> TELEPHONE: 201-946-4598

New Jersey County-Operated Facilities

Operated by individual counties primarily for residents at a very reasonable fee, they are, however, open to non-residents for a slightly higher charge in most cases.

GALLOPING HILL (Union County): Located on a golf course. Natural snow only and only one rope tow. Ski trail 800 feet, vertical drop 150 feet. Daytime only.

> LOCATION: Kenilworth Boulevard, Kenilworth, in the Galloping Hill Golf Course
> TELEPHONE: 201-353-8431

BELLE MOUNTAIN (Mercer County): One chair lift, three rope tows, four ski trails including one intermediate. Lighted for nighttime skiing. Lessons.

> LOCATION: Valley Road (off Route 29), Hopewell
> TELEPHONE: 609-397-0043

CAMPGAW MOUNTAIN (Bergen County): Main slope and two learning slopes, two double chair lifts, one T-bar, vertical drop of 255 feet. Lighted for night skiing, snack bar. Lessons.

> LOCATION: Campgaw Road, Mahwah
> TELEPHONE: 201-327-7800

The Poconos Ski Areas

SHAWNEE MOUNTAIN: Close by, but open for day skiing only. Shawnee offers four double chairlifts, snowmakers, ski school, accessory rental, cafeteria, bar and nursery. Twelve trails and 700 ft. vertical drop, plus cross-country trails. Weekends its $16 for adults, $13 for Juniors. Weekdays: $13 and $11 respectively.

> LOCATION: Take Route 80 to exit 52, then north on 209 for six miles.
> TELEPHONE: 717-421-7231

JACK FROST/BIG BOULDER: You buy a combination ticket for these two popular mountains. Eleven lifts between them, two J-bars and many trails that run the gamut from "Powderpuff" to

"Thunderbolt." Rentals, ski school, restaurant, cafeteria, nursery. For daytime the one-price ticket (no juniors) is $15 weekends, $11 weekdays. After Dec. 26 there is a 12 to 10 p.m. ticket available.

> LOCATION: Lake Harmony and White Haven, Pennsylvania. Rte. 80 Exit 42 or 43.
> TELEPHONE: 717-722-0104, 717-443-8425.

CAMELBACK: About a half-hour further on and part of the Big Pocono State Park. Camelback offers a variety of trails and attracts a pleasant crowd. 23 slopes, 11 lifts.

> LOCATION: Tannersville, Pa. Rte. 80 Exit 45.
> TELEPHONE: 717-629-1661

New York State Ski Areas

HUNTER MOUNTAIN: For ski groups and more advanced skiers Hunter is very popular. A goodly drive away, but the mountain here offers a 1,600 foot vertical drop and a large variety of trails include plenty for beginners, intermediates and those who really want to hone their skills. Nine chairlifts, six tows, 45 trails, and, according to my informant, less waiting. All services available. Daytime only. $17 ticket.

> LOCATION: Take Garden State Parkway to New York Thruway, then exit 20 to Route 32 for 19 miles.
> TELEPHONE: 518-263-4223

STERLING FOREST SKI AREA: Really close at hand, in fact it is right over the border in Tuxedo. Once the site of a popular garden, this ski area now services families and is pleasant for beginners and intermediates. Four double chairlifts, seven slopes, 450 ft. vertical drop. Cafeteria, warming hut, lessons, rentals and snowmakers. $15 for weekends; $12.50 weekdays, slightly less for juniors.

> LOCATION: Route 17 north to 17A north, just above Tuxedo, New York
> TELEPHONE: 914-351-2163

Note: Unless otherwise noted, snowmaking is available. Prices and number of trails (and trails available) change all the time. The number of chairlifts may be upgraded from one season to the next. It is always best to call first.

THE JERSEY SHORE

There are 127 miles of beach along the coast of New Jersey which offer swimming, boating and fishing. But for most people going to the shore means visiting one particular portion of that lengthy coastline. Here's a roundup of the various types of shore resorts that await the newcomer or oldtimer.

First of all, the beaches. Some are narrow, some are wide but few are free. Sandy Hook (government run) is free but can become so crowded that cars are turned away by noon. Atlantic City and the beaches of the Wildwoods are free. Island Beach State Park (State run) charges a per-car admission. Most other beaches require beach badges (which you buy from a man sitting there selling them), or admission through a private bathhouse which charges per-day admission. The price of badges varies from $2 per day to as little as $20 per season, depending on the town. If you stay at a hotel which owns its own beachfront, you don't have to bother with all this. And then there are a few select beaches which are accessible to residents only.

Cottage and beach house rentals vary according to size, closeness to beach and the social status of the town. Guest houses remain the cheapest accommodation especially if you don't mind walking a few blocks to the beach. Most motels offer efficiency apartments for those who want to cook in, but still have motel convenience. Motel rates compare well to other beach areas along the Atlantic Coast. Major amusement areas are found at Long Branch, Asbury Park, Point Pleasant, Seaside Heights, Atlantic City and Wildwood. (See chapter on Amusement Parks.)

The Upper Shore; Sandy Hook to Island Beach State Park

The closest and most accessible to the crowded urban and suburban areas of northern New Jersey, the upper shore is naturally very popular for daytime and weekend trips as well as the two-week vacation. **Sandy Hook** beach is part of the Gateway National Park and is run by the Department of the Interior. The beach is free but there are parking fees. Besides the beach, Sandy Hook offers the oldest operating lighthouse in the U.S., a nature center, a visitor's center, tours of Fort Hancock and surf fishing.

Below Sandy Hook there begins a string of beachfront communities, each with a slightly different personality. Some, like **Belmar**, cater to a young, singles crowd who share cottages and guest houses. Others, like **Deal**, are quiet and rich and interested only in full-time residents and full-summer rentals. You can find **Spring Lake** with its turreted late-Victorian homes and little old lady customers (well, some families do come, too) but there isn't a motel in sight. Just hotels in the old tradition, rental homes and guest houses.

Asbury Park is a developed area with a wide beach, large amusement area and many special events. One of the "old" resorts, it now has big rock concerts at the *Convention Hall* and the *Paramount* — quite different from its heyday. The large *Berkeley-Carteret* is boarded up, giving the area a forlorn look despite a string of boardwalk amusements. Separated from Asbury by a canal, **Ocean Grove** is quiet, reserved and primly Victorian. The stick style houses here remain from the early camp meeting days.

Further on are **Brielle** and **Point Pleasant**, towns with a large fishing fleet and many summer cottage rentals. And a bit down the strip come more reasonable rentals. At **Seaside Heights** and **Seaside Park** there are over 1200 cottages, many of them minimal comfort types with just two rooms and a couple of screened windows. Hundreds of guest houses and almost 100 motels service the many vacationers who come to this popular area, with its large amusement center. Neighboring Island Beach State Park with its State-run beach and nature area gets the daytime visitors. Parking at this popular public beach runs $4 on weekends. Even so, the lot is filled early.

Long Beach Island

For many middle executive families the place to go is Long Beach Island only an hour and a half away from North Jersey's affluent suburbs. A long, narrow strip of beach that extends from Barnegat Light to Holgate, the island is actually a series of little towns connected to the mainland by a bridge. Here you will find closely quartered beach houses and a few motels leading up to the dunes. The friendly small-town atmosphere and spanking clean air remind one of Cape Cod. Since most people rent cottages or apartments for at least two weeks, there is an air of leisure and permanence about Long Beach Island.

Courses in art, photography, Yoga and such are offered at both the *Foundation of Arts and Sciences* and at *St. Francis Center.* A dinner theater assures visitors there's more to summer life than basking on the beach and a small amusement park and water slide at Hartmann's in **Beach Haven** give the kids a break too.

Of course a trip to Long Beach Island would not be complete without a visit to "Old Barney" which is the main attraction at **Barnegat Lighthouse State Park.** The park allows swimming (although the waves are rough), picnicking, surf fishing and a view of the panorama from the red and white 122 year old lighthouse. It only takes 217 steps to climb.

The only access to Long Beach Island is the one road, Route 72 from the mainland to the center of the island. For the **Atlantic City** area (see separate chapter) you must return to Route 9 or the Garden State Parkway.

The Cape: Ocean City to Cape May

Like Atlantic City, this last strip of coastline is considered Philadelphia's shore as well as New Jersey's. However, people from all over come to these beaches, especially Canadians. **Ocean City,** the first down the line, bills itself as America's oldest family resort. It has never allowed liquor to be sold in its environs, but the beach is wide and clean and the long boardwalk very popular.

Among the Wildwoods, **Wildwood Crest** may have the advantage of getting the biggest family crowd but the beaches all along this area are very wide and kept quite clean despite the huge crowds that come on weekends. The surf is definitely milder down here and shallow enough for a toddler to wade a little without fear of imminent drowning. Both Wildwood and the Crest are solid motels from start to finish with guest houses and rental houses a block behind. **North Wildwood** and **Wildwood** have the nightclubs, the amusement park and the swinging crowd, while the Crest is more kiddie centered (although these things change from year to year). **Stone Harbor,** a bit above, is rich and quiet with just a few very good motels.

Twenty minutes down the coast and at the very tip of New Jersey lies **Cape May City.** Here is a beautiful Victorian town with whitewashed gingerbread houses and green lawns set against a placid shore. Compared to Wildwood with its many rectangular motels, Cape May presents a 19th Century dream. Quaint guest houses offer bed and breakfast and a turn-of-the-century ambience. What they don't offer is swimming pools and instant everything, although there are several hotels in town that offer at least a pool. Young couples and older folks seem to love the environment here. The beach in town, however, is brown and narrow and a poor relation to the neighboring wide swaths. Also, Cape May town has recently had a big splash of publicity so the narrow streets are now getting crowded and the automobiles are getting to be a nuisance.

One center of attraction here is the "Victorian Town," a series of renovated houses, quaint boutique shops, gaslight lamps and brick walkways. The shops lining Washington Mall offer an evening's entertainment in themselves with their art & crafts. And a visit to Roth's Candyland with its mouth-watering confections is worth a trip down here alone. Parking is a problem and the local Acme charges $4.00 for a space so get there early and look for a "free" space.

Beyond the town, **Cape May Point Beach** offers a wide beach, a picturesque lighthouse you cannot enter, and those little pieces of quartz known as Cape May Diamonds. And at the very tip of the county, the line begins for the **Cape May-Lewes ferry**, a three hour boat ride that takes you to Delaware the slow but pleasant way.

HIKING

There are any number of County Parks which offer both easy and more difficult hiking trails. Popular among these are the trails in the Watchung Reservation in Union County, the South Mountain Reservation in Essex County, the Lenape Trail in Nutley, the Mahlon Dickerson Reservation in Morris County. Almost all State Parks include hiking trails and you will find the complete list of State Parks following this article. There are, furthermore, two areas of extreme interest to outdoor enthusiasts in New Jersey — the **Pine Barrens** and the **Delaware Water Gap National Recreation Area**. Both of these include or neighbor state parks.

Information on hiking trails and other events at Delaware Water Gap is available at the Kittatinny Point Station right off of Route 80 as you travel toward the Pennsylvania border. Among the many activities sponsored by the Recreation Area are: the **Peters Valley Craftsmen** — a summer place where you may watch master potters, weavers, and jewelry makers, at work; the **Walpack Art Center** (basically an art gallery); and **Slateford Farm**, an 1800's farmhouse. The **Kittatinny Point Center** is also a staging area for canoeists (who bring their own) and includes picnic area, restrooms and lots of leaflets, including hiking trail guides. Whether you hike or take the car to an outlook point, a view of the Delaware Water Gap (which is a deep gorge cut by the river between two sets of mountains) is probably the most spectacular view in New Jersey. It should not be missed.

Stokes State Forest which is right nearby in the northern section of the State includes 17 named and marked trails plus a nine-mile stretch of the Appalachian Trail that transects the area. Here you will find Tillman Ravine. The 10,000-year-old ravine is preserved exactly as it was found with a host of natural wildflowers and trees. Five bridges have been installed to gain a better perspective for the hiker. The trails here are for the more experienced hiker.

The **Pine Barrens** offer a completely different experience. The terrain is practically flat but the flora and fauna of the region are unusual. Trails and old sand roads wind through the pines and swamps. The Batona Trail is the longest, extending from Carpenter Spring in Lebanon State Forest to Batsto in Wharton Forest, for thirty miles. Another, shorter trail in the Pine Barrens is called the Absegami. Since trails in the Pine Barrens can be confusing and people have gotten lost, it is best to start your hike at Batsto where you can talk with the Rangers at the visitor's center and obtain hiking guides.

Those interested in hiking can obtain further information by writing to the *New Jersey Division of Travel and Tourism*, P.O. Box 400, Trenton, NJ 08625. Another good place to contact, especially if you are interested in joining group hikes is: **The Sierra Club**, 360 Nassau Street, Princeton, NJ. Telephone 609-924-3141. Although this club is primarily devoted to environmental protection, their hikes and canoe trips are graded according to difficulty and led by a responsible hiker. They are very knowledgeable in the area of New Jersey trails.

FISHING

Most people think of fishing in New Jersey as off-shore fishing. Indeed, there are fleets of boats from Atlantic Highlands to Cape May, just waiting to take customers out. Party boats go out seven days a week during the summer either for half or full day excursions. They come complete with tackle, bait, food and drink although you pay for the extras, of course. These boats can handle over a hundred people and are sturdy enough to go well out into the ocean in their quest for bluefish, weakfish, tuna, fluke, and striped bass.

Charter boats are hired by groups for the day and in the busy season must be reserved weeks in advance. **Brielle,** on the Manasquan Inlet is one of the largest centers of party and charter boats in the state. Check the Sports Section of your daily newspaper (the Friday edition, especially) for the names and rates of party and charter boats.

Fresh-water fishermen have several favorite spots in New Jersey, two of them in State Parks. **Round Valley** is deemed to have the best sport fishing with 22 species of fish, including rainbow and lake trout and largemouth and smallmouth bass. The Round Valley Reservoir is part of the State Park about one mile south of Lebanon in Hunterdon County. It was created by two dams and is stocked by the State. In **Swartswood State Park** both Big and Little Swartswood Lakes are known for their fishing quality. This is a beautiful area high in the mountains of Sussex County.

The Pine Barrens is a magnet not only for hikers but for campers and fishermen as well. The **Bass River** in the State Forest of that name, the Batsto River and many lakes and inlets are dotted with fishing camps, both public and private.

While boating ramps are available at most of these state parks you must bring your own boat along. Anyone over 14 years of age must have a license for fresh water fishing. You may buy your Fishing License at any sporting goods store. The cost is $9.50 for adults, $5.50 for juniors (14-15) and $4.50 extra for a trout stamp. No license is required for deep sea or surf fishing.

CAMPING

Although there are many camping facilities in the State parks, you can also find hundreds of sites in the many private campgrounds around the State. The Pine Barrens and the southern portion of New Jersey abound with these camps which usually offer more sophisticated facilities than the State-run sites (higher rates too, of course). For a listing of both public and private campgrounds write for "Your 1980s Campsite Guide". It is available, free, from: *N.J. Division of Travel and Tourism,* CN 384, Trenton, NJ 08625 (Telephone: 609-292-2470)

STATE PARKS AND FORESTS

Following is a listing of the State Parks and Forests of new Jersey. Many of these, especially if they have swimming and boating facilities, levy a charge per car (no matter how many or few people are crammed inside). The highest charge ($4) is for weekends at such popular destinations as Island Beach State Park, Lake Hopatcong, Spruce Run and Round Valley. Rates are considerably less during the week. Others are free. Some, with historic sites, have been mentioned in greater detail elsewhere in this book.

State Parks

ALLAIRE STATE PARK, Monmouth County — 2,620 acres. Historic Howell Works and restored Allaire Deserted Village. Picnicking, hiking, nature study, horse trails, fishing, camping, old-time narrow gauge train rides. Lively calendar of events. Telephone: 201-938-2371.

ALLAMUCHY MOUNTAIN STATE PARK, Warren County — picnicking, camping, fishing. Telephone: 201-852-3790.

ATSION STATE PARK, Burlington County — Swimming, picnicking, food pavillion, boating. Telephone: 609-561-3262.

BARNEGAT LIGHTHOUSE STATE PARK, Ocean County — 172-foot lighthouse with 217-step spiral staircase. Swimming, picnicking, fishing. Telephone: 609-494-2016.

CAPE MAY POINT STATE PARK, Cape May County — fishing, picnicking, guided nature tours and tours of ruins of defense installation. Telephone: 609-884-2159.

CHEESEQUAKE STATE PARK, Middlesex County — swimming, picnicking, fishing, camping, hiking. Telephone: 201-566-2161.

CORSON'S INLET STATE PARK, Cape May County — bathing, boating, fishing, hiking. Free.

DELAWARE & RARITAN CANAL STATE PARK, Somerset County — Kingston or Bull's Island sections. Canoeing, fishing and hiking. Telephone: 201-873-3050. Free.

FORT LEE HISTORIC STATE PARK, Bergen County — spectacular view; picnicking permitted, historic sites. Telephone: 201-461-3956.

FORT MOTT STATE PARK, Salem County — fishing, picnicking, playground. Telephone: 609-935-3218. Free.

HACKLEBARNEY STATE PARK, Morris County — picnicking, hiking, fishing.

HIGH POINT STATE PARK, Sussex County — 220 ft. monument, swimming, picnicking, hiking on Appalachian Trail, fishing, camping, nature tours. Telephone: 201-875-4800.

HOPATCONG STATE PARK, Morris County — on Lake Hopatcong, New Jersey's largest. Picnicking, swimming, fishing, boating. Telephone: 201-398-7010.

ISLAND BEACH STATE PARK, Ocean County — ocean bathing, surf fishing, picnicking, wildlife sanctuary.

LIBERTY STATE PARK, Hudson County — ferry to Ellis Island and Statue of Liberty. Picnicking. Telephone: 201-435-8509. Free.

MONMOUTH BATTLEGROUND STATE PARK, Monmouth County — Visitor Center, picnicking. Telephone: 201-462-9619. Free.

PARVIN STATE PARK, Salem County — campsites, bathing, boating, hiking, picnicking, fishing, cabins. Telephone: 609-692-7039. Free.

RINGWOOD STATE PARK, Passaic County — historic mansions, botanic gardens, swimming, fishing. Telephone: 201-962-7031.

ROUND VALLEY STATE PARK, Hunterdon County — fishing, bathing, boating, wilderness camping. Second largest "lake" in New Jersey. Telephone: 201-236-6355.

SANDY HOOK STATE PARK, Monmouth County — swimming, picnicking, fishing, nature and military tours. Telephone: 201-872-0092.

SPRUCE RUN, Hunterdon County — fishing, small boating, bathing and picnicking. Reservoir area. Telephone: 201-638-8572.

STEPHENS STATE PARK, Warren County — Telephone: 201-398-7010.

SWARTSWOOD STATE PARK, Sussex County — excellent fishing, boating, camping, hiking, swimming. Telephone: 201-383-5230.

VOORHEES STATE PARK, Hunterdon County — picnicking, camping, nature study. Telephone: 201-638-6969. Free.

WASHINGTON CROSSING STATE PARK, Mercer County — museums, nature center, picnicking, outdoor theater during summer. Telephone: 609-737-0616.

WASHINGTON ROCK STATE PARK, Somerset County — picnic facilities, views of Watchung Mountains. Free.

WAWAYANDA STATE PARK, Sussex County — fishing, boating, swimming, picnics, camping.

State Forests

ABRAM S. HEWITT STATE FOREST, Passaic County — hiking and hunting.

BASS RIVER STATE FOREST, Burlington/Ocean Counties — bathing, picnicking, hiking, nature study, hunting, fishing. Cabins and campsites. Telephone: 609-296-1114.

BELLEPLAIN STATE FOREST, Cape May/Cumberland Counties— bathing, picnicking, camping, hunting, fishing. Telephone: 609-861-2402.

JENNY JUMP STATE FOREST, Warren County — picnicking, camping, nature study, hunting. Telephone: 201-459-4366.

LEBANON STATE FOREST, Burlington County — bathing, picnicking, hiking, hunting, camping. Telephone: 609-726-1191.

NORVIN GREEN STATE FOREST, Passaic County — hiking, hunting.

PENN STATE FOREST, Burlington County — bathing, picnicking, hiking, hunting, fishing.

STOKES STATE FOREST, Sussex County — bathing, picnicking, hiking, camping, fishing, hunting. Telephone: 201-948-3420.

WHARTON STATE FOREST, Burlington County — bathing, camping, picnicking, fishing, boating, hiking, hunting. Batsto Historical Area. Canoeing. Telephone: 609-561-0024, 609-561-3262.

WORTHINGTON STATE FOREST, Sussex County — hunting, fishing, hiking, picnicking, camping. Telephone: 201-841-9575.

THE
GARDEN VARIETY

Photo: Courtesy N.J. Div. of Travel & Tourism

In This Chapter You Will Find:

Longwood Gardens
The Duke Gardens
Brooklyn Botanic Gardens
New York Botanical Gardens
Hershey Rose Garden
Colonial Park
Buck Gardens
Branch Brook Park
Skylands
Frelinghuysen Arboretum
Presby Iris Gardens
The Hedge Garden

←
One of the eleven enclosed "gardens of the world" at the Duke Gardens, Somerville

LONGWOOD GARDENS

Without a doubt the most extensive and the best gardens in the area (and considered the best in the United States), this impressive display by the DuPont family offers an amazing variety. The gardens are open all year round and there is always something of interest whatever the weather. Altogether 350 acres are open to the public, including some beautifully laid out conservatories, so bring good walking shoes.

You enter through the main Visitor Center which looks like a standard institutional building from the front, but like an underground house from the back — it's cleverly concealed under a hillock of green. At the Center you purchase your tickets and watch a four-minute continuous film which introduces you to the highlights of the gardens and points out seasonal displays. There's a gift shop chock full of books and plants where you'll want to stop on your way out. But for now, be sure to get the brochure guide and map at the information desk — you'll need it to find your way around. Here are some of the highlights you will probably choose on your visit:

The *Conservatories* are huge glass-enclosed rooms that surround a patio. Inside there are hanging basket mobiles sprouting flowers; stone herons in a pond surrounded by azaleas and acacias; a ballroom featuring organ concerts spring and fall; and the hot and humid Palm House with its banana, breadfruit and traveller trees. There is one room for insect-eating plants another just for orchids. The main conservatory displays change four times a year. (The Christmas display alone, with its poinsettias and line of Christmas trees, attracts more than 100,000 people a year.)

Outside, directly in front of the conservatories (and below, because you watch from the terrace) is the main water fountain area. The fountain display, with its many spouting water jets is framed by trimmed boxwood. Tuesday and Saturday nights during the summer, colored lights and music from the *Carillion* make a spectacular *"Son et Lumiere."* The carillion, by the way, is beyond the fountain area in its own little romantic nook. A high cascading waterfall, a rock garden and the stone carillion tower look like something out of a 19th century painting. Further on, on this west side of the gardens are the *Idea Garden, Heaths of Heather*, the *"Eye of God"* (a low, circular water sculpture), a topiary and a rose garden.

The right side of Longwood boasts the flower walk — a sort of main drag bordered by seasonal flowers, and the open air theater

— a stage surrounded by sculptured trees and using a curtain of water fountains. You will also find the *Peirce-DuPont House*, open to visitors for an extra fee ($1.00). This 1730 home has had only two owners — the original Mr. Peirce, who owned the basic park from which Longwood Garden was born, and the DuPonts, who saved the property from becomming a sawmill in 1906.

Further on there are wisteria and rose gardens, forest walks and meadows, a lake with gazebo and ducks, and last of all, a complete (though miniature) *Italian Water Garden* in the manner of the Villa D'Este. Luckily there are many benches and shaded spots at which to rest along the way.

The Gardens are very strict about certain things. No food can be brought in (although there is a nice picnic area outside the Visitors Center). Smoking is forbidden. There are plenty of drinking fountains but don't expect to find a Coke machine or a Frito in the place. There are future plans, happily, for a restaurant with catering service to groups.

> HOURS: Daily. April - Oct., 9-6; Nov. - Mar. 9-5.
> Illuminated displays Tues. & Sat., 9:15 PM, Summer only.
> ADMISSION: Adults: $4.00, Children: $1.00, Under 5, free.
> LOCATION: Route 1, Kennett Square, Pa.
> TELEPHONE: 215-388-6741

THE DUKE GARDENS

Open from October to May, one of New Jersey's foremost attractions, the Duke Gardens, features a series of interconnecting hothouses with an amazing variety of plants. They are part of the Duke Estate in Somerville. Indeed, from the moment you board the little green bus in the parking lot that takes you through a winding road bordered by tall spruces you are aware you are in Rich Man's country. The administration building where you get your tickets and wait for the guide is an English style gardener's cottage replete with rich woods and carpets. From here the tour guide takes you across to the hothouses where you enter a different world.

Each hothouse contains a shortened version of an international garden. The layout, the flowers and the walkways are all planned to reflect the atmosphere of that particular garden. The first one you enter is the *Italian Romantic garden*. Here you find statuary amid overgrown plants, standing orchids, and the type of Mediterranean setting that threw nineteenth century poets into ecstasy.

Each garden is controlled for climate and humidity. As you move from one to the other you find yourself shedding coats and sweaters according to the climate. Enter the *Edwardian Conservatory* and it's warm. Here, in a hothouse with tropical plants such as sego palms and elephant ears, the English gentleman would propose to his lady love (or at least he did in all those old movies on late night television). He would probably clip an orchid and hand it to her. For there are enough big, fat orchids in the Conservatory to sent an entire graduating class to the Senior Prom.

The long *English garden*, on the other hand, is temperate. A brick walkway takes you through sedate rows of hollyhocks, primroses and manicured boxwoods. A small herb garden is here also. The *French garden* is formal, with flowers set out in greenery shaped in a fleur-de-lis pattern. Lattice work covers all, and a far statue of a goddess reminds you that this is a small version of what you might find at Versailles.

The *Chinese garden*, with its overhanging willows, stone walkway and arched bridge over a goldfish pond is for serene meditation. The scent of the fragrant tea olive permeates the air. Among the other gardens you will find an Arizona desert with succulents and tall cacti; a Japanese rustic style meditation garden; a Spanish semi-formal with decorated tiles and brilliant birds-of-paradise; and the lush foliage of a tropical rain forest with its banana trees and large ferns.

Twenty-five gardeners attend the plantings, so the Duke Gardens changes the flowers on display often, but the overall scheme remains intact. It is a favorite destination of garden clubs, but individuals enjoy the gardens as well. Advance reservations are required however. Cameras and high heels are not permitted (you'll understand why when you walk on those arched stone bridges).

HOURS: Oct. - May, 12-4 Daily. Wed., Thurs., evening hours.
ADMISSION: Adults: $2.50, Children: $1.50, Under 6 free. Students in class group, free.
LOCATION: Route 206, south of Somerville Circle.
TELEPHONE: 201-722-3700

BROOKLYN BOTANIC GARDENS

New Jerseyans often combine a trip to these gardens with one to the Brooklyn Museum (which is right next door) since parking in the museum lot can serve for both places.

The Brooklyn Gardens are known for the cherry blossom walk — a wide swath of lawn with Japanese double blossoms, white and pink, that come out in mid-April. Their other famous display is the *Japanese Gardens* which were originally designed and built in 1914, then reconstructed in 1960. Here a pagoda rising from the calm waters, the quiet meditation walks, the willow trees and the stone turtles create a duplication of a Kyoto scene set down incongruously in the midst of urban high-rises.

At this garden everything goes by natural cycles: the daffodils in March, then the lilacs, then the cherry blossoms, then the wisteria and rhododendrons in May. The rose garden is fenced off and opens only in June, so it's best you visit at the time of your favorite flower.

However, there are a number of attractions that are practically seasonless — the formal prospect that greets you as you enter from Eastern Parkway, the herbal gardens, the Shakespeare garden, the fragrance garden, the rock gardens, and the large Conservatory filled with exotic plants which are all more or less clumped together.

There are 50 acres to the gardens, and plenty of benches to sit on and brooks to meander by. They are fairly strict about behavior here — no picnicking, no bicycles, no dogs, no sitting on the grass (except in the Cherry Esplanade), and no children under 16 unless accompanied by adults — and there are patrols that enforce these rules. Perhaps that is why the Brooklyn Botanic Gardens have remained a verdant oasis throughout the years. Free. Greenhouse admission 25¢ on weekends.

LOCATION: Eastern Parkway & Washington Ave., Brooklyn, N.Y.
HOURS: May - Aug.: Tues. - Fri. 8-6; Weekends and Holidays: 10-6. Sept. - Apr.: Tues. - Fri. 8-4:30; Weekends and Holidays: 10-4:30.
TELEPHONE: 212-622-4433

Photo: Courtesy N.J. Div. of Tourism

In mid-April, the Japanese flowering cherry tree delights visitors to both Branch Brook Park (above) and the Brooklyn Botanic Gardens.

NEW YORK BOTANICAL GARDENS

These gardens are a disappointment to some because much of these 250 acres are in such a natural state you might as well be in Central Park. Still, the gardens contain several areas of interest to garden clubs and plants lovers.

One is the imposing museum building which contains a library of 400,000 books and journals plus a herbarium of 4,000,000 plant specimens for staff and scientists. The museum also offers a first rate shop which sells plants, garden books, tools and related items.

The large conservatories, within easy walking distance of the parking lot, were recently restored to their original 1901 crystal-palace look. Eleven galleries include the *palm dome, Old World* and *New World* deserts, an orangerie and one acre reserved for seasonal displays of lilacs, orchids, poinsettias, etc. Nice, but without the beauty or imagination that characterizes Longwood and the Duke Gardens.

Outside, there are many pockets of flowering displays during the spring and summer. A rose garden with a succession of blooms from June to late autumn; a herb garden; a rhododendron slope; Daffodil Hill, Azalea Glen, and a flowering rock garden with many alpine plants are scattered about the extensive acreage.

The Bronx Gardens as they are often called, have much the look of a large, well-tended city park rather than a formal garden. On the day I visited, there were people walking dogs, joggers, and what looked like picnickers, all unusual in a garden atmosphere. Since areas of interest, such as flowering displays, the pine hill and the virgin hemlock forest, occur sporadically among the many acres, be sure to arm yourself with visitor's guide. And although the gardens are across the street from the Bronx Zoo, anyone who hopes to do both in one day is either an incurable optimist or has legs of steel.

HOURS: Daily. 8-7 in summer, 10-5 in winter.
ADMISSION: Free to grounds. $2.50 parking lot fee.
**ADMISSION TO
CONSERVATORY:** $1.50 adults. 75¢ children & seniors.
Conservatory open Tues. - Sun. 10-4
LOCATION: George Washington Bridge & Cross Country Express-way east to Exit 4B, to Bronx River Parkway North. Take Bronx Zoo exit.
TELEPHONE: 212-220-8747

HERSHEY ROSE GARDENS
AND ARBORETUM

Not far from the Hershey Hotel, the Rose Garden and Arboretum began as a small 3½ acre plot devoted to roses and now covers over 23 acres with flowers, trees, lakes and shrubs. Individuals take a self-guided tour through terraces of roses and past a man-made lake filled with goldfish, ducks and swans and the statue of a *Boy with a Leaking Boot*. A holly collection, one hundred varieties of herbs, rhododendrons, and evergreens are part of the display all season long. Other major flowerings are: mid-April to mid-May — daffodils, tulips and early azaleas; May 15 - June 1 — azaleas, rhododendrons, peonies. Then, from June 1 to September 15, 27,000 rose plants bearing 1200 varieties of roses are in bloom. From September 15 to November 1 — chrysanthemums. Tapes available. Picnic area and sale shop.

HOURS: April 15 - Nov. 1: 8 AM to dusk.
ADMISSION: Adults: $1.50, Children 5-18: 50¢
LOCATION: Hershey, Pa. on Route 322.
TELEPHONE: 717-534-3531

COLONIAL PARK ROSE GARDEN

The original garden, once part of the Mettler Estate, was redeveloped and expanded by a horticulturist so that it now covers an acre and displays a wide variety of roses. 275 species, 4,000 bushes form a formal display garden which exhibits the A.A.R.S. Award Winning Roses each year. Included here are the original York and Lancaster roses, tearoses, floribunda, and more. They are all labeled to show type and date of introduction into the horticultural world. A flagstone walk makes for easy ambling.

Behind the rose garden is the new *Fragrance Garden for the Blind* which provides both braille plaques and a handrail for the handicapped. Both gardens are set inside of Colonial Park, one of those beautiful county parks that one comes upon so often in New Jersey. An arboretum and meandering stream border the gardens. Beyond that there are tennis courts, paddle boats and picnic tables for family get togethers.

Garden clubs, school classes and other groups can arrange for guided tours for a fee. Otherwise the gardens are free. Major bloomings are the first week of June and the first week of September.

HOURS: 10 AM to 8 PM daily from June 1st to Nov. 1st (for gardens)
LOCATION: Amwell Road, Millstone, Somerset County.
TELEPHONE: 201-873-2459

BUCK GARDENS

At this time, these estate gardens are open by appointment only, but Somerset County hopes to make them a public garden someday. For now, you must go by group, but the same $10 charge covers anywhere from two to fifty people.

The former estate of Leonard J. Buck, a Far Hills millionaire, the tract is informal, grassy and treed, with many rock gardens (which were Mr. Buck's specialty) along the trails. The Buck mansion still stands atop a winding, hilly path but is not open for viewing. There's plenty of walking here, with stops at various benches for the vistas. Terrain varies from low lying swamp to steep hillsides. The gardens are best seen in the spring when thousands of tiny flowers peek out from designed rock formations. There are many other plantings and unusual trees plus a pleasant lake that provides the ducks with a picturesque swimming area.

LOCATION: Far Hills Road, Far Hills, Somerset County.
TELEPHONE: 201-873-2459
or write: Somerset Park Commission
P.O. Box 837, Somerville, NJ 08876
Attention: Horticulture Dept.

BRANCH BROOK PARK

More than 2,000 cherry trees in bloom in the middle of April beautify this Essex County Park which stretches from Newark to neighboring Belleville. The cherry blossom area covers 2 miles in length but only about a quarter mile in width. Originally donated by Caroline Bamberger Fuld, these pink and white, single and double flowering trees now outnumber those in Washington, D.C. Many special events are planned to coincide with the cherry blossom festival.

CONTACT: Essex County Dept. of Parks, 201-482-6400 for events and special bus tours.

SKYLANDS

A popular springtime attraction is the Skylands preserve flowering around the mansion in one section of **Ringwood Manor State Park**. A half-mile alley of crabapple trees, 400 varieties of lilacs, azaleas and peonies and a small formal garden surround the castle-like 44-room home. There are signs pointing out flowering sections and you can also pick up a map when you pay your entrance toll. For location check Skylands Manor entry.

> **HOURS:** Daily
> **PARKING**
> **FEE:** $1 Weekdays; $2 Weekends.
> **TELEPHONE:** 201-962-7031

FRELINGHUYSEN ARBORETUM

Tulips, azaleas, rhododendrons, a rose garden and a wealth of flowering trees are part of the display at this 127 acre tract that was once the home of the Frelinghuysens. Cherry trees, crabapple and magnolia blossoms along with a lilac garden and a dogwood copse bring color and contrast to the many evergreens in the collection. Run by the Morris County Park System. At the Administration Building there is a botanical library and a meeting room where lectures, concerts and other activities take place. Free.

> **HOURS:** Daily
> **LOCATION:** 53 E. Hanover Ave. (Route 511) Morristown, Morris County
> **TELEPHONE:** 201-285-6166

PRESBY IRIS GARDEN

From the last week in May to the second week in June, an outstanding display of irises can be found in this lovely suburban park in Upper Montclair. Hilly terrain and gracious homes are the setting for this local park where a Mr. Presby began his iris beds many years ago. Every color in the rainbow is reflected in irises. The 4,000 varieties are planted in beds that line a long walk. Free.

HOURS: Daily. Display runs approximately 3 weeks, beginning May 24.
LOCATION: Mountainside Park, 500 Upper Mountain Ave., Upper Montclair, Essex County
TELEPHONE: 201-744-1400

THE HEDGE GARDEN

What started as a backyard hobby has now grown into a full-time tourist attraction. Gus Yearicks, who is almost 90 years old, has spent 53 years nurturing and shaping this topiary garden. Hedges shaped in the figures of Santa Claus or people in a baseball game, the bulk of an elephant or the outline of a ship can be seen spread out over almost two acres. For people who have seen the animal topiaries at Disney World, this is a closer look at an unusual art. No frames are used and Mr. Yearicks trains all this privet hedge himself.

HOURS: April - Nov.: 8:30 to dusk
ADMISSION: Voluntary donation
LOCATION: 185 Fishing Creek Road, Fishing Creek, Cape May County (one mile from County Airport)
TELEPHONE: 609-886-5148

See Also: Formal gardens and landscaped lawns are often attached to the historic houses treated elsewhere in this book. For outstanding examples, see in particular, *Winterthur* (Restored and Reconstructed Villages, Homes, etc.) and *Nemours*, *Lyndhurst*, and the *Vanderbilt Mansion* (Homes of the Rich and Famous).

FLEA MARKETS
AND OUTLETS

Photos by Linda Kimler

In This Chapter You Will Find:

OUTLETS
Reading, Pennsylvania
Flemington Outlets
Secaucus Outlets

FLEA MARKETS
Englishtown Auction Sales
Chester
Lambertville
Lahaska
Other Flea Markets (N.J.)
Antique Centers
Indoor Markets

Flea market dealers with urns, crafts, odds and ends. Top and left, Meyersville Grange flea market. Lower right, Archies Resale Shop.

READING, PENNSYLVANIA

Reading is a rather grim looking factory town of red brick and wood tenements. Yet every day, busloads of people pour into Reading. Why? For the outlet stores that dominate the center of town. And although buses and cars always make several stops at the major outlets, the common complaint is that there just aren't enough hours to go through all those seconds.

One reason there isn't enough time is that not all outlets are equal. A true outlet sells a manufacturer's irregulars and seconds (those slightly imperfect articles that cannot be sent to the department stores). But some of the "outlets" in Reading are simply discount houses and the bargains you find are no better or worse than those in the local discount emporiums. So time is lost in running from one store to the other as you try to sort the true bargain from the not-so-great buy.

By far the most popular store in Reading is the *Vanity Fair Outlet*. Here you can find all the robes, gowns and lingerie you want at absolutely half price. Kay Windsor dresses and Lee jeans are also sold here at 50 percent off. But one always has to remember that some of these are seconds, so checking for stuck zippers and loose threads becomes a must. Vanity Fair's quality however, seems to be good. Several other buildings are part of the Vanity Fair complex — the shoe outlet here offers good buys. There is also a Black and Decker and an Oneida Silver outlet.

Another large complex, a short drive away is the *Reading Outlet Center* (bounded by Moss, N. 9th and Douglass Sts.) A tremendous red brick building that was converted from a factory, it fills a huge square block and is jammed with many small outlet stores. I found some Van Heusen shirts at the Men's Outlet store here at fully two-thirds off the price. Take note that the packages in this place are boldly stamped "Irregular" right on front. If you're hoping to load up on Christmas presents here some fancy repacking will be in order. One shirt I bought even had "Imperfect" stamped on the inside collar. It's nice finding a $15.00 shirt for $4.95 but my husband had to spend the year not only with ring around the collar, but "Imperfect" around the neck as well.

Heister's Lane is a new area that includes the Sweater Mill, the Burlington Coat Factory and china and glassware shops.

If you visit Reading a few helpful hints are in order.

1. Take a bag lunch with you. It saves time and time is of the essence here. There apparently are few decent eating places in Reading.

2. Checks are acceptable in most places only if you have major credit cards (Visa, Mastercharge, Exxon, etc.) to show that you're honest. However, the outlets will not accept credit cards themselves so don't count on a pocketful of plastic. Cash and a checkbook should do it. Vanity Fair accepts checks with only a driver's license as identification.

3. Check local prices before you take the trip. Only when you become as expert as the contestants on "The Price Is Right" will you be sure you have a bargain.

4. The peak season for bus tours is October, November and early December. If you're not shopping for Christmas, avoid these times.

5. There is no clothing tax in Pennsylvania.

HOURS: Most stores open Mon. - Sat., 9:30-5:30 and Sun. 12-5 (except Jan. & Feb.)
LOCATION: U.S. 222, Reading, Pa.

FLEMINGTON OUTLETS

A few years ago Flemington offered a mix of outlet stores and boutiques; *Turntable Junction* boasted specialty stores; and next door you could watch the colonial craftsmen at *Liberty Village*. But as the economy changes so do the towns. Thus, Flemington, while still a quiet country town of Victorian homes, and still the seat of rural Hunterdon County, is now very heavily an outlet town.

Liberty Village, which never did too well as a colonial restoration, now has outlet shops inside those authentically restored 18th Century shells. The Vandermark Glass Manufactury is still going and you can still watch the glassblowers work over their hot furnaces, and the fanciful tulip glasses and paperweights are still on sale. A few craftsmen still craft and peddle their wares in the Liberty Village area. But most of the charm is gone — and in its place — bargains, bargains, bargains.

The largest concentration of outlet stores in Flemington is in the area bounded by Main, Mine and Church Streets, just a few blocks away from the Flemington Circle. Slightly below Turntable Junction on the other side of the Black River and Western Railroad tracks are two stores of interest. One is the *Paul Revere Shoppe* where Revereware is sold at from 40% to 70% discount. This is a true manufacturer's outlet and if you happen upon a discontinued item you can really clean up.

A few paces from the Revere Shop is *George Briard* (who also has an outlet store at Reading). Even if you don't recognize the name, you'll recognize the glassware. Briard cheesboards and ice buckets, bar glasses and accessories grace every department store in the country. You'll find them at very good discounts here and for the life of me I could not detect any flaws in the glasses. Next door is *Pfaltzgraeff* (in the old Staengl factory). In this huge shed there are clearly marked sections of "Firsts" and "Seconds" of this popular dinnerware manufacturer. The seconds were cheap but they looked like seconds.

If you cross the tracks and walk beyond Turntable Junction, you come to the *Flemington Cut Glass Factory*, which seems to be sprouting smaller outlets as a spider plant puts out sprigs. Besides the usual selection of ordinary glassware in the regular building, there is the separate Mart for decorative items, the China Closet for dishes, and a new store specializing in pewter that had some very interesting bargains.

The *Flemington Fur Company* is a huge building at 8 Spring Street where furs are abundant. There is a large selection here but no one I know has ever raved about their prices. And up near the Flemington Circle (where Routes 202, 31 and 12 all meet) some popular stores are: the *Dansk Factory Outlet* (modern cookware and some furniture), *The Shoe Factory* and the *Ladies Factory Outlet* for Ship 'N Shore blouses.

Altogether there are about thirty outlet stores in Flemington and the number is growing. In times of recession, outlets are in, and the "In" boutiques are out.

LOCATION: Route 78 to 31 south, or Route 202. From Flemington Circle follow signs for "business district."

SECAUCUS OUTLETS

Here is another area of burgeoning outlet and discount stores. Close to the Meadowlands, and beneath the shadow of the new Harmon Towers and Cove, there is a gridwork spread of industrial park warehouses, sleek new office buildings and outlet stores. In some cases one building shares the executive offices of a fashion company and the fashion outlet too. Stores vary from big and comfortable to small and basic. Ladies Rooms are a rarity and luncheon spots are non-existent, although you can track down a pleasant, casual place like nearby *Cleo's* if you ask the right salesperson.

The landscape is like a maze, although the tractor-trailers who service the industrial park all seem to know where they are going. You will need a map. Luckily you can pick one up at the first outlet you hit and proceed from there. The best way to approach the complex is to travel down Meadowlands Parkway, past the Hilton and Riverside Hospital. Make a left at American Way or Secaucus Road. These roads lead on the Hartz Way and Enterprise Avenue. Most of the outlets are dispersed here and there on these streets but there is also a nice little cluster of shops at a dead end at the bottom of Enterprise Ave. South.

As for the stores themselves — some clothing stores carry high fashion names but give only 20% off (not much different from department stores at their constant sales). Other places carry deep discounts, but the quality did not seem high. In other words, what's good is not that cheap, and what's cheap is not that good. However, there are sales on top of the discounts so you may find a worthwhile bargain after all.

Of the non-clothing stores, *The China, Glass and Gift Outlet* (25 Enterprise Ave.) seems to offer good value if you know what you want. If you are planning to buy a set of Mikasa china, you can find many lovely patterns here at 1/3 off. When you're talking about a $600 set of dishes, one-third off can make a big difference.

There are several chain discount stores in the complex — among them, *NBO* and *Linens 'N Things*. Of the clothing stores, one friend likes *Discovery* (60 Enterprise Ave.) where you can find Villager and Huk-A-Poo at nice discount. The people's favorite seems to be *Abe Schrader* (Hartz Way) where you can buy a $90 dress for $70. But from the way people were fighting over parking spaces in the rather small parking lot the day I visited, you'd think Abe Schrader was handing out the clothes for nothing.

Many of the stores here are only open from 10 to 4, although most stay open at least to 5 pm. At any rate it's best to start in the morning if you want to hit several stores. Most places take checks if you have two valid IDs, and some take credit cards. Cash, of course, is always happily accepted.

DIRECTIONS: NJ Turnpike to Exit 16W to Route 3 East to Meadowlands Parkway. Follow signs for Industrial Park.

FLEA MARKETS

The term supposedly originated in the Middle Ages when peddlers gathered at the marketplace to sell old clothing and assorted junk which came already infested with fleas. Nowadays the term covers a wide variety of sales, none of which have anything to do with insects. At Flea Markets you might find:

1. **NEW MERCHANDISE** from manufacturers overruns or seconds. Some "Flea Markets," such as the one outside of New Brunswick on Route One, are almost completely new merchandise. They are housed inside of defunct supermarkets or chain stores and the same dealers remain there all year round. Actually these are almost giant conglomerations of pushcart peddlers. Bargain hunters jam these places, especially as inflation rockets higher. But you get no guarantees of the merchandise and it's *caveat emptor* in all cases.

2. **ANTIQUE AND COLLECTIBLES DEALERS.** Both indoor and outdoor markets create a buying and selling arena for dealers of older merchandise. Traditionally, antiques must be 100 years old to be considered such and pieces dated before 1840 (the watershed date for the Industrial Revolution) are counted more valuable. Collectibles, on the other hand, include fairly recent items that have been discontinued or are considered desirable. Bubble gum trading cards, old postcards, Avon bottles in a series, Depression glass (nothing fancy — just those cheap dishes they handed out at movie theaters in the 30s), old orange juice squeezers enter this category. Prices vary drastically according to what's in and what's out.

3. **GARAGE SALE ITEMS.** Since many outdoor flea markets rent their tables for the day and often for as little as 4 or 6 dollars, it is not unusual for local people to simply hold their garage sales at a popular market. Anything goes here!

4. **CRAFT DEALERS.** Generally craft people do better at Craft Fairs than at flea markets, since bargain hunters balk at the prices for new, hand-made items. However, at certain flea markets you might find someone selling seashell decorations or duck decoys, especially if the dealer has staked out this territory for himself.

5. **FARMER'S MARKETS.** Especially in Monmouth and Ocean Counties, summer markets include a food section where fresh corn, watermelons, beans and squash are on hand in quantity and at much better prices than at the supermarket.

6. ANTIQUE CENTERS. Sometimes they abut a flea market; other times they are in the center of town; but an Antique Center can be a barn, a mall, a house, a reconverted factory. Inside the structure, you might find a series of rooms, stalls, niches or even huge quarters rented by individual dealers. Some centers are collectives with all dealers contributing to the rent, upkeep, etc. More often one dealer owns the building while the others rent. They take turns minding the store, however.

THE ENGLISHTOWN AUCTION SALES FLEA MARKET

It's advertised as the world's largest flea market, this vast dusty field set in the midst of Monmouth County's farm country, and it probably is. However, the term "flea market" is changing these days and anyone expecting acres of antiques on sale will be disappointed.

Right now, Englishtown Auction Sales consists of about 70 percent dealers in new discount merchandise and 30 percent dealers in collectibles. What you find is something like 300 garage sales going on side by side with 700 New York street hawkers all set up on tables covering a huge field. Add to that a farmer's market with tables of fresh corn, tomatoes, melons, apples and pumpkins. And then add four buildings filled with discount clothing booths, kielbasa stands, knish stands, booths selling hot dogs, hamburgers and oriental food and a complete bar and grill. Then add a cast of thousands worthy of a Cecil B. DeMille movie and you have some idea of the immensity of the place. In fact, Englishtown Auction Sales has everything but an auction — that term refers to the old days when cows were sold off too.

The Flea Market is open weekends only, but traditionally the day for "antique" bargains is Saturday, the earlier the better. The market actually opens at 5 a.m. However, chances of your finding the missing teapot to Catherine the Great's silver tea service is about the same as your chance of hitting the jackpot at Atlantic City. Even less. What you will find is a mass of memorabilia, knick-knacks, new shoes and old tires — practically anything in the world can be discovered here. A new bell for your bicycle, a collection of porcelain doorknobs, a reproduced stone plaque or garage sale "junque" all mixed in with bargain basement clothing and cosmetics.

Those who search for collectibles can certainly find something of interest. Depression glass, comic books, paper-weights and German World War I helmets and medals were some that I noticed the day I visited. However there is only one permanent dealer in collectibles and he's enscounced in the Brown Building (the other three are named Red, Green and Blue respectively). This man deals in back number Hummels and Norman Rockwell plates, and his booth is stocked with colorful figurines. He told me that in the old days hundreds of antique dealers would unload their goods early and that it was possible to find excellent values among the junk. Nowadays, he noted, the proliferation of new discount sales people has driven many antique dealers away.

Still in all, Englishtown Auction Sales offers you a chance to buy that elusive whatnot you could never find anywhere else. Perhaps it will be a kitchen sink faucet or a car seat cover that's just right, a beat-up plant-stand or the missing Avon bottle to your set. A craft table pops up here and there also — I found candles molded in the form of Venus Di Milo, conch shell lamps and personalized birthday cards.

Outdoor tables in seasonable weather (well into fall). Lots of dust and dirt so dress appropriately. And they charge either 50¢ or $1.00 for parking.

HOURS: Sat.: 5 AM - 5 PM. Sunday: 9 AM - 5 PM all year
LOCATION: Garden State Parkway to Exit 123. Route 9 South to Texas Road. Right on Texas Road to Route 527 for 3 miles. Look for signs.
TELEPHONE: 201-446-9644

CHESTER FLEA MARKET AND ANTIQUE STORES

Chester has been trying to be a quaint Revolutionary town for years now, but what finally put it on the map was the Chester Flea Market. Run by the Lions Club in a field right outside the main hub of town, the Flea Market now brings hundreds of dealers and thousands of visitors every Sunday from late April to October.

Tables are spread out on a dusty field and the mix of new merchandise to collectibles is about 50/50. One fixture of this market is the "telephone man," who sells old Bell receivers for novelty (or for real). I bought an old-fashioned black job for $3 back in 1971. His recent price for the same phone was $12. At least he's keeping pace with inflation.

Vendors here tend to book for the whole season, so there is some stability. Hot dogs and funnel cakes are available for snacking. Don't expect to find high quality antiques but there is a nice assortment of souvenir type collectibles.

As for the town of Chester: a combination of specialty boutiques and antique shops has the streets bustling here in spring and summer. On East Main Street, stores with cutesy names like *Karen's Koop* and the *Country Mouse* offer a mix of antiques, quilts, coverlets, cookware, etc. *Woodcock's Gourmet* and the *Factory Fudge Shop* make your mouth water before you even enter with their food specialties.

P.S. Now that the flea market is really popular they are talking of moving it somewhere else. Check before going.

HOURS: (For Flea Market): Sundays only, April - Oct. Antique Shops: Weekdays, Saturdays, and in most cases Sundays from 11 AM

LOCATION: Route 24, Morris County

LAMBERTVILLE

This is another town that has benefitted greatly from the presence of flea markets. Over the years it has become a genuine antique center. For years, Lambertville looked like a poor relation of its neighbor across the river, New Hope. But now the antique shops have brought a certain panache to this old canal town. The *Pork Yard Antique and Art Center*, for instance, not only has classy antiques and Delaware Valley artists, but a cute French restaurant attached to the main building. It's open for lunch only on weekends, though. Both Bridge Street, (the main thoroughfare through town), and Union Street have a number of antique stores worth looking at.

But it's the flea markets that the crowds go for and they are located outside of town, on Route 29 going south. This is where you will find both the *Lambertville Antique Market* and *Golden Nugget Antiques* side by side and causing traffic jams every summer weekend. The indoor sections of the market are extensive and some carry rather nice 19th Century items. The indoor part is open all year round, while the outdoor tables only last as long as the weather is good. One nice thing about the Lambertville market is that there is hardly any new merchandise, so you do not have to contend with tables of jeans and sneakers.

LOCATION: Routes 179 and 29, Hunterdon County

LAHASKA FLEA MARKET

Across from the boutiques and restaurants of Peddlers Village, and rivaling them in popularity, is the Lahaska Flea Market. Actually, there are two markets — the outdoor tables of collectibles and antiques and the new indoor market where better quality awaits.

The outdoor flea market here is very much like the one at Lambertville (in fact I suspect that the same dealers run over to different markets on the same weekend). The indoor market includes stores that specialize in old sheet music, records and posters plus several antique furniture places. The indoor market runs weekends while the outdoor tables are open Wed. through Sunday if weather permits.

LOCATION: Route 202, Pa. 4 miles west of New Hope.
TELEPHONE: 215-794-5000

OTHER FLEA MARKETS

NEW EGYPT MARKET: Again, a mix of old and new, with everything from foundry type to bicycle parts available. There are inside buildings which, though old, host plenty of dealers and in good weather over 100 outside tables are filled with garage sale items. Once in a while a real "find" is discovered among the junque. Antique day is Sunday when the market opens at 7 AM. Auctions at 1 PM Sunday. Open Saturday, Sunday and Wednesday. New Egypt is located 6 miles west of Great Adventure in Ocean County (take Route 528). Telephone: 609-758-7440.

HOWELL ANTIQUE VILLAGE AND FLEA MARKET: Another popular market that attracts large crowds and bus tours. Open all year on Friday, Saturday and Sunday. Located on Route 9, Howell, Monmouth County, between Freehold and Lakewood. Telephone: 201-367-1105.

COLUMBUS MARKET: A well-known farmer's market that is also a flea market. The Thursday morning market sells produce and "anything legal." The Sunday "Family Yard Sale" is for used items only — no new merchandise or produce. 70 inside stores here. Located on Route 206, Columbus, Burlington County. Telephone: 609-267-0400.

NEWTON FLEA MARKET: Outdoors in the Newton Drive-In Theater, Route 206, one mile north of Newton in Sussex County. Open Sat. & Sun. 9-5 from May through October. Telephone: 201-383-3066.

NESHANIC FLEA MARKET: Neshanic Station, Somerset County. This was considered very good, then dropped out of sight for a while. It seems to be operating again, but call first. Telephone: 201-369-3660.

MEYERSVILLE GRANGE FLEA MARKET: A change of pace since this market is indoors and runs only in the cold weather. The building is small, but there are almost 30 tables inside. Glassware, china, urns, posters and one or two craft tables that feature duck decoys or handmade quilts. On Meyersville Road, Passaic Twp., Morris County. Sundays only, Oct. - May. Telephone: 201-832-7422.

ARCHIE'S: A little further down the road is Archie's Resale Shop — a glorified junkyard that has become an institution because of Archie's Santa Claus appearance. The 3,000 ice skates in Archie's Ice Skate Exchange are a boon to local mothers. Old sleighs, roomsful of old chairs (not in the cleanest condition), everything but the kitchen sink and probably that too. In Meyersville Center, Passaic Twp., Morris County.

FLEMINGTON FAIR FLEA MARKET: Except when it is used for the county fair in the fall, the large rural fairgrounds are fair game for flea market dealers and buyers. Tables operate on Wednesdays and weekends during the warm weather. Call 201-782-7326 for exact times. Located on Route 31, a few miles north of Flemington Circle, Hunterdon County.

ANTIQUE CENTERS

For those who do not relish the trudge through the dusty fields, there are plenty of antique stores and centers where you may browse in comfort — even air-conditioned comfort. There are over two thousand antique stores in New Jersey alone. Here is a short run-down on some of the better known centers.

RED BANK: *The Antique Center* hosts about 100 dealers in four large buildings within walking distance of one another. The shops are open daily from 11-5 and are located on Front Street and the 200s block. Take Garden State Parkway to Route 109, Monmouth County.

MONTVALE: *The Antique Mall* in the Chestnut Ridge Shopping Center, 30 Ridge Road, Montvale, in northern New Jersey has a collection of quality shops in comfortable surroundings. Take Exit 172 from Garden State Parkway.

A new enclave in north Jersey is *The Mill Market* in the quaint town of **Lafayette,** Sussex County. Forty dealers run a cooperative effort in a reconverted 1842 mill. The mill is on Route 15 in the center of town and is open Friday to Monday only. There are some other interesting antique shops in Lafayette also.

Both Hunterdon and Somerset counties have a gaggle of loosely strung out country-store type antique marts. Some of these are individual dealers and some are centers that include over a dozen dealers. A few of the well-known names are: *Whitehouse Manor Antiques Center,* Route 22 West, **Whitehouse Station,** *Kitchen Caboodle* in **Mountainville,** Tewksbury Township, *Melody Cottage* in nearby **Oldwick,** *River Edge Farm, Smoke House* and *Yesterday's Barn Antiques* in **North Branch,** Somerset County and *Country Antiques* in **Pluckemin.**

In southern Jersey the village of **Mullica Hill** hosts several antique centers. Among them are shops with quaint names like *The Eagles Nest, King's Row Antiques* and *Farm House Antiques* all on Main Street. And visitors to the shore can always find antique shops open during the season, from *The Pink House Antiques* in **Cape May** to several shops on **Long Beach Island** that specialize in nautical antiques.

As I mentioned several pages before, towns like **Chester** and **Lambertville** and **Lahaska** have a full complement of antique and specialty stores besides their well-known flea markets. For neophytes, the best way to track down the antique marts is to pick up a copy of one of those free antique newspapers at the local flea market or antique dealer. Or you can subscribe yourself, since these papers list auctions as well as the better known stores, trails, centers, and of course, flea markets. A popular paper that is heavy with listings for New Jersey and eastern Pennsylvania is: *The Jersey Devil*, P.O. Box 202, Lambertville, N.J. 08530. Subscription price is $6 a year.

INDOOR MARKETS

This is a growing group of markets that is fast taking over a big share of the bargain hunters brigade. Huge indoor marts, usually abandoned supermarkets, are divided into hundreds of stalls where entrepreneurs sell everything from bells to belts. Instead of *Two Guys* you get three hundred guys all touting discount merchandise. Market days are Friday, Saturday and Sunday.

The best known is probably the *U.S. #1 Flea Market and Antiques* situated on Route #1, New Brunswick (Telephone: 201-846-0900). This one still attempts to have an antique and collectible section. Another biggie is the *Route 18 Indoor Market*, 290 Route 18, East Brunswick (Telephone: 201-254-5080) which is almost completely new merchandise. *The Union Market*, Springfield Ave. & Route 24, Union, and the *Pushcart Palace*, Route 9 & Enston Road, Old Bridge, are both examples of this new type of market where the fleas have all but disappeared from the flea market scene.

Often customers find good buys at these places. Whether the alligators on the Izod shirts and the swans on the Gloria Vanderbilt jeans are real or fake is a question that bothers the manufacturers a lot more than the customers. It is by no means the norm, but once in a while, a pirated item ends up at a flea market or an indoor market.

OTHER OUTINGS

Photo: Courtesy PA Dutch Visitors Bureau

In This Chapter You Will Find:

Planetariums (N.J.)
School Tours
U.S.S. Ling Submarine
Black River & Western Railroad
Other Excursion Railroads
Twin Lights Lighthouse
Bushkill Falls
Renault Winery
Other Area Wineries
The Meadowlands
Other N.J. Racetracks
Other N.J. Arenas and Auditoriums

←

A steam train excursion — this one at Strasburg, Pennsylvania.

PLANETARIUMS (NEW JERSEY)

Aside from the planetariums you find within major museums, (such as The American Museum of Natural History, the Newark Museum, etc.) there are a number of places star-seeking New Jerseyans can visit for sky programs. Children under seven are usually not admitted to programs for good reason — once those doors shut in darkness, there is no escape. Luckily, many planetariums feature special "Stars for Tots" shows. Here's what is available.

OCEAN COUNTY COLLEGE: College Drive, Toms River. Robert J. Novin Planetarium. Outside the main hurly-burly of Toms River on a large campus, this planetarium not only schedules public shows all year round but has a special astronomy curriculum for school grades 1-6 during the public school year. (And this attracts students from outside counties as well.) Public shows are on Thursday, Friday and Saturday at 8 pm and Saturday at 2 pm. They do shut down every once in a while to prepare a new show, (although *not* when the college does) so call first. The planetarium holds 117 people and is quite modern. Admission: Adults $1.50; Children $1.00. Under 6 not admitted. Telephone: 201-255-4144.

TRAILSIDE PLANETARIUM: Coles Avenue and New Providence Road in Mountainside, Union County. Part of the Watchung Reservation's Trailside Nature and Science Center, this simple "down home" building is worth tracking down (it's just down the hill from the big Nature Center). Although it only seats 35 people, it is rarely overfilled on Saturdays and offers the same slide presentations, manufactured by a scientific company, that you see anywhere else, plus their own local star show. Weekends at 2 and 3:30 pm. Weekly after-school shows for groups — such as scouts —who reserve in advance. 50¢ admission. Telephone 201-232-5930.

MORRIS COUNTY COLLEGE: Route 10 & Center Grove Road, Randolph. This automated 80-seat planetarium offers not only several free programs to the local citizenry but two courses for those who really want to delve into the subject. Since the shows are created by the College Planetarium staff they may run longer than the average. Shows follow the school schedule so are closed during August and certain holiday weeks. Otherwise: Fridays: 7:30 pm, Saturdays: 1:30 and 3:30 pm, and a special 10:30 am showing for groups. Reservations required. Telephone: 201-361-5000. Ext. 206.

SPERRY OBSERVATORY, UNION COLLEGE: 1030 Springfield Ave., Cranford. Not a planetarium but an observatory with large telescopes that is run by Amateur Astonomers, Inc., in conjunction with Union College. Fridays from 7:30 to 10:30 pm (except the third Friday of the month) everyone is welcome to shoot for the stars. Children should be accompanied by parents. Telephone: 201-276-7827.

SCHOOL TOURS

Almost any museum, zoo, historic house or park mentioned in this book is open to reserved guided tours for school groups, scout groups and members of adult schools. Here are a few more places, popular with school groups, that did not fit in the above-mentioned categories:

NEW JERSEY STATE HOUSE: Tours through the gold-domed State House, where the legislature meets, are geared for school children from the fourth grade up. Tours can emphasize history, government, etc., according to the needs of the class. The building itself is quite impressive. Parking space is at a premium here at the State Cultural Complex, so bus tours have a distinct advantage. Location: State St., Trenton. Contact: School Reservation Service, N.J. State Museum, 205 W. State St., Trenton, N.J. 08625. Telephone: 609-292-6347.

HAYFORD STATE FISH HATCHERY: A new hatchery is in the offing, but this 1912 structure still serves for the moment. The fish that stock the state lakes and streams are hatched and bred here. These include different varieties of trout and some warm water species. Guided tours are by appointment and are quite popular with schoolchildren. The hatchery also hosts a once-a-year Open House in April for the general public. Location: Grand Avenue, Hackettstown, Warren County. Telephone: 201-852-3676.

THE U.S.S. LING SUBMARINE

The U.S.S. Ling is only 312 feet long and 27 feet wide, and when you consider that ninety-five men and twenty-four torpedoes were aboard during its short career as an active sub in 1945, you realize that this is no place for someone with claustrophobia. Nowadays, most of the torpedoes and many of the berths have been removed to allow for tour groups to move about. Indeed the inside seems surprisingly spacious compared with the outside.

Tickets are bought at the outside trailer museum which also houses pictures and paraphernalia — including the periscope of a Japanese sub. Tours leave about every 15 minutes and last about 45 minutes, depending on your guide.

You begin in the torpedo room where there are still two of these sleek weapons left. (No, they are not active). I learned that torpedoes do not go off by accident since they are activated only after they leave the tube. They also had to be aimed right, since a miss would give away the sub's position to an enemy ship.

I also learned that much of the time on the sub was devoted to eating and cooking. Besides three meals a day and night for all shifts, sailors could raid the refrigerator at any time. When the Ling first left port, space was so dear that fresh fruit and vegetables were stacked in one of the showerheads.

Since it was hot and cramped in on the sub, showers were popular, as was Lifebuoy soap. And a huge laundry room throbbed night and day, cleaning the sailor's clothes. Smoking was allowed, surprisingly, until the air became so stale that the cigarette would not light.

Tours include the Control Room, Maneuvering Room, Main Engine Room, sleeping quarters and more; but the Conning Tower with its periscope is off limits. You are allowed to handle certain equipment, including the wheels and gauges, and the guide does sound the diving signal (memorable from a host of old war movies starring Cary Grant and John Garfield).

While modern submarines are larger and sleeker, this black, fleet-type vessel is a memorial to the World War II submariners who must have been a hardy lot. An interesting place, both for older children and ex-servicemen.

HOURS: 10:15 AM - 4 PM Daily except major holidays.
ADMISSION: Adults $2.00, Children: $1.00
LOCATION: Court & River Streets, Hackensack, Bergen County
TELEPHONE: 201-488-9770

BLACK RIVER AND WESTERN RAILROAD

Here is an old-fashioned train ride that runs through the pretty countryside between Flemington and Ringoes in Hunterdon County.

The trip takes about an hour and includes a twenty-minute stopover at Ringoes. For kids and adults who have never ridden a steam-driven train (with its resulting soot and nostalgia) this is the only full-scale excursion train now operating in New Jersey. The train leaves from Turntable Junction in Flemington.

> **HOURS:** Weekends from April to December 1st. Several trips a day.
> **ADMISSION:** Adults: $4.00; Children 5-12: $2.00; Children 3 & 4: $1.00.
> **TELEPHONE:** 201-782-6622.

OTHER EXCURSION RAILROADS

A popular attraction at *Allaire State Park* in Monmouth County is the **Pine Hill Railroad** which runs a ten-minute trip. The train ride and a railroad museum are part of the several attractions at this large park. The ride operates on weekends during the summer season. Check the *Allaire Village* listing for further information.

Another train ride, this one well into Pennsylvania Dutch territory (and therefore, technically, beyond the periphery of this book) is the **Strasburg Railroad.** Located on Route 741, Strasburg, in Lancaster County, Pennsylvania, the ride is so well known that it attracts tourists from across the border. The 45-minute ride offers a steam train with pot belly stoves in the coaches and an observation car straight out of "Hello, Dolly!". It operates on weekends during March, April, November and December. Weekdays on May 1 through October 31. Call 717-687-7522 for time schedules.

As for the **Morris County Railroad** in Newfoundland, which used to run a scenic ride complete with holdup men, please be advised that this train ride is **not** operating at this time. However, there is a small museum *(The Pequannock Valley Transportation Museum)* which is open at the depot, located at Green Pond Road (Rte. 513) Morris County. The museum is open weekends and holidays 12-4:30 from April to October.

TWIN LIGHTS LIGHTHOUSE

An unusual brownstone building that looks more like a castle than the lighthouse it once was, Twin Lights is perched on a mountainous bluff in Atlantic Highlands and affords a sweeping view of the ocean and coast. The "twin" lights, (one is square and one octagonal) are towers on either side of the main building. The first Fresnel lights were used here in 1841. The present fortress-like structure was built in 1862 and was the scene of many "firsts".

The museum inside includes exhibits on early life-saving equipment, a replica of the first rowing skiff to cross the Atlantic and displays concerning Marconi's first demonstration of the wireless in America.

Naturally part of the enjoyment of visiting a decommissioned lighthouse is making the climb up the stairs. The ascent up the spiral staircase involves only 167 steps and leads to an excellent view of Sandy Hook and the ocean. Downstairs, there is a small gift shop and outside you will find a picnic area and several historical markers. A look at the original Fresnel lens which is housed in separate area, is also available. Free.

HOURS: Daily May 1 - Sept. 30; 9-5. Closed Mon. & Tues., Oct. 1 - April 30.

LOCATION: Atlantic Highlands, Monmouth County, Take Route 36E make right turn just before Highlands Bridge, then another right. Follow signs.

TELEPHONE: 201-872-1814

BUSHKILL FALLS

For families who wish to avoid the hurly-burly of amusement parks there are many scenic attractions which offer a day in the country with the simpler amusements of an earlier day. One of these is Bushkill Falls, set in a primeval forest in the foothils of the Poconos. The forest is cool in the summer and colorful in the fall, and while the main waterfall is nowhere near Niagara in width or grandeur, it does present both photographers and easy hikers with a pleasant outing. How long Bushkill Falls can compete with nearby *Magic Valley* (which offer smaller waterfalls but also a full-fledged amusement park) is a matter of conjecture. But for Pocono tourists and visitors to the Delaware Water Gap area, the Falls have long been a standard attraction. A small fishing pond, miniature golf and paddle boats offer extra recreation.

The entrance pathway through a hushed forest is near the top of the falls, so although you get a good view of the cascading water from up top, it is more impressive to see it from below. That however, requires a climb up and down a "natural" log stairway. The Main Falls drop over the edge of a 100-foot cliff to a deep pool below. From that point the water now drops another 70 feet through a large gorge strewn with gigantic boulders. The falls are fairly narrow, but the drop is spectacular.

There are three routes to follow to the falls. The short route, with a green trail marker, takes only 15 minutes to walk. It is the "chicken" trail to a lookout where you can drink in the vistas, take a picture then sit down. The second or "popular" route takes 45 minutes and is for those who want their money's worth. This takes you down and around the bottom of the main falls, where from a bridge across the creek you get a full view from below of the majestic spill of white water.

The third route takes one and a half hours. Here you pass the series of three pretty, mist-laden falls on your trek through the virgin forest. Following this path you also come upon a lookout where you can enjoy a panoramic view of the Delaware Valley. Actually, the path is not much more rugged than the previous trails, but it is absolutely necessary for one to wear good walking shoes. Wedgies, Dr. Scholls, clogs and such are a disaster on these paths.

When visiting the Falls be sure to check the map in the brochure you receive with your ticket. It clearly marks the trails to follow. Senior Citizens and young children could probably do without the huffing and puffing on the longer trails.

HOURS: April - mid-November, Daily.
ADMISSION: Adults: $2.50; Children 6-12: 75¢; Under 6, free.
LOCATION: Bushkill, Pa. Take I-80 to Exit 52, then 209 N. Follow signs.
TELEPHONE: 717-588-6682

RENAULT WINERY

Let's face it, a winery tour is just about the most popular kind of industrial tour there is. The art of winemaking is so ancient, the slightly fermented air in the cellars so heady and the little old winemaker is usually so jolly that there is always a party air about these tours. And since wine-tasting is involved, no wonder everyone seems to have a good time.

Historic Renault Winery calls itself the best little tour-house in New Jersey and for good reason. It's fun! Yes, you learn about the early wine presses and dosage machines, but the tour leader also plays to the crowd, threatening to send the women in to stomp the grapes or the men in to clean the barrels. The tour begins in the hospitality room, an oak room ringed by casks. Here you get a sip of wine and some history of the place. The winery is not run by the Renault family, by the way, but by third family to buy this thriving business. It is situated way out in the Pine Barrens about 16 miles northwest of Atlantic City. Apparently this sandy soil lends itself well to grape production.

After the hospitality room there are various stops in rooms full of antique wine-making equipment and small wine-tasting rooms. Then it's into the cellars where giant vats store the wine. These oak and redwood vats are fifty and sixty years old and would have to be replaced today by stainless steel as the old cooper's craft is lost. The guide explains how the wine poured off and facts of vineyard life. If I learned one salient fact here it was to never-more buy cooking wine at the supermarket. It seems that food companies buy the wineries' rejects, then add salt to the already bad wine (that's a law), bottle it and sell it. It's best to use your leftover open bottles for your cooking. As the tour leader mentioned — no cookbook every says to add cooking wine to your recipe.

Before or after your tour, you are invited to inspect the glass museum which is a collection of fanciful wineglasses, many from the 16th and 17th Centuries and some from Venice. After the tour there is, of course, the gift shop where you can buy wine and accoutrements. Many vineyards make at least one third of their sales from the tours so the last stop is a most important one to them.

Aside from regular tours, Renault Winery also arranges group lunches and dinners at a very reasonable price. The food is cooked there and of course a good number of the dishes are *"au vin"*. For the best view of winemaking the optimum months to visit are in September and October when the grapes are harvested and processed.

HOURS: Daily. Tours are Mon. - Sat.: 10-5:30
ADMISSION: $1 for tours. Under 18 free.
LOCATION: Bremen Ave., Egg Harbor City, Atlantic County. Take Garden State Parkway exit 44 (if coming from north only!) and right onto Moss Mill Rd., then 6 miles to Bremen Ave. From Atlantic City: Route 30 to Bremen Ave.
TELEPHONE: 609-965-2111

OTHER AREA WINERIES

Another Atlantic City sidetrip is the one to **Gross' Highland Winery.** Champagne tanks and equipment a specialty. Gift shop includes a wide selection of glassware. Hours: Mon. -Sat.: 9-6. Location: Absecon Highlands. Take Route 9 to Route 561 (Jim Leeds Road) look for winery on left. Telephone: 609-652-1187.

In New York State, about one-half hour north of West Point you can find the **Brotherhood Winery** which bills itself as America's oldest and most historic winery. Guided tasting tours last about 1½ hours. No charge for the tour but there is a $3 parking fee. Hours: 10-4 daily except major holidays. Take Route 17 to Exit 130, then right onto Route 208 into town. Telephone: 914-496-9101.

Over in Pennsylvania, just 3 miles west of the Delaware River, a new winery has been attracting tourists on the New Hope-Lahaska trail. **Bucks County Vineyards** offers guided tours, wine tasting and a museum which includes costumes worn by Broadway stars as well as the usual wine presses. Hours: weekdays: 11-5; Saturday: 10-6; Sunday: 12-6. Location on Route 202 west of New Hope. Admission: weekdays, free; weekends, $1. Telephone: 215-794-7449.

And the newest addition to New Jersey viticulture is the **Tewksbury Wine Cellars,** tucked in the Hunterdon County hills. Started only a few years ago, this small vineyard hopes to produce "estate bottled" wines. Tours are available on Saturdays 10-5 or Sunday 1-5 or by appointment. Located at Burrell Road, Lebanon. Take Rte. 78 to Oldwick exit, then 517 north to Burrell Road. Telephone: 201-832-2400.

THE MEADOWLANDS

You have only to drive through the battle-scarred South Bronx on your way to Yankee Stadium to realize what a stroke of genius it was to build the Meadowlands Sports-Arena Complex in the middle of a wide open area. It may have been a wasteland once, but now the sports-entertainment complex is breaking all box-office records. In fact, the biggest problem now is traffic tie-ups, especially when all three buildings are holding events. The complex consists of:

1. THE RACETRACK: Both harness and flat racing have their season at this modern, sparkling facility. The glassed-in, climate controlled Grandstand can hold up to 35,000 people. There are several restaurants here for those who want to combine a night out with dining out. The Tracksider restaurant offers good though unexciting food at moderate prices. The tables are set on tiers so you can watch the race while you eat. The Handicapper also provides food, while the Pegasus restaurant, up on the top level of the track, gives you a bird's eye view of the race and a fancier place to eat with its two buffets, sitdown section and high prices.

For those watching the race from the grandstand a large 15 x 36 foot video matrix screen allows you to watch the action on the far side of the field and also flashes the results almost immediately. The Meadowlands Racetrack has now become the number one track in harness racing and is among the top ten in thoroughbred racing in attendance and wagering. General Admission is $1.75. Clubhouse admission is $3.

2. GIANTS STADIUM: So named because the football team of that name makes its home there. However, the Cosmos' soccer games sell out just as well. The stadium has a seating capacity of 76,000, color coded seats and a video matrix scoreboard that delights the kids. The stadium is used not only for sports events for special concerts, antique shows and other extravaganzas as well.

3. THE ARENA: (Officially the Byrne Arena). The newest addition to the Meadowlands Complex boasts a striking modern design that arches eleven stories high. The arrangement of seats (approximately 20,000) allows good viewlines. However, a shortage of personnel often closes off the lower concourse so you may have quite a hike if you go for snacks. The Arena hosts the N.J. Nets, college basketball games, ice shows, Ringling Brothers Circus, rock shows and many other entertainments that New Jerseyans used to travel to Madison Square Garden to see.

FOR THE MEADOWLANDS COMPLEX:
    PARKING: $1.00; Valet Parking: $2.00. Come early to avoid jamups.
    LOCATION: East Rutherford, Bergen County
    DIRECTIONS: From N.J. Turnpike northbound - take Exit 16W for direct access. From Turnpike south - take Exit 18W. From Garden State Parkway northbound - Exit 153A to Route 3 East. From G.S.P. south-Exit 163 to Route 17S to Paterson Plank Road East.
    TELEPONE: 201-935-8500

OTHER NEW JERSEY RACETRACKS

MONMOUTH PARK: Oceanport, Monmouth County. Telephone: 201-222-5100. Thoroughbred racing at this track close to the Jersey shore runs from May through September.

FREEHOLD RACEWAY: Park Avenue, Freehold, Monmouth County (Take Route 9 and 33). Telephone: 201-462-3800. Harness racing continues from January through December.

ATLANTIC CITY RACE COURSE: Junction of Route 40 and Route 322, Atlantic County. Telephone: 609-641-2190. Thoroughbred racing June 1 - September 30.

OTHER NEW JERSEY ARENAS & AUDITORIUMS

GARDEN STATE ARTS CENTER: A beautiful white concrete ampitheatre designed by Edward Durell Stone is the setting for nightly concerts and loads of special events throughout the summer. The "shell" is covered and offers seating for 5,000 while an additional 4,000 people can be accommodated on the lawn. The lawn people, however, must bring their own blankets and chairs and risk the weather.

The shell is open on all sides so that there is easy access to seats and a delicious breeze from the nearby seashore wafts through the auditorium. Shows at the Garden State range from pop singers to symphony orchestras with a few ethnic festivals thrown in. The season runs from late June to early September.

LOCATION: Holmdel, Monmouth County. Take Exit 116 off Garden State Parkway, follow signs.
TELEPHONE: 201-264-9200

OCEAN GROVE AUDITORIUM: A cavernous 7,000 seat auditorium built in the late Victorian age is one of the attractions of this quiet camp-meeting town right next to Asbury Park on the shore. The Great Auditorium, with its majestic organ, has recently been refurbished and restored. It is now home to many family-style entertainments plus a lecture series. Typical attractions are singers (including pop singers) choral groups and festivals. Again, this is for the summer season only.

LOCATION: 54 Pitman Avenue, Ocean Grove, Monmouth County.

WATERLOO VILLAGE SUMMER MUSIC FESTIVAL: Mentioned in the chapter on Restored Villages, this festival has plans afoot to build a permanent shell next to the historic village. Classical music, jazz and bluegrass are featured here. A new food pavilion provides an alternative to picnics for visitors to the festival.

LOCATION: Waterloo Village, Stanhope, Sussex County.
TELEPHONE: 201-347-4700

INDEX

A

Abram S. Hewitt State Forest 175
Acorn Hall 76
Allaire State Park 70, 173, 208
Allaire Village 70
Allamuchy State Park 173
Allen House 76
American Museum of Immigration 121
American Museum of Natural History 103
Amusement Parks 131-144
Antique Centers 201
Archie's Resale Shop 200
Arrowhead Ski Area 164
Art Tours of Manhattan 13
Asbury Park 143, 168
Atlantic City 3, 143
Atlantic City Race Course 214
Atsion State Park 173
Aviation Hall of Fame 94

B

Bainbridge House 56
Ballantine House 50
Barnegat Lighthouse State Park 169, 173
Barnes Foundation 112
Bass River State Forest 172, 175
Batsto 68, 70
Bell Labs Exhibit 91
Belle Mountain Ski Area 165
Belleplain State Forest 175
Beach Haven 169
Belmar 168
Bergen Community Museum 85
Bergen County Wildlife Center 159
Bertrand Island Amusement Park 144
Big Boulder Ski Area 165
Black River and Western Railroad 207
Boardwalk Amusements 142-143
Bordentown Walking Tour 16
Boscobel 54
Bowcraft Amusement Park 144
Boxwood Hall 35
Branch Brook Park 186
Brandywine Battlefield Park 37
Brandywine River Museum 114
Brielle 168, 172
Brigantine Castle 143
Brigantine National Wildlife Refuge 157
Bronx Zoo 147

Brooklyn Botanic Gardens 182
Brotherhood Winery 212
Buccleuch Mansion 35
Buck Gardens 186
Bucks County Playhouse 8
Bucks County Vineyards 212
Burlington County Prison-Museum 18
Burlington Tour 17
Bushkill Falls 209
Buten Museum of Wedgewood 113
Byrne Arena 213

C

Camden County Historical Society 100
Camelback Ski Area 166
Campbell Museum 94
Campgaw Ski Area 165
Camping 172
Cannonball House 38
Cape May, Town 169
Cape May County Musuem 99
Cape May County Park Zoo 154
Cape May - Lewes Ferry 170
Cape May Point State Park 170, 173
Center for Environmental Studies 159
Cheesequake State Park 173
Chester Flea Market 197
Chinatown 10
Chinese Museum 10
Chocolate World 133
Circle Line Tour 125
Clara Barton Schoolhouse 17
Clementon Lake Park 144
Cleveland, Grover, Birthplace 49
Clinton Historical Museum Village 64
Cloisters, The 104
Cohansic Zoo 154
Colonial Park Rose Garden 185
Columbus Flea Market 200
Cooper, James Fenimore, House 18
Cooper Mill 75
Corson's Inlet State Park 173
Covenhoven House 34
Craigmeur Ski Area 163

D

Deal 168
Delaware and Raritan Canal State Park 173
Delaware Water Gap 170
Dey Mansion 25
Drake House 37

Drew University Archeology Museum 88
Dreyfuss Planetarium 83
Duke Gardens 180
Durham Boat House 31

E

East Jersey Olde Towne 67
Edison Labs 44
Edison Memorial Tower 95
Ellis Island 121
Empire State Building 125
Englishtown Auction Sales Market 196

F

Fairmount Park Historic House Tours 20
Ferry Museum 31
Fishing 171
Firestone Library 6
Flat Rock Brook Nature Center 158
Flea Markets 195-200
Flemington Fair Flea Market 200
Flemington Outlets 192
Fonthill Museum 114
Force House 75
Ford Mansion 24
Forests, State 175
Fort Lee State Park 37, 174
Fort Mott State Park 174
Fosterfields 73
Franklin Court 128
Franklin Institute 107
Franklin Mineral Museum 88
Freehold Raceway 214
Frelinghuysen Arboretum 187
Frick Collection 105

G

Galloping Hill Ski Area 165
Garden State Arts Center 214
Giants Stadium 213
Gilder House 16
Glenmont 47
Gloucester County Tour 19
Golf House 90
Great Adventure 131
Great Adventure Safari 148
Great Falls, Paterson 15
Great Gorge Ski Area 163
Great Swamp 155, 159
Great Swamp Outdoor Education Center 157, 159

Greenfield Hall 76
Gross' Highland Winery 212
Guggenheim Museum 106

H

Hacklebarney State Park 174
Hagley Museum 78
Hancock House 37
Hartshorn Arboretum 159
Haunted Mansion 142
Hayden Planetarium 103
Hayford State Fish Hatchery 206
Hedge Garden 188
Hershey Rose Gardens 134, 185
Hersheypark 132
Hidden Valley Ski Area 163
High Point State Park 174
Hiking 170
Historic Cold Spring Village 71
Historic Gardner's Basin 5
Historic Washington Crossing Park 31
Hoboken Walking Tour 13
Holly Mountain Ski Area 164
Holmdel Park 73
Homewood 31
Hopatcong State Park 174
Hopewell Museum 97
Howell Antique Flea Market 199
Hunter Mountain Ski Area 166
Hunter-Lawrence House 19
Hunterdon Art Center 65
Hyde Park 42

I

Independence Hall 128
Independence Mall 127
Indian King Tavern 34
Indoor Markets 202
Island Beach State Park 174
Israel Crane House 74

J

Jack Frost Mountain 165
Jenny Jump State Forest 175
Jersey City Museum 87
Jersey Shore 167-170
Jockey Hollow 23
John Woolman Memorial 18

K

Keansburg Amusements 142
Kittatiny Point Center 170

L

Lafayette Antiques 201
Lahaska 9, 199
Lahaska Flea Market 199
Lambert Castle 51
Lambertville Flea Markets 198
Land of Make Believe 140
Lawrence House 18
Lebanon State Forest 175
Liberty Bell 128
Liberty State Park 120, 174
Liberty Village 72
Lincoln Center Tour 12
Long Beach Island 168
Long Branch 142
Longstreet Farm 72
Longwood Gardens 179
Lorimar Nature Center 158
Lucy, the Margate Elephant 5
Lyndhurst 53

M

Macculloch Hall 54
Magic Valley Amusement Park 137
Marlpit Hall 76
Marshall House 76
McKonkey Ferry Inn 31
Meadownlands Sports Complex 212
Mercer Mile 113
Mercer Museum 114
Metropolitan Museum of Art 101
Meyersville Grange Flea Market 200
Miller-Cory House 74
Monmouth Battlefield Park 33, 174
Monmouth County Historical Museum 99
Monmouth Museum 86
Monmouth Park Racetrack 214
Montclair Art Museum 83
Montvale Antiques 201
Moravian Pottery and Tile Works 114
Morris County College Planetarium 205
Morris Museum 84
Morven 55
Mount Holly 19
Mullica Hill Antiques 201
Municipal Art Society 13
Museum of American Life 134
Museum of Early Trades and Crafts 95
Museum of Glass, Wheaton 66
Museum of Holography 12
Museum of Modern Art 106

N

Nassau Hall 6
Nast, Thomas 54
National Broadcasters Hall of Fame 92
Nature Centers 158-160
Nemours 41
Neshanic Flea Market 200
New Egypt Market 199
New Hope 8
New Jersey Historical Society 99
New Jersey Shore 167-170
New Jersey State House 206
New Jersey State Museum 81
New York Aquarium 154
New York Botanical Gardens 184
New York Stock Exchange 13
Newark Museum 82
Newton Flea Market 200
Norvin Green State Forest 175

O

Ocean City 143, 169
Ocean City Historical Musuem 98
Ocean County College Planetarium 205
Ocean County Historical Museum 97
Ocean Grove 168
Ocean Grove Auditorium 214
Odgen Belcher Mansion 76
Old Barracks 28
Old City Hall, Bordentown 16
Old Dutch Parsonage 27
Osborn Cannonball House 75
Outlets 191-194

P

Parks, State 173-175
Parry House Mansion 8
Parvin State Park 174
Paterson Museum 87
Paterson Tours 14
Peapack Ski Area 164
Pearson How House 18
Penn State Forest 175
Pennsbury Manor 57
Pennsylvania Academy of Fine Arts 109
Pequannock Valley Transportation Museum 208
Peters Valley Craftsmen 170
Philadelphia Museum of Art 108
Philipsburg Manor 63
Phillip's Mushroom Museum 115
Pine Hill Railroad 208

Pine Barrens 170, 171
Plainfield Tour 15
Planetariums 81, 83, 103, 107, 205
Poconos Ski Areas 165-166
Point Pleasant 143, 168
Poricy Park Nature Center 160
Presby Iris Gardens 187
Princeton 6
Princeton Art Museum 7, 88
Princeton Battlefield Park 37
Princeton University Tour 6
Putnam Sculptures 7

R

Racetracks 212, 214
Radio City Music Hall 12
Raggedy Ann Doll Museum 93
RCA Building 125
Reading Outlets 191
Red Bank Antiques 201
Red Bank Battlefield Park 34
Renault Winery 210
Revolutionary War Museum 24
Riker Hill Geological Museum 159
Ringwood Manor 51
Ringwood Manor State Park 51, 174, 187
Rockefeller Center Tour 13
Rockingham 27
Rogers Exhibit 15, 100
Roosevelt Library and Museum 43
Rosenbach Museum and Library 110
Round Valley State Park 172, 174
Rutgers Art Gallery 87
Rutgers Geology Museum 87

S

Salem Generating Station 95
Salem Tour 19
Sandy Hook 160, 167, 174
Sandy Hook Visitors Center 160
Schoolhouse Museum 97
Schuyler-Hamilton House 38
Seaside Heights 143, 168
Seaside Park 168
Secaucus Outlets 193
Sesame Place 136
Shawnee Mountain 165
Ski Mountain 164
Skiing 163-166
Skylands 52, 187
Sleepy Hollow Restorations 53, 62-64

Smithville, Historic Towne of 65
Smithville Mansion 18
Soho Tour 11
Somers Mansion 76
Somerset County Environmental Education Center 159
Space Farms Zoo 153
Speedwell Village 47
Sperry Observatory 206
Spring Lake 168
Spruce Run 174
Spy House Museum 98
Squibb Headquarters 92
Staten Island Zoo 151
Statue of Liberty 120
Sterling Forest Ski Area 166
Stevens State Park 175
Stokes State Forest 171, 175
Stone Harbor 169
Strasburg Railroad 208
Sunnyside 53
Swartswood State Park 172, 175

T

Terry Lou Zoo 152
Tewksbury Wine Cellars 212
Thompson-Neely House 31
Trailside Nature Center 159
Trailside Planetarium 159, 205
Trent House 56
Turtle Back Zoo 150
Twin Lights Lighthouse 208

U

United Nations Headquarters 119
United State Mint 19
University Chapel, Princeton 6
University of Pennsylvania Archaeology Museum 111
Urban Archaeology 12
U.S.S. Ling 206

V

Vail House 47
Valley Forge 32
Van Cortlandt Manor 62
Van Riper-Hopper House 76
Van Saun Park Zoo 154
Vanderbilt Mansion 43
Vernon Valley Action Park 134
Vernon Valley Ski Area 163
Von Steuben House 36
Voorhees State Park 175

W

Wallace House 26
Washington Crossing Park (N.J.) 30
Washington's Headquarters, Morristown 24
Washington Rock State Park 175
Waterloo Village 61
Waterloo Village Music Festival 61, 215
Wawayanda State Park 175
West Point 126
Wharton State Forest 175
Wheaton Village 66
Whitman, Walt, House 57
Wick Farm House 23
Wild West City 141
Wildlife Refuges 155-158
Wildwood 143, 169
Wildwood Crest 169
Windmill Museum 93
Winterthur 77
World Trade Center 123
Worthington State Forest 175

Z

Zoos 147-154

REGIONAL INDEX

NEW JERSEY

ATLANTIC COUNTY

Atlantic City
  Casinos and boardwalk
  Atlantic City Race Course
  Historic Gardners Basin
Brigantine Castle
Brigantine National Wildlife
  Refuge
Gross' Highland Winery
Lucy, Margate Elephant
Smithville, Historic Towne of
Pine Barrens
Somers Mansion

BERGEN COUNTY

Aviation Hall of Fame,
  Teterboro
Bergen Community Museum
Bergen County Wildlife Center
Campgaw Ski Area, Mahwah
Flat Rock Brook Nature Center
Fort Lee Historic State Park
Lorimar Nature Center
Meadowlands Sports Complex
Montvale Antiques
Schoolhouse Museum, Paramus
U.S.S. Ling, Hackensack
Van Saun Park
Von Steuben House

BURLINGTON COUNTY

Atsion State Park
Bass River State Forest
Batsto Village
Bordentown Tour
Burlington Tour
Columbus Flea Market
Lebanon State Forest
Mount Holly Tour
Penn State Forest
Pine Barrens
Rancocos State Park
Wharton State Forest

CAMDEN COUNTY

Camden
  Camden County Historical
  Society
  Campbell Museum
  Walt Whitman House
Clementon Lake Park
Greenfield Hall, Haddonfield
Indian King Tavern,
  Haddonfield
Ski Mountain, Pine Hill

CAPE MAY COUNTY

Belleplain State Forest
Cape May County Museum
Cape May County Park Zoo
Cape May—Lewes Ferry
Cape May Point State Park
Cape May (town)
Corson's Inlet State Park
Hedge Garden
Historic Cold Spring Village
Ocean City
Ocean City Historical Museum
Stone Harbor
Wildwood
Wildwood Crest

CUMBERLAND COUNTY

Belleplain State Forest
Cohansic Zoo, Bridgeton
Pine Barrens
Wheaton Village, Millville

ESSEX COUNTY

Center for Environmental
  Studies
Grover Cleveland Birthplace
Edison Labs/Glenmont
Force House, Livingston
Hartshorn Arboretum

Montclair
  Israel Crane House
  Montclair Art Museum
  Presby Iris Garden
Newark
  Ballantine House
  Branch Brook Park
  New Jersey Historical Society
  Newark Museum
  Riker Hill Geological Museum
  Turtle Back Zoo

GLOUCESTER COUNTY
Gloucester County Tour
Hunter-Lawrence House,
  Woodbury
Mullica Hill Antiques
Red Bank Battlefield Park

HUDSON COUNTY
Hoboken Tour
Jersey City Museum
Liberty State Park
  Ellis Island
  Statue of Liberty
Secaucus Outlets

HUNTERDON COUNTY
Clinton Historical Museum
  Village
Hunterdon Art Center, Clinton
Flemington
  Black River and
    Western Railroad
  Flemington Fair Flea Market
  Liberty Village
  Outlets
  Raggedy Ann Doll Museum
Lambertville Flea Market
Marshall House, Lambertville
Round Valley State Park
Spruce Run State Park
Tewksbury Wine Cellars
Voorhees State Park
Windmill Museum

MERCER COUNTY
Belle Mountain Ski Area
Hopewell Museum

Princeton
  Bainbridge House
  Morven
  Princeton Art Museum
  Princeton Battlefield
  University Tour
Squibb Headquarters
Trenton
  New Jersey State House
  New Jersey State Museum
  Old Barracks
  Trent House
Washington Crossing State Park

MIDDLESEX COUNTY
Cheesequake State Park
East Jersey Olde Towne
Edison Memorial Tower
New Brunswick
  Buccleuch Mansion
  Rutgers Art Gallery
  Rutgers Geology Museum

MONMOUTH COUNTY
Allaire State Park
Allen House
Arrowhead Ski Area
Asbury Park
Belmar
Brielle
Deal
Englishtown Auction Sales
Freehold
  Covenhoven House
  Monmouth Battlefield
    State Park
  Monmouth County Historical
    Society
  Freehold Raceway
  National Broadcasters
    Hall of Fame
Garden State Arts Center
Haunted Mansion, Long Branch
Howell Antique Flea Market
Keansburg Amusements
Longstreet Farm, Holmdel
Marlpit Hall
Monmouth Museum, Lincroft
Monmouth Park Racetrack
Ocean Grove

Poricy Park Nature Center
Sandy Hook
Spring Lake
Spy House Museum
Twin.Lights Lighthouse

MORRIS COUNTY

Archie's Resale Shop,
  Meyersville
Bertrand's Island Amusement
  Park
Chester Flea Market
Cooper Mill
Craigmeur Ski Area
Drew University Archeology
  Museum
Fosterfields
Frelinghuysen Arboretum
Great Swamp Outdoor Center
Hacklebarny State Park
Hopatcong State Park
Meyersville Grange Flea Market
Morris County College
  Planetarium
Morris Museum of Arts and
  Sciences
Morristown
  Acorn Hall
  Ford Mansion
  Jockey Hollow
  Macculloch Hall
  Shuyler-Hamilton House
Museum of Early Trades and
  Crafts
Speedwell Village

OCEAN COUNTY

Barnegat Lighthouse State Park
Great Adventure
Island Beach State Park
Lebanon State Forest
Long Beach Island
New Egypt Flea Market
Ocean County College
  Planetarium
Ocean County Historical
  Museum
Point Pleasant
Seaside Heights
Seaside Park

PASSAIC COUNTY

Abram S. Hewitt State Forest
Dey Mansion, Wayne
Norvin Green State Forest
Paterson
  Great Falls
  Lambert Castle
  Paterson Museum
  Paterson Tour
  Rogers Exhibit
Ringwood Manor State Park
Skylands
Van Riper-Hopper House,
  Wayne

SALEM COUNTY

Fort Mott State Park
Hancock House
Holly Mountain Ski Area
Salem Generating Station
Salem Tour
Parvin State Park

SOMERSET COUNTY

Buck Gardens
Colonial Park Rose Gardens
Delaware and Raritan Canal
  State Park
Golf House, Far Hills
Great Swamp
Neshanic Flea Market
Peapack Ski Tow
Somerset Environmental
  Education Center
Somerville
  Duke Gardens
  Old Dutch Parsonage
  Wallace House
Washington Rock State Park

SUSSEX COUNTY

Delaware Water Gap
Franklin Mineral Museum
Great Gorge Ski Area
Hidden Valley Ski Area
High Point State Park
Newton Flea Market
Space Farms Zoo
Stokes State Forest

Swartswood State Park
Vernon Valley Action Park
Vernon Valley Ski Area
Waterloo Village
Wawayanda State Park
Wild West City
Worthington State Forest

UNION COUNTY
Bell Labs Exhibit
Bowcraft Amusement Park
Boxwood Hall, Elizabeth
Cannonball House, Springfield
Drake House, Plainfield
Galloping Hill Ski Area
Miller-Cory House

Ogden Belcher Mansion
Osborn Cannonball House
Plainfield Tour
Sperry Observatory
Terry Lou Zoo
Trailside Nature Center
Trailside Planetarium

WARREN COUNTY
Allamuchy State Park
Delaware Water Gap
Hayford Fish Hatchery
Jenny Jump State Forest
Land of Make Believe
Stephens State Park

NEW YORK STATE

HUDSON VALLEY AREA
Boscobel
Brotherhood Winery
Hunter Mountain Ski Area
Hyde Park
Lyndhurst
Philipsburg Manor
Sterling Forest Ski Area
Sunnyside
Van Cortlandt Manor
Vanderbilt Mansion
West Point

NEW YORK CITY

Manhattan
American Museum of
   Natural History
Art Tours of Manhattan
Chinatown
Circle Line Tour
Cloisters, The
Empire State Building

Frick Collection
Guggenheim Museum
Lincoln Center Tour
Metropolitan Museum of Art
Municipal Arts Society
Museum of Modern Art
N.Y. Stock Exchange
Radio City Music Hall
RCA Building
Rockefeller Center Tour
Soho Tour
U.N. Headquarters
World Trade Center

Brooklyn
Brooklyn Botanic Gardens
N.Y. Aquarium

Bronx
Bronx Zoo
N.Y. Botanical Gardens

Staten Island
Staten Island Zoo

PENNSYLVANIA

BRANDYWINE VALLEY AREA

Brandywine Battlefield
State Park
Brandywine River Museum
Longwood Gardens
Phillips Mushroom Museum

BUCKS COUNTY

Bucks County Vineyards
Lahaska
Mercer Mile, Doylestown
New Hope
Pennsbury Manor
Sesame Place
Washington Crossing Park

PHILADELPHIA AREA

Barnes Foundation (Merion)
Buten Museum (Merion)
Fairmount Park Houses
Franklin Institute
Independence Mall

Pennsylvania Academy of
Fine Arts
Philadelphia Museum of Arts
United States Mint
University of Pennsylvania
Archeology Museum

POCONOS AREA

Big Boulder Ski Area
Bushkill Falls
Camelback Ski Area
Delaware Water Gap
Jack Frost Ski Area
Magic Valley Amusement Park
Shawnee Mountain Ski Area

OTHER PENNSYLVANIA AREAS

Hershey Rose Gardens
Hersheypark
Reading Outlets
Strasburg Railroad
Valley Forge

DELAWARE

Cape May-Lewes Ferry
Hagley Museum
Nemours
Winterthur